The Rise and Fall of the Knights Templar

The Order of the Temple, 1118–1314
A True History of Faith, Glory, Betrayal and Tragedy

THE RISE AND FALL OF THE KNIGHTS TEMPLAR

THE ORDER OF THE TEMPLE, 1118–1314
A TRUE HISTORY OF FAITH, GLORY, BETRAYAL AND TRAGEDY

by

Gordon Napier

SPELLMOUNT
Staplehurst

British Library Cataloguing in Publication Data:
A catalogue record for this book is available
from the British Library

ISBN 1-86227-199-2

First published in the UK in 2003 by
Spellmount Limited
The Old Rectory
Staplehurst
Kent TN12 0AZ

Tel: 01580 893730
Fax: 01580 893731
E-mail: enquiries@spellmount.com
Website: www.spellmount.com

1 3 5 7 9 8 6 4 2

Typeset in Palatino by MATS, Southend-on-Sea, Essex
Printed in Great Britain by
TJ International Ltd, Padstow, Cornwall

Contents

Map		vii
Acknowledgements		ix
Introduction and Historiography		xi
PART ONE *BEAUSEANT!*		1
I	Holy War	3
II	The Early Templars	15
III	The Templars' Rule	25
IV	The Fortunes of War in the Holy Land	37
V	Powers and Accomplishments	43
VI	The Loss of Jerusalem	55
VII	The Third Crusade and its Aftermath	69
VIII	The Fate of the Holy Land	79
PART TWO *BAPHOMET*		93
IX	The Aftermath of Acre	95
X	The Sleep of Reason	99
XI	The Downfall	105
XII	The Destruction of the Temple	109
XIII	Possible Non-Catholic Influences on the Templars	123
XIV	Trial and Terror	147
XV	The Templars Beyond France	155
XVI	Abolition and Aftermath	171
Epilogue	The Shadow of the Crusades	179
Appendix A	Modern Templars – Survival or Revival?	183
Appendix B	Grand Masters of the Knights Templar	191
Appendix C	Timeline	193
Addendum		196
Bibliography		197
Index		201

But will God indeed dwell
on the earth? behold, the heaven and
heaven of heavens cannot contain
thee; how much less will the house that
I have built?
(Solomon's prayer, 1 Kings 8:27)

Non nobis, non nobis, Domine, sed nomini
tuo da gloriam

Not unto us, not unto us O Lord, but unto thy name
give the glory

(Psalm spoken by the Knights Templar on the eve of battles)

CONSTANTINOPLE
Black Sea
NICAEA
BYZANTINE EMPIRE
(ANATOLIA)
EPHESUS
SULTANATE OF RUM
Tigris
COUNTY OF EDESSA
EDESSA
Dodecanese
Rhodes
ARMENIAN CILICIA
TARSUS
ATABEGS OF MOSUL
ANTIOCH
ALEPPO
NICOSIA
PRINCIPALITY OF ANTIOCH
EMIRATE OF ALEPPO
Cyprus
FAMAGUSTA
TORTOSA
RUAD
LIMASSOL
HOMS
Euphrates
TRIPOLI
Mediterranean Sea
BEIRUT
DAMASCUS
TYRE
ACRE
HAIFA
TIBERIAS (Lake Galilee)
EMIRATE OF DAMASCUS
CAESAREA
Hattin
NABLUS
Jordan
ALEXANDRIA
DAMIETTA
JAFFA
ASCALON
JERUSALEM
GAZA
BETHLEHEM
La Forbie
Dead Sea
MANSURAH
KERAK OF MOAB
TRANSJORDAN
CAIRO
KERAK OF MONTREAL
ARABIA
Nile
EGYPT
Red Sea
THE·HOLY·LAND·
·IN·THE
·MIDDLE·AGES·
·c.1150 AD.
DS ·2003·

Acknowledgements

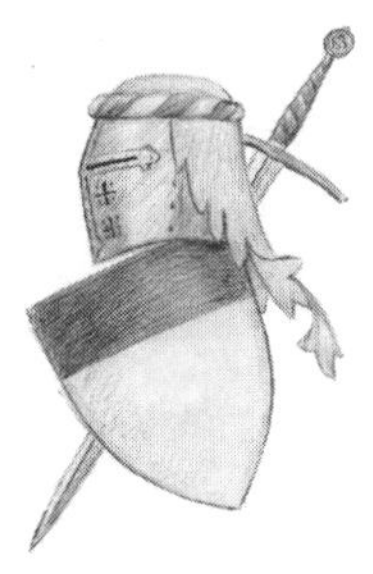

My thanks go to Jamie Wilson and everyone associated with Spellmount Publishing, especially David Grant, the editor. Appreciations also to my mother, Helen, for those laborious hours going through all this and for her help in straightening it out. I also wish to thank the history department at University College, Worcester, in particular Dr Darren Oldridge. To all of the above, and to the memory of my grandmother, Nancy, this book is dedicated.

Introduction and Historiography

The Knights Templar were a religious brotherhood founded in Jerusalem, in AD 1118, in the wake of the mysticism and bloodshed of the First Crusade. They were made up of idealistic European knights, who elected to live as warrior-monks. Their avowed purpose was to protect Christian pilgrims in the Holy Land, and to fight to safeguard the territory conquered by the Crusaders. According to the twelfth-century chronicle of Richard of Poitiers, the Templars:

> . . . live as monks, take vows of chastity, observe discipline at home and on the battlefield, eat in silence, and hold everything in common. They fight only against the infidel, and have spread themselves far and wide . . . They are called 'Soldiers of the Temple' because they have fixed the seat of their Order in the Portico of Solomon.[1]

To many they were the dutiful and courageous defenders of Christianity, and their dedication to the doomed cause of the Crusades was to become legendary. In battle after fierce and bloody battle against the Muslims, in Syria, Palestine and Egypt, the Templars fought to the brink of their own extinction. Then new brethren came to replace the dead – equally proud and equally ready to die for the Cross. Widely acclaimed for their boldness and tenacity, the Order received many gifts from devout Catholic nobles, and powers and accolades from admiring Popes.

The Grand Masters of the Knights Templar, at their height, were among the most highly honoured men in Christendom: advisers to princes, guardians of national treasuries, commanders of armies, lords of countless castles and internationally respected diplomats. Even at the turn of the fourteenth century, after the final failure of the Crusades, the brotherhood survived throughout Europe as an august landed elite, retaining unity, great wealth and political power.

Then suddenly, in 1307, they were set on by the regime of King Philip IV (known as Philip the Fair) of France – the land where the Order of the Temple was most extensively based. With shocking speed and seeming ease the King brought the Temple down. Soon Philip, who had extended his power over the papacy, had the Templars condemned and destroyed for crimes, astonishing to hear of, against the very faith they were supposed to defend. Ecclesiastical trials were convened, presided over by bishops and friars of the Mendicant Orders but dominated by the Inquisition. There, the Templars were revealed by their own testimony to be duplicitous heretics, Devil-worshippers, sodomites and traitors. They had conducted secret, nocturnal rituals involving spitting on the Cross, denying Christ, idolatry, and bestowing obscene kisses. Numerous Templars confessed to all these practices. By 1314 the Order was no more. In that year, after revoking his confession, the last Grand Master was burned alive.

Evidently, however, the royal jailers and Dominican Inquisitors, as was their proclivity, had used protracted torture in the obtaining of these damning depositions. Their agenda, perhaps always, was to seal the fate of the Knights Templar. Many contemporaries, including the poet Dante, maintained the Order's innocence. Philip's extensive debts and his imperialistic ambitions were both common knowledge, and destroying the Templars (and seizing their assets) provided a convenient solution to the former concern, while eliminating a potential barrier to the latter. However, it must have been a dangerous thing to voice this opinion too loudly. For many it was easier to accept the allegations as true, especially when they took into account the secretive ways of the Templars. Raimon Lull, the Mallorcan poet and mystic (who had learned Arabic and sought to convert the Muslims to Christianity), was among those who ultimately came to accept the Templars' guilt.

The issue remained politically controversial, as Templar innocence had consequences for the reputations of the monarchies of France and elsewhere, and for the infallibility claimed by the Supreme Pontiff. Therefore, the dark guilt of the Templars found its way as fact into official chronicles. The seventeenth-century writer Pierre Du Puy, librarian of the *Bibliothèque Royale*, wrote a history of the Templars affirming their guilt, and so defended the French monarchy from any posthumous slur by vindicating Philip IV.

Protestant–Catholic arguments, and the contention of Freemasonry, later fuelled the controversy. Some Protestant writers asserted the Templars' guilt, in the context of Catholic nefariousness. It was, therefore,

Catholic writers who began to question the matter. Canon R P M Jeune, Prior of Etival, championed the Order's innocence in 1789.

Then came the esotericists, such as orientalist Joseph von Hammer-Purgstall and Freemason Friedrich Nicolai, who, for very different reasons, linked the Templars with the Essenes and the ancient heresy of Gnosticism. Freemasonry is an esoteric society pledged to mutual support. Its initiates meet in lodges to conduct arcane rituals. Exiled Scottish Jacobite and Freemason Andrew Ramsey became Chancellor of the French Grand Lodge in the 1730s, and traced his society to the masons who built the Crusader castles. George Frederic Johnson, another Scotsman, was prominent in German Freemasonry. He believed the Templars had recovered profound secrets in the east, and that a number of them had escaped from Philip's clutches to Scotland, where they afterwards went underground as Freemasons. Meanwhile various rumours went around concerning the nature and the likely hiding place of the Templars' legendary treasure.

The theology within Freemasonry (and its revolutionary politics on the continent) led to hostility with Roman Catholicism. Von Hammer-Purgstall, a servant of the Catholic Austrian Chancellery, wrote of the guilt of the Templars, apparently wishing to discredit Freemasonry by association. He reproduced obscene Gnostic ceremonies, and mystic symbolism found in Templar buildings, and tried to prove links between the two. He suggested that the Knights Templar were originally orthodox, but at some stage were converted or corrupted. He supposed there to have existed a secret Rule, containing their *secret knowledge*, perhaps of ancient Egyptian origin. The Order gave itself over to pride and cupidity, selling out to the Infidel and the Devil. This Devil, in the Templars' trials, took the name of Baphomet. The occultist Elephas Levi produced a fatuous illustration of Baphomet as a hermaphroditic, winged demon, with the head of a goat. After this image entered wider circulation, the diabolical image of the Templars found popular acceptance.

W F Wilcke, meanwhile, believed the Templars secretly practised Islamic-style monotheism. Another writer of the nineteenth century, Hans Prates, believed the alleged practices of spitting on the Cross and denying Christ were simply tests of obedience, the purpose of which was later forgotten under the influences of various heresies – the failure of the Crusades having undermined the brotherhood's faith in Christianity.

After the French Revoluton of 1789, the last prison of the French royal family was the dungeon of the Paris Temple, the medieval tower which had been the Templars' chief stronghold in Europe. In 1808 the tower was demolished, ironically, because it had become a shrine for Royalists. Two years later, following Napoleon's conquests in Italy, the papal archives were brought to Paris. The playwright, lawyer and historian François Raynouard spent years scouring them for references to the Templars, finding nothing conclusive regarding mystical practices or Gnostic religious rites.

There was never conclusive material evidence for a secret, fearful and wicked cult within the Order. Subsequent archaeological finds, such as those from Templar-related sites in England, have been questionable. In 1837 one Dr Oliver excavated the Preceptory at Temple Bruer, which stood in ruins in Lincolnshire. He claimed to have found hidden vaulted chambers of stone, containing burnt and mutilated skeletons, which he linked to monstrous Templar rituals. Subsequently, however, any trace of these skeletons vanished. It seems the site was re-excavated by one William St John-Hope, who found the trapdoor Oliver described, although the stairs to the vault appeared to have been mysteriously removed. He saw a small oblong chamber and oven, but recorded no human remains. An underground room found in the Temple Church, London, has, meanwhile, been identified variously as a secret treasury or Chapter house, where secret rites may have been performed. Then there is the cave at Royston, near Baldock, Hertfordshire, carved in medieval times with curious religious imagery and arcane symbols, and approached through a passage, reminiscent of those described in some of the testimonies given at the trials of the Templars. Similar, bell-shaped caverns were to be found in the Holy Land, their purpose and function long forgotten.

In 1842 Charles G Addison, a Member of the Middle Temple (one of the two law societies that took over the former headquarters of the Knights Templar in London), wrote an accomplished history of the Templars, arguing with much common sense in their defence. He called von Hammer-Purgstall's charges 'extraordinary and unfounded', whilst Wilcke's German history seemed to have incorporated 'all the vulgar prejudices against the fraternity'. The Templars, Addison concluded, were 'plundered, persecuted and condemned to a cruel death by those who ought in justice to have been their defenders and supporters'.[2] Henry Charles Lea, the American writer of a history of the Inquisition, and H Finke sought, likewise, at the turn of the century, to prove the Templars' innocence; that the Templar confessions, as Bologna, their advocate, had said, proved only '. . . the helplessness of the victim, no matter how highly placed, when once the fatal charge of heresy was pressed against him . . . through the agency of the Inquisition.'[3]

Modern scholarship has generally continued to view the accusations made against the Order as false – the grafting of a pre-existing concept of a secret Devil-worshipping conspiracy onto an organisation innocent of such things. Instead, the Templars are seen as having been guilty of arrogance, intransigence and obsolescence. Norman Cohn argues that similar defamatory allegations had been falsely made to demonise earlier groups, such as the Waldensian and Cathar sects, and the Jews. Cohn attributes Philip IV's motives to deluded religious mania.

Malcolm Barber shows that the French Templars confessed after appalling suffering. He concludes that their confessions proved only the power of torture over an individual's mental and physical resistance. He, like Addison, cites the relationship between the confessions made in France and the denials from elsewhere (where less torture was applied) as proof of Templar innocence. He concludes that the notorious rituals, described in the articles of accusation, were merely appropriated from folklore concerning heretical groups. Barber attributes Philip IV's conviction that the Templars were heretics to self-deception. His diabolism veiled his true agenda – that of gaining land, power and money.

Yet there was always a clandestine aspect to the Templars, cloaking the Order in mystery. The brethren did close themselves off from society, and conducted their ceremonies and Chapters with all outsiders excluded, and thereby they invited sinister conclusions to be drawn. Moreover, the accusations made against the Templars, as we shall see, contained a peculiar aspect absent from the accusations made either against any earlier heretics or against later 'Witches' and 'Satanists'. This singular allegation, the adoration of a sacred, severed head, will be one of the things that this book will endeavour to explain, as well as addressing the circumstances surrounding the trials of the Templars. However, the story of the Order's rise to prominence is no less intriguing, or revealing of the times, than that of their fall. The story must be explored in order to account for the Templars' eventual demise. It begins with the ancient cult of Jerusalem, the Holy City, the capital of the Promised Land, without which the Templars would never have come to be.

NOTES

1 Maxwell-Stuart, P G, *Chronicles of the Popes*, p. 96.
2 Addison, Charles G, *The History of the Knights Templars*, p. 25.
3 Barber, Malcolm, *The Trial of the Templars*, p. 139.

Part One

Beauseant!

CHAPTER I
Holy War

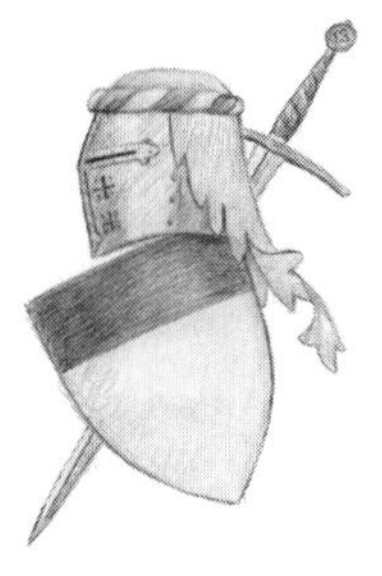

The Biblical King David, after smiting numerous enemies, conquered Jerusalem from the Jebusites, in the tenth century BC. Under his rule, the city became spiritually important for the Jews. It was not merely a capital city, it was the centre of the world. David brought to Jerusalem the mythical Ark of the Covenant, a box overlaid with pure gold, associated with Moses and invested with the power of the God of Israel. It contained the two stone tablets bearing the Ten Commandments that Moses had received from God, after he brought the Hebrew nation out of Egypt (Exodus 25:10–21). The Ark itself was given miraculous attributes: it could bring victory in battle against the enemies of the chosen people, bring blessings to the godly, or smite the ungodly with supernatural plagues and pyrotechnics. Guarded by winged cherubim of gold, it was installed by Solomon, the son of David, in a fabulous Temple above the city, built with assistance from Hiram, King of Tyre. Innumerable animals were sacrificed at its consecration, and the glory of the Lord filled the Temple in the form of a cloud.

In 722 BC the Assyrians crushed the northern kingdom of Israel. They later conquered all the surrounding lands, even Egypt. The small kingdom of Judah (later called Judaea) stood alone and encircled. The population of its capital, Jerusalem, swelled with refugees from the north. This was perhaps the first real holy war. The Hebrews destroyed the shrines of all other gods on their land, and put all their faith in their God. Yet, by the turn of the seventh century BC, the time of Jeremiah, Jerusalem alone remained defiant. At this time the Torah (holy book) of God first emerged; writings telling that the land was the Lord's gift, but that if the people disobeyed God and committed sins 'the land itself [would] vomit out her inhabitants' (Leviticus 18: 25).

The Assyrian Empire was eventually swallowed up by that of Babylon. Judah also fell. In 587 BC Solomon's Temple was demolished by Nabuchadnezzar, who took the Jews into exile in Mesopotamia. It was at this time that the remaining Old Testament books were largely written, but nowhere was the fate of the Ark recorded. On the Jews' return from exile, King Zerubbabel built a new, but presumably Arkless Temple on Mount Moriah, the site of the old. This Temple, in turn, was plundered by the invading Syrians in 169 BC. Jerusalem was recovered for the Jews by Judas Maccabeus, but lost to the Romans who invaded under Pompey in 63 BC. The greatest and last Temple was that of Herod the Great, who ruled the Jews as a client of the Roman Empire. Levite priests were even trained as masons and carpenters to build the edifice (according to Josephus), so that the new shrine need not be profaned by laymen.

Herod's Temple was the scene of a massacre as the Jewish revolt began. In AD 70 the Roman general and later Emperor, Titus Vespasianus, put down the Zealots and the Jews, who had temporarily won back their land, soaking Jerusalem in blood. He demolished the Temple, but for a portion of the west wall of its outer court, which he left as a monument to the Jewish defeat. (This remnant, known as the Wailing Wall, has remained deeply sacred in Judaism to this day.) Rather than submit to the Romans, the last Hebrew rebels, besieged at their mountain fortress of Masada, selected ten men to kill all their company; which they did before killing themselves. The remaining Jews, banished from Zion, were dispersed throughout the Empire.

In Jerusalem a sect had existed called the Nazarenes, or the Jerusalem Church. They adhered to the teachings of Jesus, who they believed had been a descendant of David and the long-prophesied Jewish Messiah. Jesus's message boiled down to 'Love God, love your neighbour'. He had wandered Galilee healing, performing miracles, teaching forgiveness and preaching repentance, so that souls might become worthy of the expected Kingdom of Heaven. His career, however, had ended with his crucifixion by the Jewish priests and the Roman authorities, as a blasphemer and rabble-rouser. His body was taken down from the Cross, and put in a tomb given by a wealthy Jew named Joseph of Arimathea. Christians believe he rose again, appearing first to Mary Magdalene, then to the disciples, delivering the teachings that could save mankind from death and the Devil, before ascending to Heaven.

Paul of Tarsus was an individual somewhat estranged from the original Christians, whom he had actively persecuted before his conversion, following his vision on the road to Damascus. Subsequently, he began preaching about Jesus Christ, who was Lord God, who had become man, lived a faultless life, and died in an act of sacrifice that made eternal life possible for mankind. Paul believed Jesus had literally risen from death, a view by no means unanimously upheld in the Jerusalem Church. Paul preached tirelessly to the Gentiles, and won converts in Rome, Greece and Asia Minor. The creed he espoused was, however, influenced by his own prejudices. It reflected, for example, some of the misogyny inherent in both Classical and Hebrew culture:

> Let your women keep silent in the churches: for it is not permitted unto them to speak; but they are commanded to be under obedience, as also saith the law. And if they learn anything, let them ask it of their husband at home . . . (1 Corinthians 14: 34–35).

Paulian Christianity began to spread through the Roman world. Christians, as they became more numerous, were periodically persecuted by the pagan authorities, and driven underground. By their refusal to acknowledge the divinity of the Emperor, and to fight in his wars, they were guilty of sedition. They were additionally accused of conducting ghastly rituals, where obscene kisses were exchanged, child-sacrifice, cannibalism and blood drinking occurred and wild orgies were engaged in. The insane Emperor Nero inaugurated a general persecution of Christians in AD 67, blaming them for a fire which had earlier destroyed much of Rome. Hundreds were tortured, crucified and burned, or fed to wild beasts.[1] Saint Paul himself was beheaded, that same year, in Rome. Many Christians died bravely for their beliefs, and inspired others by the way they embraced martyrdom. Christianity's spread continued, therefore. Believers in Christ formed a Church across the Empire, with priests emerging to administer to the spiritual needs of their flock, and to preach what they regarded as the word of God.

The Gospels of the evangelists Matthew, Mark and Luke appeared after about AD 70, containing accounts of the life and teachings of Christ. Mark's was the oldest, the others derivations produced in Syria, though all were based on a vanished original. Later came the more mystical Gospel of John, probably a Greek, who also wrote the book of Revelation, containing cryptic prophecies about the reign of the demonic Antichrist, the Last Judgement, the Heavenly Jerusalem and the Second Coming of Jesus; subjects that would obsess Christian minds through the centuries, and that would significantly influence their actions. These texts were accepted, along with the Jewish Old Testament, for inclusion in the Christian Bible. Other writings were rejected as apocryphal.

Tertullian, in the second century, defined heresy as putting one's own judgement above the teachings of the priests of the Church, and deviating in one's beliefs from the doctrines which the apostles received from Christ. In AD 330, under the Emperor Constantine, Christianity became the official religion of the Empire. Constantine gave the Empire a new,

Christian capital in Byzantium on the Bosphorus, which he renamed Constantinople. Here he presided over a succession of religious councils, to establish the doctrines of the Church. Church fathers built on the work of St Paul to construct a hierarchical ideology that supported the established social order, thereby gaining acceptability with the conservative ruling classes. The priesthood, especially bishoprics, became a preserve of the aristocracy. Obedience was a central tenet.

From Peter's and Paul's fear of women arose a belief that sex was of the Devil. Therefore Eve's daughters were soon forbidden to be priests, and priests and the religious were expected to be celibate. Meanwhile others, including the disenfranchised poor, and many women, were drawn to other forms of faith, such as Arianism, Montanism, Gnosticism and Manichaeism. These could offer a more direct spirituality (free of highly structured, mediating priesthoods) and put less emphasis on the knowing of one's place. Catholic Christianity saw such ideas as dangerous and heretical.

One former heretic was Augustine, who was turned from his early ways by reading St Paul's warnings against sexual licentiousness. Augustine became Bishop of Hippo in North Africa in AD 391. Hitherto, the Church had advocated absolute pacifism. Christ had said:

> You have heard that it hath been said, An eye for an eye and a tooth for a tooth: But I say unto you, That ye resist not evil: but whosoever shall smite thee on thy right cheek, turn to him the other also. (Matthew 5: 38–39).

Christ's message was to love your enemies, bless them that curse you and do good to them that hate you. Therefore, as St Martin expressed it a century before Augustine's time: 'I am a soldier of Christ, I must not fight.' Augustine, however, argued that a defensive war could be justified, and that God also sanctioned holy wars against unbelievers.[2] Augustine went on to influence monasticism, where communities of brothers could live apart from the temptations of society, armed in Christ to conquer the cravings of the body. Augustine's writings later inspired a Rule (set of instructions) to govern the conduct of these monks. His writings became enormously influential, especially on St Benedict, who in AD 529 founded the first Monastic Order to become part of the Church in the west. Certain clerics, meanwhile, began to accuse the members of rival sects of the same abominable rites as the pagan Romans had accused the early Christians of, and soon the Christian establishment, likewise, began to persecute its theological and political foes.

With the conversion of Emperor Constantine, Jerusalem became Christianity's foremost Holy City. There was a desire among the faithful to trace the course of Christ's Passion on Earth. Pilgrims journeyed there to pray at the Holy Sepulchre, the tomb of Christ, and to venerate the True Cross, miraculously unearthed nearby in AD 289 by Constantine's mother, the Empress Helena. The Emperor soon ordered the building of a great church, housing both the Cross and the tomb. It was called the Church of the Resurrection. Many also beat a path to the Church of the Nativity in Bethlehem, enshrining the birthplace of Jesus.

The Roman Empire gradually lost its western provinces to invading tribes of pagan Goths – Germanic peoples whom the Romans considered barbarians, displaced from their own lands north of the Imperial frontier by the marauding Huns. Rome itself was sacked by one such tribe, the Visigoths, in AD 400. After the fall of Rome, however, Jerusalem and the Holy Land remained in the hands of the Eastern, or Byzantine Empire, and the traffic of pilgrims continued without interruption. Rome, meanwhile, survived as the seat of the most powerful bishops, called Popes, who dispatched monks to convert the Frankish and Germanic chiefs, and to re-establish Christianity in the west.

The Arab prophet Muhammad began preaching in AD 622 in Mecca. This was the holy city of the Quraysh tribe, containing an ancient shrine called the Ka'ba, that was supposedly built by the prophet Abraham. Muhammad claimed to have received revelations from the Archangel Gabriel – revelations that were subsequently set down in the Holy Book, the Koran. Acting on his divine inspiration, Muhammad purged the Ka'ba of all idols, except for a black stone, sacred to a singular God, Allah. The Koran directed believers to have no qualms about resisting evil:

> Fight for the sake of God those that fight against you, but do not attack them first, God does not love aggressors. Slay them wherever you find them, drive them out of the places from which they drove you. Idolatry is more grievous than bloodshed. Do not fight them in the precincts of the holy mosque unless they attack you there. If they attack you put them to the sword. Thus shall the unbeliever be rewarded. But if they mend their ways, know that God is forgiving and merciful.
>
> Fight against the unbeliever until idolatry is no more, and God's religion supreme. But if they desist, fight none except against evil-doers. (The Koran, The Cow or *Al Baqarah* 2: 182–3)

In time the Meccans drove Muhammad and his followers out of the city, forcing them to remove to Medina. However, Muhammad returned to Mecca with an army, as an aggressor, raiding their camel caravans, then taking Mecca itself by storm. Peaceful means had failed to win people over to Allah. Muhammad decided that it was necessary to convert them by force.

In the years that followed, his preaching inspired the nomadic peoples of Arabia to embark on their great enterprise of evangelical imperialism. Islam, the new religion, emphasised submission to the will of Allah, moral behaviour, ritualised prayer, pilgrimage to Mecca, fasting during Ramadan, charity and hospitality. It also subordinated women. 'Men have authority over women because God has made the one superior to the other and because they spend their wealth to maintain them' (Koran, Women, or *Al Nisa*, 4:34). The religion also permitted slavery and blood vengeance: 'Believers, retaliation is decreed for you in bloodshed, a slave for a slave, a female for a female . . .' (Koran, The Cow; 2: 178–9).

Jihad was the holy war that Muhammad's preaching unleashed. Some Muslims interpreted their duty to Allah, the beneficent, the merciful, as being to convert the world to his worship by the sword. *Jihad* promised these holy warriors material rewards: booty, concubines and slaves, while greater rewards awaited the fallen. Many envisaged a paradise harem where seventy alluring houris would ensure that each martyr would live eternally in bliss. On all sides they would be offered golden vessels and cups filled with all that their appetites could desire.

Muhammad's successors began by conquering Persia. Byzantium at this time was already beset from the north by the Avars and Bulgars, and could not defend its middle-eastern provinces against the Muslims. Moreover the Syrian, Palestinian and Egyptian Christians mainly adhered to Monophysitism, the doctrine that Jesus had a singular, divine nature (as opposed to the prevailing orthodoxy that Christ had both a human and a divine nature; the human aspect necessary for his sacrifice to have meaning). The Byzantine Emperor Justinian had tried and failed to reconcile these views which had threatened the religious unity of his Empire, and subsequently the Monophysites had been persecuted as heretics. Such was the resulting resentment of the Byzantine Greeks among their middle-eastern subjects that the Monophysites did little to resist the invading Muslims.

After Muhammad, the spiritual and temporal rulers of Islam were the Caliphs. Caliph Omar conquered Syria in AD 636, taking Jerusalem the following year. It became a Holy City for Islam. Omar's successors built the Dome of the Rock Mosque, where once had stood Solomon's Temple. The rock it enclosed, once the foundation stone of the Jewish Temple's Holy of Holies, was sacred to Muslims also. From it, they believed, Muhammad had flown in spirit to Heaven. Omar's succesor, Othman, captured Cyprus and attacked Constantinople itself, burning the Byzantine fleet into the water.

The succeeding Umayyad Empire, centred on Damascus, spread Islam as far as Afghanistan in the east, while in the west it overwhelmed north Africa and, by AD 711, Spain. The *Jihad* advanced well beyond the Pyrenees. Muslim armies sacked Bordeaux in 732, and burned its churches. They were only checked by the Franks at the Battle of Poitiers. Moslem pirates, meanwhile, harried the coastal regions of Italy. They took Sicily and, in 846, even landed an army of raiders in Italy and drove the Pope from Rome.

For all their militancy, the Umayyads and later the Abbasids, the dynasty of Caliphs who ruled Islam from Baghdad, permitted their conquered people to practise their chosen religions – at the price of paying an extra tax. The Koran forbade believers to have friendships with Christians and Jews. It did, however, accord them some respect as fellow 'people of the book' and conceded that the Bible contained some light. Omar had formally guaranteed to Patriarch Sophronius the safety of Christians and to respect the sanctity of their churches. His successors had the wisdom to leave alone the pilgrims, who continued to visit the Holy Sepulchre, and were a useful source of revenue. Meanwhile, heterodox varieties of Christianity actually flourished in Islamic dominions, free of persecution by the established Churches of Byzantium and Rome.

Christian Europe initially did little to stave off the encroaching forces of Islam. Although there were campaigns to expel the Arabs from northern Spain, in which Norman knights participated, the concept of a Christian holy war was not yet born. Rather there was increasing tension between the western lands, who looked to the Pope in Rome for their spiritual leadership, and the Greek Byzantines, with a divinely appointed Emperor and an Orthodox Patriarch in Constantinople. A schism divided the churches of east and west in 1054. After this rift the hostilities festered. Norman mercenaries had made themselves powerful, championing the Pope in Italy, and taking Sicily for themselves from the Arabs. They began to covet the wealth of Byzantium also, and plotted an invasion of Greece.

In the meantime, the Seljuk Turks were overwhelming the Middle East. The Turks were warlike marauders, one of the nomadic tribes periodically belched out of the Steppes of Asia. They adopted Islam after their conquest of Baghdad. The Arab Caliph became a mere figurehead, with a Turkish Sultan taking the real power in a Great Seljuk Empire. In 1065 the Turks became masters of Jerusalem, decimating the population. They began to persecute, rob and terrorise Christian pilgrims. Stories were told that Turkish swordsmen turned devotees back from the gates of the Holy Sepulchre, if they could not pay the gold demanded. It was also said that they dragged the Partiarch away by his hair, and held him for ransom. Soon other Turkomans had moved into Anatolia (central Turkey). They slaughtered the Byzantine army at Manzikert in 1071, and soon afterwards consolidated their domination of Asia Minor by capturing Nicaea. They called their state the Sultanate of Rum, because the Byzantines they subjugated had considered themselves Romans. The Turks were on the doorstep of Constantinople, the greatest Christian metropolis. The Byzantine Emperor Alexius wrote to Pope Urban II, requesting western military aid, emphasising the plight of Jerualem and the threat to all Christendom posed by the Turks.

The response was the First Crusade, called in AD 1095 by the Pope at the Council of Clermont. The huge crowds massed in a field to hear him speak. Urban II called for an armistice between Christian barons so they could unite and fight for Christ. They should abandon sinful wars and embark on a holy war which in itself would cleanse away all their sins. The property of those who 'took the Cross', that is to say those who swore to fight in the Crusade, would be protected by the Church. The Church would exempt them from taxes and guarantee their salvation. Zion, the mystical Holy City, waited for them, the birthright of Christ, usurped by the *Saracen* or foreigner. The Pope's audience responded with shouts of 'God wills it!'

Some 30,000 knights and civilians, monks, holy hermits and ordinary people answered the call, of which around two thirds ultimately perished. Among those who sewed cloth crosses to their clothes and left for the Holy Land were the mighty, who had kingdoms to gain, and the meek, who had nothing to lose. Some participants were opportunistic knights, in it primarily for plunder and glory. For such men, the Crusade offered a timely outlet for their passion for warfare (the defining characteristic of the Frankish ruling class) as well as a moral justification for it. For ages the knightly cult of warrior pride, with its code of honour that demanded violent retribution in kind, had been irreconcilable with the teachings of the Church. Ironically it would have accorded more easily with the Islamic attitude to fighting. Now, though, any religious dilemma had been conveniently removed, and many knights were eager to start killing the Infidel on behalf of Christ. Many Crusaders, however, undertook the enterprise at great cost. Knowing and dreading the risks involved, and how they would suffer, they fought for the Holy Sepulchre as a pious sacrifice. They were motivated by sincere religious conviction, and saw the Crusade as a divine mission. Others probably just did not want to miss the great adventure. Most of them knew little about the Muslims, except that they had been the enemies of the legendary heroes Charlemagne and Roland and had a particular reputation for ferocity and courage. The Muslims were also erroneously supposed to be idol worshippers.

The first Crusaders to set off were a mass of ordinary civilians, led by a ragged visionary from Picardy named Peter the Hermit. Many poor peasants went, leaving regions ravaged by famine, and taking their whole families. The cult of poverty was chrystalising, and some knights had sold up in order to accompany the poor pilgrim army, and to protect 'God's poor'.[3] The 'People's Crusade' stole from and killed the Jews and others they found on their route through the Rhineland and the Near East, to fund their progress. Most of Peter's followers were in turn killed by the Turks in Anatolia, two months before the more organised armies of the warrior barons began to muster at Constantinople. The Byzantine Emperor sought oaths of allegiance from the Latin commanders before ferrying their forces to Anatolia, surely aware that they privately desired to conquer principalities for themselves.

Somehow the ill co-ordinated venture progressed. Initially the Latin Crusaders co-operated with the Byzantines, whose fleet assisted in the capture of Nicaea. Then the Turks, who had scorched the earth before the Christians, attacked in force at Dorylaeum. The Normans, under the warlord Bohemond, were trapped by the Sultan's mounted archers, but held firm until relieved by the armies of Godfrey de Bouillon, Duke of Lorraine and Raymond de Saint Gilles, Count of Toulouse, who routed the enemy. Several other battles followed, as the Crusade pushed on through Anatolia and Armenia. Early in 1098, however, Alexius heard false reports from deserters (including Stephen of Blois, the cowardly son-in-law of William the Conqueror) that the Crusaders had been wiped out by hunger and fighting, outside the formidably defended city of Antioch in northern Syria. Alexius turned back to Constantinople with his reinforcements. In fact, the half-starved Crusaders had gained entry to Antioch, only to be besieged in turn by a Muslim relief-force. Inspired by visions of saints, the Crusaders launched out and, by some miracle, repulsed the enemy. In January 1099 they marched on to their goal, believing that God was with them still, even if the Byzantines were no longer there. The Crusaders carved out four Latin Christian realms around Edessa, Antioch, Tripoli in Syria and, eventually, Jerusalem.

Temporary Muslim disunity was a considerable factor contributing to this otherwise unlikely outcome. The Turkish (Sunni Muslim) rulers of Damascus, Mosul and Aleppo, were jealous of each other, and bore little love for the Fatimid (Shi'a Muslim) Egyptians, who had recently taken Jerusalem, with tacit Byzantine approval. Many lesser Emirs (Muslim lords), meanwhile, simply bribed the Crusaders to pass on, such was the terror these invaders inspired. The beleaguered pilgrim-army reached the Holy City on 7 June 1099.

By this time, the Muslims, to thwart the invaders, had poisoned every well in the area outside the city, felled all the trees and expelled all the native Christians. The Crusaders besieged Jerusalem in the summer heat for over a month, without adequate food or water, and lacking siege equipment. They processed barefoot around the Holy City, and visited the Mount of Olives, praying and singing psalms. To taunt them, the Muslim soldiers of the Egyptian governor raised on the walls crosses, torn from the city's churches. They spat on them, and subjected them to abuse and mockery.

Some fresh supplies arrived by sea, from English and Genoese ships that sailed into Jaffa, a Levantine port abandoned by the Muslims. Wood was found and siege towers built. The Crusaders commenced a determined assault, but were repeatedly repelled by burning pitch called 'Greek fire' being hurled down at them from the walls. Several days later, on 15 July 1099, Jerusalem fell bloodily to the armies of Geoffrey de Bouillon and Raymond de Saint Gilles. The preachers had aroused in the Crusaders an uncontrollable hatred of the unbelievers. This hatred had been inflamed by the suffering they had endured and the sacrilege they had witnessed during the siege. The victorious Crusaders rampaged through the Holy City, killing and looting. The chiefs could not or would not control the bloodlust of their men. Some of them massacred the Muslims who retreated to the Al-Aqsa mosque on Temple Mount. The Mount had been captured by a Norman knight, Tancred de Hauteville, a nephew of Bohemond. Tancred had seized the treasures of the mosques there, and had accepted offers of a great ransom in exchange for the lives of the refugees. He had raised his banner over the sanctuary to show that it was under his protection. It did not stop other Crusaders turning the mosque into a slaughterhouse.

Other men, in their morbid frenzy, set fire to the Jews in their synagogues, or killed indiscriminately in the streets. 'They desired,' wrote Fulcher of Chatres, 'that this place so long contaminated by the superstitions of the pagan inhabitants, should be cleansed from their contagion.'[4] Accounts tell of mountains of mutilated and dismembered bodies. With the massacre still raging, the Crusader nobles went to the Holy Sepulchre to offer up thanks to Heaven. Of the Muslims, only the Egyptian Governor and his men, who surrendered the Citadel of David and its treasure to Count Raymond, were spared.

Raymond refused the throne of Jerusalem. Geoffrey declined to call himself King in the city where Jesus had worn the Crown of Thorns, but reigned with the title of Protector of the Holy Sepulchre. Geoffrey was succeeded a year later by his brother, Baldwin of Edessa, who had no such scruples. King Baldwin ruled until 1118 when he died, leaving the throne to his cousin, Baldwin of le Bourg.

A Catholic Patriarch was installed in Jerusalem, and a feudal kingdom rapidly established, dominated by the race the Turks knew as the *Firenj*. These Frenchmen, through faith and arrogance, imagined they could rule a faraway land, between two great and greatly affronted Muslim powers, on their own. The territory was also called the Latin Kingdom (Latins here meaning the people of western European stock, Roman Catholic as opposed to Eastern Orthodox Christian in faith). These latest conquerors of this troubled region rejected any assistance or interference from Constantinople. Thus they snubbed the only local ally they might have had. It became clear that European commitment to the Holy Land could not end with the victories of the First Crusade.

NOTES

1 Read, Piers Paul, *The Templars*, p. 23 (citing the Roman historian Tacitus).
2 Ibid., p. 74; also, Oldenbourg, Zoé, *The Crusades*, p. 47. Oldenbourg discusses the religious effects of the concept of Christ as a warrior King. In *Revelation*, Jesus appears as a vanquisher of evil leading armies of angels, as well as the more usual metaphor of the martyred lamb.
3 Oldenbourg, op. cit., p. 49. The cult of sacred poverty was probably related to popular apocalypticism – poverty was spiritually desirable. It seems the poor Crusaders believed that God had called them to Jerusalem to bring about and witness the triumphant second coming of Christ.
4 Jones, Terry, and Ereira, Alan, *Crusades*, p. 53 (quoting Fulcher of Chatres).

CHAPTER II
The Early Templars

When news of victory was brought back to Europe, there was a fresh wave of pilgrims to the Holy Land (known by the Crusaders as *Outremer,* or 'overseas'). People believed that God's will had triumphed, and naturally assumed that the undertaking would be less dangerous now. However, those bringing the news were most likely to be the returning veterans of the campaign who had done their sacred duty and now dreamed of home. Thus, in the aftermath, there was a critical shortage of fighting men in the Crusader states – certainly too few to both defend their borders and keep order within. This resulted in a perilous situation for the pilgrims. The Turks were still masters in Anatolia, so most of the pilgrims arrived by sea, usually on ships chartered from Genoa or Venice. Crowds of people of all sorts trod the road from the coast to Jerusalem, only to fall easy prey to bands of fugitive Muslims and bandits based in the mountains bordering the coast. Hostile Muslim elements remained at large within other parts of the Crusader state additionally, making it dangerous for pilgrims to pass on to Bethlehem, with its Church of the Nativity, or Nazareth and the Jordan, where Jesus had lived and been baptised.

William of Tyre, a later Levantine Bishop and statesman, writing in the 1170s, chronicled the birth of the Knights Templar as follows:

> In this same year [1118] certain noble men of knightly rank, religious men, devoted to God and fearing him, bound themselves to Christ's service in the hands of the Lord Patriarch. They promised to live in perpetuity . . . without possessions, under vows of chastity and obedience. Their foremost leaders were the venerable men Hugues de

> Payens and Godfroi de St Omer. Since they had no church or fixed abode, the King gave them for a time a dwelling place in the south wing of the palace, near the Lord's Temple . . . Their primary duty . . . enjoined upon them by the Lord Patriarch and other Bishops, for the remission of sins, was that of protecting the roads and routes against attacks of robbers and brigands. This they did especially in order to safeguard pilgrims.[1]

Presumably Hugues de Payens (or, as his name is sometimes given, Payns) and his eight identified companions were not alone in this devout work. Hardy and resourceful as the medieval knight was, a mere nine of them could scarcely have made much difference to the security of such a kingdom. They may have had common soldiers under them whom the chroniclers considered unworthy of note.

The nine knights were of noble birth, and hailed from the vicinity of Champagne and Burgundy. Their attitudes would have been formed by their native culture, feudal and warlike, but their conviction in Christianity, as they understood it, would have been absolute. The cult of sacred poverty also evidently impressed them. This spirit had earlier been exemplified by Peter the Hermit and Walter Sans-Avoir, a knight who had given away all his possessions to the poor, and who had died outside the walls of Nicaea during the Crusade. The concept was blossoming at this time into the finest ideal of Christian Chivalry: that instead of might automatically being right the great should serve the weak. The pilgrims were widely admired as people who had sacrificed worldly security for the dangers and discomforts of the journey, becoming strangers in strange lands. Pilgrimage makers became God's poor, and in serving them, such well-born knights as the Templars aspired to serve God. Or at least, that seems to have been a major part of it.

Hugues de Payens was a vassal (and probably cousin) of Hugh the Count of Champagne, and came from a village near Troyes. He had visited Jerusalem at least twice previously, once in the company of the Count himself, in 1104. There is some contention concerning whether de Paynes had fought in the First Crusade, and whether he had gone on pilgrimage after the death of his wife (a lady who was, according to a Scottish Masonic tradition, a member of the Norman branch of the noble St Clair/Sinclair family). The Count of Champagne was certainly one of the greatest aristocrats of the time, and his lands were all but independent of the King of France. The Count's dynasty would contribute substantially to the leadership of later Crusades, marry into the royal houses of France and Jerusalem, and patronise great poets such as the author of the first French Grail romance, Chrétien de Troyes. They were also generous patrons of the Cistercian monks.

Hugues de Payens, as the leader of the knights on Temple Mount, was styled the Master of the Temple. The brotherhood came to be known as the Knights Templar, or in full, the Poor Knights of Christ and the Temple of Solomon. They were otherwise known as the Militia of the Temple, or simply as Templars. Emulating the pilgrims, the original Templars embraced lives of poverty. They took vows before the Patriarch, in the Church of the Resurrection, to live the lives of monks, but also to combat the Bedouin bandits and the raiders on the passes between Jaffa and the Holy City.

Baldwin II, King of Jeruslem, granted the Templars the former Al-Aqsa mosque, to use as their base. A decade after the Crusaders massacred the Muslim faithful there, the fourth most sacred shrine in Islam thus became the headquarters of a Christian brotherhood that existed primarily in opposition to Islam. The size and importance of this building, which the King, by some accounts, had earlier planned to make his own palace, makes it all the harder to believe that the original Templars were so few in number (unless the knights had an undeclared purpose that Baldwin was party to). Adjacent stood Beit Allah, the Dome of the Rock, Islam's third most sacred shrine, likewise converted for Christian use, with a great gold cross erected above it where the crescent had formerly risen. Catholic priests celebrated Mass there daily. The court between these buildings was also granted to the Templars. A number of local barons and prelates pledged to support the knights with various revenues. Whatever else they were doing in Jerusalem, they surely had been seen to be acting in accordance with their professed cause.

As well as taking up arms in defence of pilgrims, and striving to lead pure and exemplary lives, the original Knights Templar apparently became involved in the politics of the region from an early stage. They were trusted by the King as envoys and, perhaps, as advisers. A decade after their formation, the King sent a number of Templars to Europe, on a diplomatic mission. He charged them, among other things, with persuading Fulk, Count of Anjou, to come east and to marry Baldwin's heiress, Melisende. Fulk, gruff and middle-aged,was one of the most powerful lords in France. He was a veteran warrior, who had already visited the Holy Land and become an honorary associate of the Templars. He would certainly have met Hugues de Payens, whom he now entertained at Le Mans, in April 1128. He may have encountered the young princess too. Fulk's son by an earlier marriage, Geoffrey Plantagenet, had married Matilda, the heiress to the English throne, so the Anjevin dynasty was on the make. By marrying the beautiful, half Armenian Princess Melisende, Fulk himself would become heir to the Kingdom of Jerusalem. He would bring with him the protection of his own overlord, the Capetian King of France. Baldwin II needed such a man to succeed him in Jerusalem, to prevent one of the ever ambitious barons of the Crusader states from making a bid for power.

Baldwin II also desperately required fighting men. The Templars needed to recruit more soldiers for the 'good fight' as a matter of some urgency.[2] Baldwin saw the extension of the Order of the Temple as critical in preserving the Latin kingdom, by keeping alive the Crusading enthusiasm of the west. Lands in Europe would be essential too, for raising money and, to some extent, for producing supplies for armies to the east. The Templars might become independent of Baldwin's power once their European estates were established, but this would at least mean that the King would not have to pay them. The need for men to police the pilgrim routes was also pressing. At Eastertide in 1119, three hundred pilgrims were killed and sixty enslaved by Saracen insurgents, at a pool, on the road from Jerusalem to Jordan.

Another influential personality in France and beyond was Abbot Bernard of Clairvaux, a highly persuasive preacher and a spiritual force to be reckoned with. Bernard was related to André de Montbard, who was one of the nine founders of the Templars and who would become their fifth Grand Master. King Baldwin dispatched André and a companion with a letter to the Abbot, containing the following:

> Baldwin by the Grace of the Lord Jesus Christ, King of Jerusalem, Prince of Antioch, to the venerable father Bernard, Abbot of Clairvaux, health and regard.
>
> The brothers of the Temple, whom the Lord hath deigned to raise up . . . for the defence of the kingdom, desiring to obtain from the Holy See the confirmation of their institution, and a rule for their particular guidance, have decided to send you these two knights André and Gondemar, men as much distinguished by their military exploits as by the splendour of their birth, to obtain from the Pope the approbation of their Order, and to dispose his holiness to send succour and subsidies against the enemies of the faith, reunited in their design to destroy us, and to invade our Christian territories.
>
> Well knowing the weight of your mediation with God and his vicar on earth . . . we have thought fit to confide in you these important matters . . . The statutes we ask of you should be so ordered and arranged as to be reconcilable with the tumult of the camp and the profession of arms.[3]

Bernard of Clairvaux was born in 1090. His father was the aristocratic Burgundian Crusader Tiscelin Sorrel, and his mother was Aleth, probable half sister of André de Montbard. Bernard had been well educated before doing a stint of military service in a fortress of the Duke of Burgundy. Perhaps it was then that he formed his low opinion of secular warriors and grew obsessed with personal purity. As a youth (according to a later book of Saints' 'Lives') he had jumped into a pool of freezing water, to 'cool from the heat of carnal longing'. Later Bernard went to pray before a wooden statue of the Virgin, whilst suffering a crisis of faith. As he came to the words in his chant '*monstram esse matrem*' (show thyself a mother), Sainte Mary appeared to him in a vision, and let three drops of milk fall to his mouth from her divine breast.[4] This mystic experience inspired Bernard's lifelong faith, and caused him to become a monk. He went on to revive the moribund Cistercian Order, based in the monastery of Cîteaux, modelling it in his own image.

Bernard sought purity through the most austere poverty and absolute chastity. He reacted against the indolence and luxury that had come to pervade mainstream Cluniac Monasticism, and advocated obeying the Rule of St Benedict to the letter. He deliberately founded his monasteries, such as Clairvaux, in the most barren of places, which his colonies of monks, in their white habits, would transform by working the land themselves, rather than employing servants. Bernard founded one hundred and sixty such monasteries. The Cistercian ideology was reflected in their church architecture – geometric, pure and austere, and normally bare of towers, painting or sculpture. The Count of Champagne paid for much of this building work.[5]

Bernard was impressed by the mission of the Templars. He saw the brotherhood as a way to spiritually regenerate a caste of men whom he believed to be vain, brutal, worldly and greedy. The knightly Order he envisaged would bring these errant cavaliers humility, discipline, salvation and purpose, and channel their violence towards the service of the Church. These knights, armed with faith, would fear neither demon nor man. Bernard worked on the Templars' behalf to obtain the convocation of an ecclesiastical council. Meanwhile Hugues de Payens and the other Templars (Brothers Geoffroi de St Omer, Payen de Montdidier, Goral, Bisol and Archembald de St Amand) were received by the Pope in Rome. These men were present again, along with a papal legate, several archbishops, and the various prelates at the Council of Troyes, in 1129. Abbot Bernard chaired the council. Despite the fever that gripped him, he dominated the proceedings. Thanks to the formidable Abbot's enthusiastic support, the Knights Templar were officially incorporated into the Church. The only voice of dissent came from the Bishop of Orléans, a 'succubus and sodomite', in the judgement of one scathing chronicler.[6]

The first Templars were experienced knights, with blood connections to powerful families. This to some extent explains their favourable reception from the partisan King of Jerusalem.[7] Several great nobles joined the Templars as honorary members, even before their official sanction. Fulk d'Anjou did so in Jerusalem in 1120, as a married brother, or lay associate. He bequeathed thirty pounds of silver to them yearly. Such men hoped to gain the spiritual rewards of the Temple through their patronage of it, while being spared the need to submit to the harsh discipline of the Order, or to give up too many of the pleasures of the flesh. The Count of Champagne, likewise, joined as an honorary member in 1125, whilst on his third pilgrimage. As Hugues de Payens (the knight who became leader of the Templars) was from the Count's land, this meant that the Count, in theory, by joining the Templars, was swearing allegiance to his own vassal. Abbot Bernard of Clairvaux praised the Count's deed as one of eminent merit in the sight of God.

Important backers such as the Count were a power behind the scenes, together with Abbot Bernard, and possibly the Scottish Sinclair/St Clair Earls of Rosslyn (apparently relations of de Payens' estranged/late wife, Catherine). The backers' initial design could simply have been to found a Cistercian community in Jerusalem, but, as Baldwin's letter showed, Jerusalem needed soldiers before monks. Another agenda of the aristocrats, some believe, related specifically to the Temple of Solomon. The knights were often taciturn, especially about their activities on Temple Mount, and it has been suggested that they might secretly have carried out certain excavations. Templar artefacts have allegedly been discovered in a tunnel below the site, dug or discovered during the knights' first years there, seeming to lead towards the centre of the outcrop.[8] Possibly they were seeking lost religious texts or holy relics for the Cistercians. Relics were credited with miraculous spiritual and healing powers. Because of these, they attracted pilgrims and were worth more than their weight in gold. Recent writers have speculated that behind the Templars' public activities was what amounted to a secret quest for some object of power, such as the Ark of the Covenant, or the Holy Grail. Crusaders were indeed always on the hunt for relics, although these tended to relate to New Testament personalities and Christian saints. Many Crusaders had ascribed their deliverance at Antioch to the 'Holy Spear' that appeared by providence there. The 'True Cross', actually just a bigger than average fragment of it, was found in Jerusalem, and encased in a gorgeous, crucifix-shaped reliquary of gold and precious stones.

Medieval people were not all as blindly credulous, or superstitious, when it came to relics, as they are often portrayed. The Norman contingent at Antioch, for example, showed some scepticism, when the Holy Spear was unearthed miraculously by a visionary peasant affiliated to the Provençal faction, at that critical moment during the First Crusade.[9] Religious relics were enormously important, however, and were a preoccupation of the age, especially objects from Christ's Passion, and the bones of saints. The greatest cathedrals were often built to house them. The desire to obtain such artefacts had been among the motivating factors for the Crusade. Later Crusaders would march out to war behind the True Cross, in its bejewelled reliquary, as if it possessed the talismanic potency of the Ark of the Covenant, and would bring victory over the Saracens.

The Knights Templar would share with the Knights Hospitaller the honour of escorting the Cross into battle. It could be said that the Ark from the Temple was the prototype for all holy relics, the first object in the Judaeo-Christian tradition to be held to accommodate heavenly power here on earth, to be physical proof of the divine, and that could be possessed only by those chosen by God for the honour.

During the first-century Jewish war, the Temple of Herod was one of the places where the patriots made a desperate stand against the mighty Roman legions of Titus. It is true that elsewhere Jewish groups, such as the Essenes, buried important texts and other treasures in a bid to keep them from the Romans. Titus (completing the work of Vespasian, his father) demolished the Temple, and paraded its treasures through Rome in triumph, but there could have been other things hidden below. It does not seem, though, that the Templars were any more destined to discover the Ark than the Romans had been. Whether they sought it, and whether they found anything else remains subject to conjecture. It has been suggested, without direct proof, that besides a cache of treasure, the knights discovered scrolls written in ancient times, revealing to them such information as may have changed the foundation of their faith – perhaps including the 'true' teachings of Christ, or some new insight into His relationships with John the Baptist, or Mary Magdalene. They may, alternatively (or at the same time), have stumbled across the lost knowledge of ancient Egypt, transmitted through Moses or King Solomon, or the Gnostics. Others suggest that they may have found the embalmed head of St John, or even of Jesus himself, and that this would inspire a new occult focus within their Order, or at least among their inner circle. Of all these far-fetched ideas, perhaps the most plausible is that the Order truly hoped to locate the Ark of the Covenant, and that this remained an undeclared interest of theirs throughout the two centuries during which they constantly professed and died for Catholic Christianity.

In 1119 a Crusader army was wiped out by a Muslim force under Ilgazi, the Emir of Mardin, at the 'Field of Blood'. At this battle, a Christian army from Antioch, moving to meet the enemy forces from Aleppo, was surrounded in the night and slaughtered in the morning. According to the Muslim chronicler Kemel ed-Din, only twenty Franks (western Christians) escaped, while those who were captured faced torture and execution by the Turks. This defeat coincided with the establishment of the Knights Templar. It rendered Latin Jerusalem (as the Crusader state was also called) particularly vulnerable. Ilgazi died three years later of alcoholic poisoning, but his nephew, Balak, kept up the pressure on the Christians, making a prisoner of King Baldwin for a time in 1123.

Unfortunately for Islam, Balak died at the siege of Tyre, after which the city fell to the Crusaders, leaving them masters of most of the Levantine coast. Help was also given to the Frankish cause by the murders of a dozen prominent Sunni Muslim leaders in Syria by the Assassin sect. However, with the rise of the Muslim leader Zenghi, the Emir of Aleppo and Mosul, Islamic unity became more of a reality. In Zenghi, the Crusader state faced its greatest peril since its inception. Whatever was originally envisaged for the Templars therefore, the priority now became to supply committed military reinforcements.

NOTES

1 William of Tyre, *Historia rerum in partibus transmarinis gestarum* (medieval sourcebook). See also Oldenbourg, Zoé, *The Crusades*, pp. 283–95. Not all pilgrims were poor and vulnerable. Those who were represented the wave in popular piety that surged at the time. During the First Crusade, many paupers followed Peter the Hermit and his donkey, even from regions that could not understand his preaching. Very few of them were as lucky as him and lived to see the capture of Jerusalem.
2 Read, Piers Paul, *The Templars*, p. 99. Why the Templars sought no official recruits in this early period, if indeed that is the case, remains a matter of speculation. When Hugues returned to Europe, he travelled far and wide recruiting Crusaders and enlisting Templars for a projected campaign against Damascus.
3 Addison, Charles G, *The History of the Knights Templars*, p. 65.
4 Frayling, Christopher, *Strange Landscape*, pp. 125–9.
5 Read, op. cit., p. 101. Cîteaux was the only Cistercian monastery when Bernard de Fontaines-les-Dijon joined the Order, taking with him a number of his kinsmen. Abhorring the laxness of Cluniac monasticism, Bernard founded Clairvaux ('valley of light') and re-invigorated the moribund Cistercians. By the time of his death (1153) some three hundred monasteries existed, in several countries.
6 Ibid., citing Ivo of Chatres.
7 Dafoe, Stephen (website), *A History and Mythos of the Knights Templar*. The sensitively guarded plot perhaps dated back to the eve of the First Crusade, when Godfrey de Bouillon sold up much of his property and set off on the quest that would result in his becoming Protector of the Holy Sepulchre. He recoiled from the title 'King', in the city where Christ had worn the Crown of Thorns. His brother, Baldwin of Edessa, did not. In 1118 Baldwin of Le Bourg, a cousin who had led the First Crusade, succeeded. These Lorraine nobles might have belonged to the coterie behind the establishment of the Templars. Dafoe mentions a shadowy 'Troyes Fraternity'.
8 Hancock, Graham, *The Sign and the Seal*, pp. 94–7. Hancock argues that the Templars sought the Ark of the Covenant, keeping their true quest secret. The tunnels extend into the heart of the mount. Templar finds included a crude leaden cross, a spur, a broken sword and a lance tip, all in poor condition. A team under Royal Engineer Lt Charles Warren, in 1867, had lobbied the Ottoman regime for permission to excavate within the sacred precincts. Muslim worshippers drove Warren out, pelting his party with stones. Hancock neglects to mention that Warren, a Freemason, later became the Commissioner of the Metropolitan Police, resigning after failing to catch Jack

the Ripper. See also *The Survey of Western Palestine* by Warren and Conder (1884).

9 Oldenbourg, op. cit., pp. 126–7. The Holy Lance was supposedly the tip of the spear with which the Roman centurion Longinus had pierced the side of Jesus on the Cross. According to a Christian myth, the blood that spurted out cured the centurion's blindness, causing him to recognise Jesus as the Son of God.

CHAPTER III
The Templars' Rule

Bernard of Clairvaux supervised the drafting of the Latin Rule, the ordinances that the Templars would have to abide by. He grafted Benedictine monasticism onto a knightly band, to ensure that their standards of godliness remained high and that they might not disgrace the Church. In the process he created, perhaps unwittingly, the first disciplined, regulated and uniformed standing army since antiquity.

The Rule document outlined a sombre and austere way of life. The evident world-hating aspect shows the influence on Cistercian thinking of St Augustine of Hippo, who, as a former Manichaean, retained a mistrust of the flesh and all things material. These things, implicitly, were within the domain of Satan. The Rule, therefore, urged discipline, moral purity and self-denial. It began by promising salvation for all those who fought for Christianity. It also emphasised the monastic aspect of the Order – the necessity of prayer and of attending services.

> You who renounce your own wills ... serving the Sovereign King with horse and arms, for the salvation of your souls, strive everywhere to hear matins ... God is with you if you promise to despise the deceitful world in perpetual love of God, and scorn the temptations of the body. Sustained by the food of God and watered and instructed in the commandments of Our Lord, at the end of the divine office, none shall fear to go into battle if he henceforth wears the tonsure.[1]

Obedience was to be of paramount importance in the Order, as several clauses made clear:

> It is to be holden that when anything shall be enjoined by the master, there be no hesitation, but the thing must be done without delay, as though it had been enjoined from heaven . . .
>
> In this house ordained by God, no man shall make war or make peace of his own free will, but shall wholly incline himself with the will of the master, so that he follow the saying of the Lord 'I came not to do mine own free will, but the will of him that sent me'.

Erring Templars were told they must admit their faults to their Master and submit to his discipline. The Order's constitution gave the Master wide powers, but advised him to be neither too lenient nor overly severe. His rod/staff of office was to support the weak and needy, as well as to strike down the vice of sinners.

Despite the colourful scenes conjured up by Sir Walter Scott in his novel *Ivanhoe*, Templars were unlikely to attend tournaments, and would have been forbidden to compete in the often deadly jousts and melées which their secular counterparts often engaged in, to impress other knights and the fair ladies watching with their prowess. The Church regarded such mock warfare as vain and sinful. Contemporary illustrations show devils claiming the souls of the fallen.

Such worldly pleasures as falconry and hunting for sport were similarly singled out for censure in the Rule of the Templars. Brethren were directed to speak sparingly and to behave 'decently and humbly, without laughter'.

Though the Templars were to be forbidden private possessions, the Rule allowed them collectively to own property, servants and land:

> Under divine providence . . . this new kind of religion was introduced by you in the holy places, that is to say the union of warfare with religion, so that religion, being armed, maketh her way by the sword and smiteth her enemies without sin. Therefore . . . since you are rightly called Knights of the Temple, for your renowned merit and especial gift of godliness, ye ought to have lands and men and possess husbandmen and justly govern them.

Men were not to be received into the Order lightly. Supplicants seeking to become Templars had to prove themselves worthy before the council. The Rule forbade the admission of children, as new brethren were expected to be already trained and equipped for battle. Aged and sick brothers were to be looked after as if it were Christ himself suffering. Some of the largest Templar establishments in the west were, in fact, hospitals for infirm and elderly members and associates of the fraternity. Examples of such foundations included Eagle in Essex and Temple Denny in the Fens, near Cambridge.

The excommunicated, secular knight, after absolution by a bishop, could be admitted, 'for the eternal salvation of his soul'. A married man could become an honorary associate of the Order, as we have seen, but could not wear the white habit of a full Knight Templar. When he died, he would leave a portion of his patrimony to the Order. His widow would receive a maintenance, but would be expected to depart from the property, it being 'improper that such women remain with the brethren who have promised chastity unto God'. Clauses of the Rule demanded celibacy, and the avoidance of feminine company:

> It is moreover exceedingly dangerous to join sisters in your holy profession, for the ancient Enemy has led many from the straight path to paradise through the society of women. Heretofore, very dear brothers, that the flower of chastity is always maintained among you, let the custom henceforth be done away with.

The implication of this last passage would seem to be that the Templars had admitted a few females, prior to the drafting of the Rule. If this is the case, it poses questions about who these sisters were and what happened to them. The passage could otherwise be read, however, as a warning against keeping company with nuns, who were sisters in their holy profession in a broader sense.

The Templars' dormitories were to be lit throughout the night, and brothers were to sleep in their shirts, belts and pantalons. This may have been intended to deter sexual activity of any sort, as well as to render the knights constantly prepared for military mobilisation. Purity was a very important concern. The Templars were given the exclusive right to wear white mantles, over their chain mail. These signified their having 'abandoned the life of darkness'. Ornamentation was forbidden, as it was deemed to show pride. Hair was to be cut short, though beards were allowed.

The Rule also regulated when and what to eat and pray. Even after meals, it gave the brethren '. . . no permission to speak openly except in emergency . . . For it is written: *In multiloquio non effugies peccatum,* that is to say that to talk too much is not without sin'. Another strange clause was as follows:

> Let him with whom they lodge be a man of the best repute . . . Let not the house of the host be without a light lest the Dark Enemy (from whom God preserve us) should find some opportunity. But when they shall hear of knights not excommunicated meeting together, we order them to hasten thither, considering so much their temporal profit as the eternal safety of their souls.

Altogether the Rule was predominantly concerned with religious and social issues, rather than with military matters, which hardly featured. The rule ended with another bleak warning against the charms of the female of the species:

> Lastly, we hold it dangerous for all religious to gaze too much on the countenances of women; and therefore no brother shall presume to kiss neither widow, nor virgin, nor mother, nor sister, nor aunt, nor any other woman. Let the Knighthood of Christ shun feminine kisses, through which men have very often been drawn into danger, so that each, with a pure conscience, may be able to walk everlastingly in the sight of God.

The original Rule was signed by Johannes Michaelensis, a Cistercian scribe who was commissioned by Abbot Bernard.

Bernard also penned *De laude novae militiae* (*In Praise of the New Knighthood*), at the request of Hugues de Payens. In it, he extolled, in rhetorical language, the ideal Militia of Christ. He contrasted these holy champions with their secular counterparts. His secular knights fought only for greed and vainglory. Addressing them, Bernard wrote:

> If fighting with the desire of killing another thou shouldst chance to get killed thyself, thou diest a man slayer: if, on the other hand, thou prevailest, and through a desire of conquest or revenge killest a man thou livest a man slayer. O unfortunate victory, when in overcoming thine adversary thou fallest into sin and anger and pride having the mastery over thee, in vain thou gloriest over the vanquished.
>
> What therefore, is the fruit of the secular, I will not say *militia* but *malitia* if the slayer commit a mortal sin and the slain perish eternally . . . ? What insufferable madness is this – to wage war with so great price and labour and with no pay except death or crime?
>
> Ye cover your horses with silken trappings and I know not how much fine cloth hangs from your coats of mail. Ye paint your spears, shields and saddles. Bridles and spurs ye adorn with gold and gems; and with all this pomp and with a shameful fury and a reckless insensibility ye rush on to death. Are these military ensigns or are they not rather the garnishments of women? Will the sword blade of the enemy respect gold, spare gems, be unable to penetrate silk?
>
> But the soldiers of Christ securely fight the battles of the Lord, fearing sin neither from the slaughter of the enemy nor danger from their

> own death. When indeed death is to be given or received from Christ, it has naught of crime in it but much of glory . . .[2]

The new knighthood humbly served God, fighting both the earthly Infidel and spiritual battles against the demon of Hell.

> They are wary of all excess in food or clothing, desiring only what is needful. They live together in common without wives, children or property . . . in one house, under one Rule . . . Each one in no respect follows after his own will or desire but is diligent to do the will of the Master . . . Such hath God chosen for his own . . .

They did not gamble or go hawking, play games or grow their hair:

> Knowing that according to the apostle, it is not seemly for a man to have long hair. They never comb and seldom wash, but appear rather with rough, neglected hair, foul with dust, and with skins burned by the sun and their coats of mail . . .
>
> There is indeed a Temple in Jerusalem, where they dwell together, unequal, it is true, to that . . . of Solomon, but no inferior in glory. For truly, the entire magnificence of that consisted in corrupt things, in gold and silver, in carved stone, in variety of woods; but the whole beauty of this resteth . . . in the Godly devotion of its inmates, and their beautifully ordered mode of life. God . . . regardeth pure minds more than gilded walls. The face, likewise of this Temple is adorned with arms, not with gems, and the walls, instead of the ancient golden chapiters [sic], are covered around with pendent shields . . . bridles, saddles and lances . . . demonstrating that the Soldiers of Christ burn with the same zeal for their house of God as that which formerly animated their great leader, when, vehemently enraged, he entered the Temple and . . . drove out the merchants, poured out the money changers' money, most indignantly condemning the pollution of the house of prayer . . .
>
> The devout army of Christ, incited by the example of its King, think indeed that the holy places are much more impiously and insufferably polluted by the infidels, than when defiled by merchants. They abide in the holy houses, with horses and with arms, that from that as well as all other sacred places, all filthy and diabolical madness of infidelity being driven out, they may occupy themselves in honourable and useful offices. They . . . honour the Temple . . . with constant devotion, not indeed with the flesh of cattle after the manner of the ancients, but peaceful sacrifices: brotherly love, devout obedience, [and] voluntary poverty . . .

Bernard portrayed the liberation of Jerusalem, which he had never visited, as assistance from on high. His epistle ended with mystical exhaltations of Zion:

> Hail, land of promise, which, formerly flowing only with milk and honey for thy possessors, stretches forth the food of life and the means of salvation for the entire world . . . glorious things are spoken of thee, city of God!

Armed with this endorsement, and the papal bull (proclamation) confirming the Rule of the Temple, Hugues de Payens toured France enlisting support. The *Anglo Saxon Chronicle* records his meeting with Henry I of England:

> This same year [1128] Hugues of the Temple came from Jerusalem to the King in Normandy and the King received him, with much honour, and gave much treasure in gold and silver, and afterwards he sent him to England. There he was well received by all good men, and all gave him treasure, and in Scotland also, and they sent a great sum in gold and silver by him to Jerusalem, and there went with him so great a multitude as was not seen since the days of Pope Urban.[3]

Hugues de Payens was welcomed by King David I of Scotland. Hugues probably visited the St Clair estates, where it seems the first Templar commandery was established at Ballentradoch (now Temple), near lands owned by the St Clairs.[4] It was a clear policy of the Scottish King to encourage the landowners of Norman blood to settle in his realm, to help him establish a feudal state. In time the Templars would gain territory in Ireland too, but most of the brethren, as in Scotland, seemed to be of Anglo-Norman origin.

Before his departure from the British Isles, Hugues de Payens appointed a Prior of the Temple. The Prior's tasks were to manage the estates that aristocrats had already donated, to supervise the admittance of those deemed worthy of entering the Order (having settled their debts with the outside world), and to manage the transfer of funds to the Holy Land.

By this time the Templars had been given land in Paris and London. These sites became administrative centres and staging posts. Hugues de Payens also visited Spain, where he was equally well received. It seems from the number of men who followed the Master of the Temple back to Jerusalem, that his mission was a resounding success. The Knights Templar were already the great cause of the European nobility.

Eventually, the monks of the Order of the Hospital of St John of Jerusalem also began recruiting fighting knights. It thus evolved into a rival Military Order. The Hospital was based near the Holy Sepulchre and provided refuge and care for thousands of pilgrims. The Hospitaller Order predated the Templars and was recognised by the Pope in AD 1113. However, it only began to operate in a military capacity, in imitation of the Templars, some time around 1136, when the Pope sanctioned its warlike activities. Both expanded rapidly, developing heirarchical organisation and administrative structures. The Hospitallers wore black mantles with a white cross on the breast, and their knights fought under a red banner.

Pious aristocrats continued to endow both Orders with land and largesse. Western European society was still of a warrior temperament, and it admired courage as much as piety. Aiding the perpetual Crusade was also becoming inextricable from Christian devotion, and patrons of the Crusader Orders hoped to gain spiritual rewards for their support. As monks, the Military Orders could pray for the souls of the departed and, it was believed, shorten their time languishing in purgatory. Many nobles donated land, therefore, for the sake of dead relatives.

The Temple and the Hospital allowed knights to pursue their martial calling whilst serving Christianity. Rather than sinners, they could become warrior saints. As well as these spiritual idealists and restless adventure seekers, the Orders later attracted fairly significant numbers of repentant criminals, disappointed or bereaved lovers, and men who simply did not fit in anywhere else. The personal sacrifices were great, however, for those who sought the honour of initiation. The brethren had to forsake the secular world, renounce family ties, and surrender all they owned to their Order.

The initiation rite

A man who wished to become a Knight Templar was required to be of noble and legitimate birth, free of debt, fit to fight, and unmarried. Before the reception ritual he would be asked questions, to establish that he met these criteria. Secrecy surrounded the initiation ceremony, and it seems that in the majority of cases nobody from outside the Order was present. By some accounts, on reception, the postulant would be admonished by the Master thus:

> Good Brother, you ask a very great thing, for of our Order you see only the outside. On the surface that you see we have beautiful horses and harnesses and eat and drink well, and have fine clothes, and it seems to you as if you would be most at ease there. But you do not know the harsh commandments which are within: for it is a hard thing that you, who are master of yourself, should make yourself serf of another.

The candidate knelt with his hands on a Bible. He pledged obedience to God and to the Blessed Mary, and swore to live in poverty and chastity, and to fight for the Holy Land. He would then be received with the 'Kiss of Peace'. The receptor then warned him that unending imprisonment would reward simony, sodomy, or betrayal of the Order's secrets. He explained various aspects of Templar discipline. Brothers were to wear a cord about them, always, as 'a sign of chastity'. They were to speak little, and be courteous when they did. The brethren were warned to avoid women and forbidden to kiss females. Finally, the receptor would say: '. . . And so we promise you bread and water and the poor robe of the house and much hardship and labour. Go – God make you worthy men'.[5]

Once in the Holy Land a Templar might be deployed as a guide and armed escort for civilian pilgrims, as part of an army fighting the Infidel, or be stationed in a garrison in a desert castle, watching for the enemy. When not active in the field, the brethren followed a monastic way of life, structured around prayer. They rose at four in the morning and heard the Rosary for the office of Matins, then went to tend their horses. Before eating breakfast, during which silence was observed, they heard the offices of Prime, Terce and Sext and took part in the prayers and chants these offices involved. Nones was at 2.30 p.m. The evening meal was again taken in silence, during which Bible readings were heard. These often included the Old Testament chapters telling of the original Hebrew conquest of the Promised Land, translated into the vernacular; selected, no doubt, to encourage the knights to see themselves as the new chosen people:

> I will send my fear before thee, and will destroy all the people to whom thou shalt come, and I will make all thine enemies turn their backs unto thee. And I will send hornets before thee, which shall drive out the Hivite, the Canaanite and the Hittite, from before thee . . . And I will set thy bounds from the Red Sea even unto the sea of the Philistines, and from the desert unto the river, for I will deliver the inhabitants of the land into your hands, and thou shalt drive them out before thee. Thou shalt make no covenant with them, nor with their gods. (Exodus 23:27–32)

This was followed by the office of Vespers at 6.00 p.m., and after Compline the brethren observed silence until the next day.

The Grand Master, as the Order's leader soon became known, presided from the Jerusalem Temple (and later from Acre when Jerusalem was lost). Elected internally, he answered only to the Pope. There were constraints on his power, however. He ruled along with a council, the General Chapter, and he did not have independent access to the Order's treasury. The rank of 'Visitor' was created for his deputy in Europe, responsible for making sure rules and decrees were adhered to, and for overseeing the supply of men and provisions to the east. Seneschals and Commanders/Preceptors were lower in rank, and managed the Order's many regional outposts. Knights were invariably nobles and wore white mantles bearing red crosses. They were allowed three horses each – two spares for battle (the Templar device of two riders on the same steed, as it appeared on the Order's early seal, was purely symbolic and represented unity). Sergeants, or serving brothers, were the common soldiers in the Order, and wore brown tabards. They had no Squire, and, according to the Rule, were allotted only one horse each.

Chaplains were clerics and wore green robes. They presided over religious ceremonies, acted as scribes and administrators, and heard the confessions of the knights, but they had no say in the government of the Order. The Templars also employed retainers, and mercenaries, called Trucopoles. These were made up of Syrian Christians, and provided a light cavalry who fought in the manner of the Muslims. Templar bases were called preceptories or commanderies. For administrative purposes, Templar territories were divided into eight *langues*, or linguistic regions. The chief house of each *langue* was the Grand Priory. The supplementary French Rule of 1140 mentioned ten Provinces: Jerusalem, Tripoli (Syria), Antioch, France, England, Poitou, Anjou, Portugal, Apuilia and Hungary. Each had a Master, or Grand Prior/Preceptor, who was the deputy of the Grand Master in his particular land, and a person of great power and influence.

The Templars fought under a half-black and half-white war-standard, that was named *Beauseant* (this being also their battle-cry, meaning 'Be fine!'). The flag was carried by a standard bearer called the Balcanifer, who enjoyed a position of honour within the Order. The flag's colours represented the two faces of the Order, good and kind to Christians, terrible and deadly to the Infidel. Templars could expect no mercy from their enemy in return. Templars captured by the armies of Islam invariably faced beheading, for none would forsake their religion. Often the eagerness with which they reputedly embraced martyrdom shows how much faith they put in their creed, of how little value they gave their own lives. Though the Order became highly wealthy, individual Templars were forbidden to offer ransom for their release, any ransom, that is, except their belt and dagger, which were not likely to suffice.

Templars carried no genealogical heraldry, having relinquished their secular identities. Their graves were likewise usually anonymous, marked by stone slabs, each carved singularly with a cruciform sword. The Templars, though powerful, existed on the fringes of society, a society they themselves repudiated. They disowned their own families, and lived apart from the world. They were stricter in this than the Hospitallers. Clerics never truly accepted the brethren because they were knights, for the most part unlettered and hardened by war, seeking salvation through bloodshed and blind obedience. Secular knights, perhaps, never accepted the Templars, meanwhile, because they were monks, and could be given to being sombre, puritanical and self-righteous. If people admired them, few loved them. Their willing isolation surely contributed much to their eventual fate.

At the same time, the Templars' exclusivity made membership of the Order a great privilege, for all its austerity. Applicants not only had to meet the criteria, but had to prove themselves worthy of entry. An English knight named Adam de Wallaincourt once quit the Order, but returned to it remorsefully. He sought this reinstatement though aware of the penance they would subject him to for his apostasy. They made him eat for a year off the ground with the dogs, fast on bread and water for four days out of five, and each Sunday appear before the high altar to be flogged by the officiating priest in punishment.[6] It emerges that the Master would also whip transgressing knights before the Chapter (assembly), where strict discipline and penances would be imposed. Erring Templars might otherwise be confined in penitential cells. There is one such cell, a 4 ft. 6in. by 2 ft. 6 in. space, to be found in the wall of the Temple Church in London, with holes through which the incarcerated man might watch the service. There, in all likelihood, perished the Templar Preceptor of Ireland, one of its last inmates, through the severity of his confinement. He had been excommunicated by his superiors in the Order and summoned to London to answer charges of embezzlement of Templar property.

When it came to the suppression of the Order, a number of Templars testified to a certain terror within the institution, arising from the threat of harsh punishments and death for those who tried to leave, or dared to betray the Order's secrets. There was reported to be a sinister prison at Merlan from which no one came out alive. Given the on-going state of war (and the diseases that mortally afflicted armies of the time), the occasional disappearance might not have caused too many questions to be asked. It is not easy, however, to establish whether a climate of fear existed beyond what one would expect from a normal religious Order concerned with discipline and an army concerned with preventing desertion in the field.

One legend from Scotland describes the tragic consequences for a Templar called Godfrey Wedderburn, when he transgressed the authority of his superiors. According to the legend, Wedderburn went from the Preceptory of Maryculter to fight in the Holy Land. On the eve of battle, he was challenged to single combat by an Emir, and was terribly wounded. He stumbled to a well where he fell unconscious. He woke to see the Emir's beautiful daughter, watching him (no doubt) with the dark eyes of a houri. She helped him to a secret cave, where she nursed him back to health, and gave him a gold ring. Wedderburn fell in love with her, but remembered his vows and returned to his brethren, eventually returning to Maryculter. Somehow the Emir's daughter followed him. The Master found her in the Preceptory and roughly ejected her. Wedderburn witnessed the discourtesy, and in his anger knocked his Master to the ground. He was then sentenced to death for his insubordination. His brethren dragged him to the place where he was to be stabbed to death with his own dagger.

The mountains resonated to a great scream, and the Emir's daughter appeared. She took the gold ring from Wedderburn's dead hand and challenged the Master to put it on if he dared. As the Master put it on his finger, so the story went, a bolt of blue fire struck him. The Emir's daughter then seized her dead lover's dagger and killed herself. Ever since then, the spot was cursed, and, on certain nights, haunted by blue light. Wedderburn was buried in the Templar chapel, where, reputedly, the bloodless ghost of the Emir's daughter was, many times afterwards, seen hovering over his tomb. Meanwhile, the knight's ghost was supposed to ride over Kingussi Hill, calling for her. It was also said that the ghost of the Emir's raven-haired daughter appeared by the beds of the dying in Maryculter.[7]

NOTES

1 *The Primitive Rule of the Templars* (trans. Upton-Ward, J). The full text of the Rule of the Templars is also available at ORB, The Online Reference Book for Medieval Studies. Tonsure refers to the shaving of the crown of the head, as practised by monks.
2 Bernard of Clairvaux, *In Praise of the New Knighthood*. Bernard was keen that the new knighthood avoid worldly pride. Templars were to be spiritually clean, though outwardly covered with the grime of the desert.
3 Addison, Charles G, *The History of the Knights Templars*, p. 51 (quoting the *Anglo Saxon Chronicle* of 1128).
4 Knight, Christopher and Lomas, Robert, *The Hiram Key*, pp. 296–316; also Lord, Evelyn, *The Knights Templar in Britain*, p. 150. Henry I's daughter was married to Fulk d'Anjou's son, so a favourable response was found in England. Henry I granted Hugues de Payens safe passage to proceed to Scotland. Hugues' supposed wife Catherine was a St Clair. Knight and Lomas wrote as if the lady was still alive at this point, though it seems unlikely. The St Clair/Sinclair clan maintained close links with the Templars, and some believe they offered refuge to fugitive knights after 1307. However, Evelyn Lord wrote that two St Clairs actually testified against the Knights Templar at the trial for heresy that took place in Scotland.
5. Cohn, Norman, *Europe's Inner Demons*, p. 86. Cohn concludes that 'nothing could be more sober' than the true initiation ritual. Also, Barber, Malcolm, *The Trial of the Templars*, pp. 253–7. Barber's second appendix provides the description of an orthodox reception described by Gerard de Caux in 1311.

6 Barber, op. cit., p. 149. The story of Adam de Wallaincourt was told by the Templars defending the Order to the papal commission of 1309. They hoped it would demonstrate the purity of the Order, on the grounds that nobody would leave a corrupt organisation and accept all these punishments simply in order to be re-admitted. De Wallaincourt had left the Templars for the Carthusians, apparently seeking a harsher Order, then regretting the move and wishing to return.
7 Lord, op. cit., p. 150. The legend was apparently recorded in 1892 by one J A Henderson.

CHAPTER IV
The Fortunes of War in the Holy Land

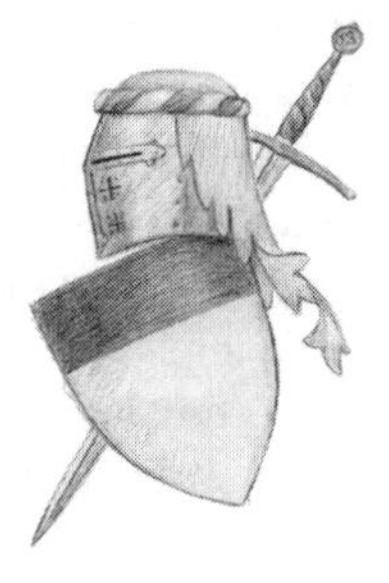

Hugues de Payens returned to Palestine in 1229, along with Fulk d'Anjou, who was married to Melisende. A council was held, to determine how to consolidate the Christian territory. The Muslims were rallying under Imad-ed-deen Zenghi, the Turkish Emir of Aleppo and Mosul, and the Crusaders were under attack. Zenghi had begun his career by putting down an Arab revolt against the Turks, inspired by the Caliph at Baghdad. However, he was soon widely hailed as the champion of Islam, as an Arab chronicler saw it: 'Before he came to power the absence of a strong ruler to impose justice and the presence of the Franks close at hand had made the country a wilderness, but he made it flower again.'[1]

In fact, Zenghi was ambitious and brutal – he sought to spread his power over the Damascene Emirate too. When he took the town of Baalbek from them, he had thirty-seven of the Damascene garrison crucified, and the commander burnt alive. The Damascenes seemed obvious allies for the Franks, against Zenghi. Odd, then, that Baldwin II and Fulk d'Anjou set off at once on an ill-fated expedition *against* Damascus.

Baldwin died in 1131. Fulk d'Anjou, soon after succeeding as King, found himself ambushed by Zenghi's forces, and retreated to a fortress near Tripoli where, having been reduced to eating their horses, the Christians had to pay ransom to get away. Byzantine reinforcements under Emperor John Comnenus appeared just too late. The Byzantines, soon alienated, withdrew under a cloud of acrimony.

Hugues de Payens led the Templars into action at this time. He died in 1136, and was succeeded as Grand Master by Robert de Craon, a

Burgundian nephew of the Archbishop of Canterbury, who had joined the Knights Templar after the death of his wife. At this time an alliance was forged with Unur, the Governor of Damascus, who still regarded Zenghi as a cruel enemy equally dangerous to both kingdoms. Together, these unlikely allies drove Zenghi's forces from Banyas, which the Franks took possession of without massacring or plundering the population. Later, however, for all their zeal, the Crusaders and their allies were overpowered by the numbers of their equally fanatical enemy at several battles. Fulk died following an accident in 1143, leaving the realm to his young son, Baldwin III, with Queen Melisende in regency.

Zenghi took various cities from the Christians. These included finally, at Christmas 1144, Edessa. Zenghi had tricked the inept Count Joscelin de Courtenay of Edessa into leading his army elsewhere. Joscelin had left the city in the protection of mercenaries who had not been paid for months. Zenghi's engineers dug tunnels that brought down the city's massive fortifications. His armies swept in and the citizens retreated to the citadel, only to find themselves locked out by the notoriously heartless Archbishop Hugo. In the event, all the Franks of Edessa, including the Archbishop, were massacred by Zenghi, save for the women, whom the Turks sold into slavery. Two years after his victory, Zenghi, sleeping in his camp after gorging himself with wine, was stabbed to death by his own eunuch.

A Crusader army lead by Joscelin, Count of Edessa, who had been lured away, went to recover the city. His faction re-established themselves for a time, but were soon slaughtered by the mighty forces of Nur ed-Din, the new, self-proclaimed *Sultan* of Aleppo. Again it was the 'helpless throng of unwarlike citizens' who suffered, as William of Tyre recorded, with some being crushed as they fled, and others falling 'under the merciless swords of the Turks'.

Nur ed-Din, Zenghi's second son, also saw his cause as holy – 'Jihad and Unity' was his slogan. An Arabised Turk, he was fanatical in his belief in Islam, and rigorously observed his fasts and prayers. He mirrored St Bernard, in discouraging frivolous conversation, wine and music, and encouraging the study of the Holy Book among his men, who were equally willing to die for God. 'Alas,' he is quoted as having once said, 'it is now a long time that I have been seeking martyrdom without being able to obtain it . . . Who can save Islam and our country but the great God who has no equal?' Nur ed-Din lost Baghdad and the Iraqi heartland of his empire to his older brother, and with it some of his father's army. He made up the numbers with Kurdish tribesmen, ironically driven from their homelands by Christian 'Crusaders' from Georgia, who had been inspired to imitate the Latins. Nur ed-Din also employed Mameluke warrior-slaves from Egypt, who had a particular reputation for ruthlessness.

News of Edessa's fall prompted Bernard of Clairvaux to appeal for a Second Crusade. In 1146 he commenced his stirring preaching at a Mass in a field outside Vézelay in Burgundy. (Vézelay lay on a popular pilgrim route and its cathedral claimed the miracle-working relics of Mary Magdalene.) Bernard's appeal caused Crusade fever to break out afresh – the mystical cause of the Holy Land became again one of the concerns that united Catholic nations, something Bernard encouraged the faithful to personalise. Men, little comprehending the political situation in the region, but fired up to fight for Jesus, flocked to take the Cross as private Crusaders. Others joined the Templars, whilst yet others made generous donations to them. Meanwhile Everard des Barres took his place as Grand Master of the Order, having previously been Prior of France. At a general Chapter in Paris, attended by Pope Eugenius III and King Louis VII, the Templars were awarded the honour of wearing the red cross, the *croix patée*, on their white mantles. They prepared to play a leading part in the second great Crusade.

Louis VII left on Crusade in 1146, accompanied by his formidable wife Eleanor of Aquitaine (who would fall out with her priggish husband, and, it was rumoured, have an affair with her uncle, the Count of Tripoli, during the course of the Crusade. She would later be divorced by Louis for her apparent inability to produce a son). Templar courage and discipline saved Louis' expedition from annihilation in Anatolia, and earned the respect even of their enemy. King Louis was impressed by the Order, and recommended them as a model for the rest of his army. The King put a Templar in charge of each section. Louis wrote to Abbot Suger of St Denis, to whom he had entrusted his realm:

> I cannot imagine how we would have subsisted for even the smallest space of time in these parts; had it not been for the Templars' support and assistance . . . a succour ably afforded and generously preserved in . . . They have lent us a considerable sum of money which must be repaid to them quickly, that their house may not suffer, and that we may keep our word.[2]

The German Emperor, Conrad III, also took an army through Anatolia. However this ran into Turkoman forces who butchered the inexperienced Crusaders. The Emperor himself escaped by sea with only a small contingent. The German Crusaders had earlier quarrelled with the Byzantines, and accused them of standing by whilst they were ambushed. Relations between the western Europeans and the Greeks deteriorated further. Louis, Conrad and the Grand Master, meanwhile, arrived in the Holy City, having already lost perhaps half of their men. At first the idea of an attack on Aleppo was projected. However, the decision to attack Damascus was taken instead, perhaps for fear that the city's population were coming around to the cause of Nur-ed-Din. This ambitious and controversial undertaking ended in disaster. The Crusading armies were trapped in the tangled orchards surrounding Damascus, and decimated. The surviving Christians retreated.

Despite such defeats, the prestige of the Templars remained high. The Baron Roger de Mowbray was so impressed by their deeds he witnessed during the siege, that later he gave them several extensive estates in England. King Stephen and Queen Matilda, though fighting a civil war at this time, each gave the brethren numerous manors. These including Crowley in Oxfordshire, and Withan and Eagle in Essex, where the Templars established a retirement hospital for veterans.

Accompanying a disheartened Louis, Everard des Barres returned to France, from Outremer, in 1149. The Christians who remained in the Holy Land continued to suffer. Nur ed-Din captured the Lord of Antioch in a battle in which all his nobles died. The Sultan cut off his head and right hand, and sent them to the Caliph in Baghdad. Combined Muslim forces then tore through northern Syria, and overran Antioch. The Templars sent a messenger from Jerusalem, imploring their Grand Master to return with reinforcements. There was a sense of urgency in their message. 'The great part of those we led to the succour of Antioch are dead.' By the time help arrived, they said, the Holy Land could be already lost.

The Templars had by now built a number of formidable castles, including Baghras, and taken charge of the city of Gaza as a critical part of the defence of the Holy Land. The Second Crusade achieved little in the east, however, besides martyrdom for those participants who died fighting it. Its only earthly gain for the Christians was the city of Lisbon in Portugal, taken from the Arabs by English and Frisian knights on their way east. The failures of the Crusade dented the confidence of Europe in the venture, and damaged St Bernard's standing. Failing to enlist the desired support, des Barres abdicated the Grand Mastership of the Temple, and died doing penance and mortifying his body among the monks in Clairvaux.

The Templars elected the Burgundian noble Bernard de Tremelay as their new Master in 1151. By this time the armies of the Crescent were camped within sight of Jerusalem. The Crusaders managed somehow, however, to push these vastly superior forces back, driving them beyond the Jordan river, and leaving five thousand dead. The following year saw the outbreak of civil war caused by Queen Melisende's refusal, with Templar backing, to yield up the throne to her son.

In 1153, from his death bed, Abbot Bernard wrote three letters commending the Templars; one to the new Templar Grand Master André de Montbard, the others to the Patriarch of Antioch and to Queen Melisende of Jerusalem, urging them to continue to support the Order. Meanwhile, the Templars tried to go it alone in an attack on Ascalon (a city on the road to Egypt) which proved disastrous. Many of their number were taken and hung from the city walls.

In 1154 Bertrand de Blanquefort succeeded as Grand Master. Even William of Tyre, who had many grievances with the Templars, noted his piety and god-fearing. He led the Templars from the forefront at every ensuing encounter with the Muslims. Cardinal de Vitry, the Bishop of Acre, admired the Templars, who he said were kind and gracious to Christians, but were inexorably ferocious to the enemy of Christ. Monastic chroniclers praised these knights for the number of infidels they sent to damnation. It did not prevent Nur ed-Din taking Damascus. 'Jihad and Unity' moved a stage closer.

There was clearly great attrition on both sides. Both religions tended to consider their own dead blessed martyrs and their fallen enemies destined for Hell. Both imagined themselves the elect of God. It was simple logic, however, that Islam could more easily replace its martyrs. This was especially so when a holy warrior for the Crescent could have multiple wives and concubines, to produce sons to follow him, whereas a Templar or Hospitaller could have had neither, even had Christian women been in greater supply. Meanwhile, the Pope's repeated calls for more Crusades largely went ignored in Europe. Already the feeling may have been growing that the Military Orders should have the resources to defend the Holy Land on their own. There was a trickle of support to the Holy Land, but no more mass migrations.

In a battle near Tiberias in 1156, Bertrand de Blanquefort was captured, whilst the Muslims overwhelmed and slew three hundred of his brethren. They took eighty-seven others prisoner. It was recorded that then, in a surprise attack on Nur ed-Din's camp, a mere thirty surviving Templars, led by the English knight Robert Mansel, put to flight and killed two hundred Saracens, salvaging the prestige of their Order. The Sultan himself was forced to flee half naked. (This vivid detail, however, reappears with some regularity in accounts of various Crusader engagements and should probably be taken with a pinch of salt.)

The Grand Master was later freed at the behest of the Byzantine Emperor, Manuel Comnenus. Blanquefort soon wrote to Louis VII of France, listing misfortunes, including a spate of earthquakes that had shattered Crusader castles and swallowed towns, and the strength of the Infidel who was poised to capitalise on the situation. It seems the Temple managed to replace its losses, however. William of Tyre recorded that by his day there were three hundred of these white knights in Jerusalem, commanding countless sergeants. They were established in every province, with wealth that 'equalled the treasures of kings'.[3]

NOTES

1 Jones, Terry and Ereira, Alan, *Crusades*, p. 75 (quoting Ibn al-Athir).
2 Addison, Charles G, *The History of the Knights Templars*, p. 120 (quoting King Louis' letter to Abbot Suger of St Denis).
3 Ibid., quoting William of Tyre, *Historia rerum in partibus transmarinis gestarum* (1170s).

CHAPTER V
Powers and Accomplishments

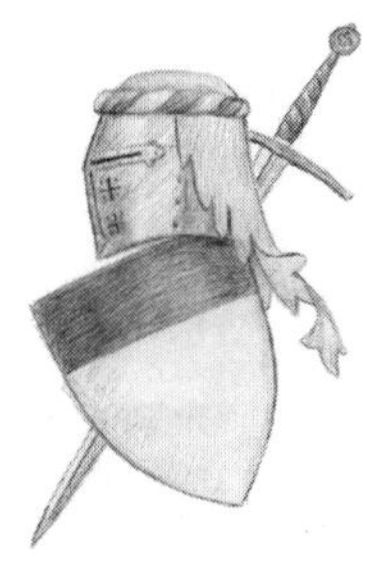

The twelfth century was a time of social stabilisation in Europe and growing international trade. Wealth was shifting from feudal hands to mercantile hands – the hands of traders, agriculturalists, cloth producers and bankers. Roads were being built, fairs and markets opening. Though the Templars owed their origins and character to the old Europe of war and religion, as landlords they played an active part in the creation of the new Europe of peaceful business. In this new society, loans replaced pillage and legal litigation replaced bloodshed in the settlement of disputes.

The Catholic Church continued to hold considerable power in society. Rome put the Templars under its protection – spiritual and political. It granted them numerous privileges, including immunity from excommunication by local clergy, and exemption from feudal duties. They could collect tithes, even from interdicted regions, build their own churches and bury their own dead.[1] The Templars also had the right to execute criminals at the gallows. They hanged a man in 1277, near Baldock, the market town the Order had founded in Hertfordshire (Baldock may derive its name from 'Baldak', which was Old French for Baghdad). In 1286 they hanged Gerard de Clifton and John de Trickhill for stealing silver spoons and a chalice from the priest at Temple Dinsley, also in a remote part of Hertfordshire. Dinsley was their second most significant compound in England, and the scene of many secret chapter meetings. The Templars likewise hanged one Peter, son of Adam, having convicted him of taking and torturing a woman near there.

The papal bull of 1139, *Omne Datum Optimum*, placed the Order above secular or episcopal jurisdiction and entitled them to keep the spoils of battle in order to advance the Crusade.[2] Templar wealth and prestige grew rapidly. Soon some nine hundred estates existed across Christendom.

> We . . . concede to you constructing on the oratories in the places bestowed on the sacred house of the Temple, where you and your retainers may dwell, so that ye may be able to assist at the divine offices, and there receive the rite of sepulture, for it would be very dangerous for the soul of the religious brethren, if they were mixed up with a crowd of secular persons, and be brought into the company of women on the occasion of going to church.

The Templars were only supposed to know one Lady, and she was the Blessed Mary, to whom they dedicated the majority of their churches.

The papal bull, in order to preserve the autonomy of the Knights Templar from the influence of secular rulers, forbade the election of an outsider as Grand Master, or the changing of its statutes without the consent of the Master and Chapter. The Order were also freed from the duty to pay tithes (church taxes). This privilege was confirmed in the later bull *Milicia Dei.*

The bull *Milites Templi* established the Templars' right to perform 'divine office' once yearly in regions under interdict (where the Pope for whatever reason had forbidden the holding of church services, as a spiritual punishment for the people there). This the Templars could do when they were collecting money. At around this time the Rule was translated into French, with new clauses added governing the hierarchical structure of the Order.[3]

Some of these bulls may have taken generosity too far, giving the Order unprecedented levels of power and independence. This apparently made them arrogant, and engendered the envy and resentment of many churchmen and secular rulers. Evidence for this emerged at the Council of Rome in 1179, where the Military Orders in the west were accused of abusing their privileges and usurping power. They were reprimanded and their privileges were curbed, but resentment of them probably remained.

Architecture and Property

The Templars built extensively. Their constructions included the great castles in the Holy Land, churches, domestic buildings, mills, bridges, city walls and numerous industrial and agricultural structures. To build the churches and fortresses, there seems to have been a class of 'Mason brothers', the only members aside from priests to be allowed to wear leather gloves. Medieval masons were a secretive guild, who had developed a theology of 'sacred geometry'. They devised various symbols which they carved as identification signs, one of which was the pentagram. Their predecessors were the master masons who had worked with the monks who commissioned the great Romanesque abbeys and cathedrals. These masons were possibly linked with their counterparts in the Islamic world, and may have exchanged certain ideas with them.

The Templars extended their base, the former Al-Aqsa mosque, on Temple Mount, from an early date. The German Monk Theodoric, who visited Jerusalem in 1169–74, saw the Templars' residence, which was like a church, with a circular roof supported by pillars, and filled with weapons, clothing and provisions. Below it the Order had built or adapted massive vaulted buildings and vast underground halls, commonly called the 'Stables of Solomon'. According to Theodoric's (perhaps somewhat wild) estimations, these artificial caverns could hold ten thousand horses and their grooms, and a bolt shot from a crossbow would hardly reach from one end of the building to the other.

The Templars erected numerous castles in the Holy Land. Many of these were earlier castles, Arab or Byzantine, taken over and enlarged, but others were newly built. At times the Military Orders nearly bankrupted themselves with their castle building. These structures were remarkable for their scale and sophistication, and comprised the earliest concentric castles. They included Saphet, one of a chain of castles in the Jordan valley guarding against Damascus. The accounts for its construction have survived, and reveal that the first two years of building it cost the Templars the equivalent of £40m in today's money. Annual maintenance cost nearly £2m. The walls were sixty feet thick and some 170 feet high, with seven towers, seventy-two feet higher than the walls. The pallisade was surrounded by a fosse (ditch) thirty-six feet wide and forty-three feet deep, cut from solid rock. The garrison was intended to be around 2,000 strong.

Such castles could accommodate thousands, and local populations might seek shelter there when Islamic armies were at large. There were cavernous undercrofts to store sufficient food to withstand years of seige. Pilgrim's Castle (also called Atlit) stood near Jaffa. Bagras was north of Antioch, guarding the northern frontier. It survives in spectacular ruins, above a rocky outcrop. Belvoir was another great castle, strategically situated near the Sea of Galilee. To enter it one had to pass along the side of a deep ditch that, again, had been hewn from the living rock. The Order also had fortified bastions in Jaffa, Sidon and Acre, among other places. They also manned castles in the Iberian peninsula, where they played an active part in the *Reconquista* – the ongoing war with the Moors. In Paris, meanwhile, they built a tall keep with four corner turrets, called the Temple, which became their European headquarters.

The norm for Templars in the west, however, was not soldiering, but estate management and semi-monasticism. They built and ran a network of Preceptories and manors across Europe, in towns and on the great estates which their noble patrons had granted. They continued a Cistercian tradition of colonising uninhabited regions, bringing wastelands into viable productivity. Perhaps part of the need for this was that much of the best land was already taken. They ran farms with military efficiency, storing grain in vast wooden tithe barns, like the two surviving examples at Temple Cressing in Essex. They also founded entirely new towns, such as Baldock in Hertfordshire, with markets for their products – most of which were cash crops, raising money for rather than directly supplying the Crusade. Templar foundations brought land hitherto unused into production. The Templars were pragmatic landlords, who even rented urban property to Jewish tenants. As they gained territory in Spain, meanwhile, during the *Reconquista*, they allowed Muslim farmers to retain their religion, as an incentive to keep them on the estates.

Most Preceptories included a chapel, as well as domestic buildings and some rudimentary fortifications. The layout of many Templar shrines has caused a degree of speculation regarding their understanding of 'sacred geometry', and also about secret codes and ancient wisdom imbued in the stonework. The relationship between the geographical locations of their sites has been made much of – as if through it, the Templars deliberately left clues to the location of their secret treasure, or the nature of their secret knowledge. In fact, the most grandiose constructions of the Templars were their oriental castles, evidence that their primary preoccupation was more military than mystical – which is not to say that they did not have a mystical approach to warfare. Their religious buildings in Europe tended to be relatively modest in terms of scale and decoration.

The Romanesque churches of the Templars were commonly circular, or polygonal in plan, and fittingly austere externally. The early Templars possessed a portable shrine or Tabernacle called the *Custos Chapellae*, a round tent which was pitched in the centre of their camp. It was always carried into the field by the Order, along with its altar ornaments. The *Custos Chapellae* could have been the inspiration behind the round-planned churches of the Templars. The round Church of the Holy Sepulchre, built by the Byzantines and much extended by the Crusaders, was also an influence. Round Templar churches survive in Loan in France, in Tomar in Portugal, and in London and Canterbury in England. Hugues de Payens founded the original London Temple at Holborn, a humble establishment from where fresh knights were quickly dispatched to Palestine. As the organisation grew in size and wealth, it bought the extensive site of the New Temple, near Fleet Street. There they built the round Temple Church in a transitional Romanesque style. Later, in the reign of Henry III, they added an oblong Gothic nave with side-aisles of equal height, reminiscent of an Islamic prayer hall. The church was surrounded by monastic buildings, including the cells of the knights and serving brothers, a chapter house and two halls. The enclosure also included a bakery, a brewery and an orchard.

In Temple Church in London, an arcade runs around the interior of the round part, with carved heads in the spandrels between the arches. Some of these are of kings and queens, some of grotesque demon-like creatures, others are of grimacing men, some suffering from toothache, others having their ears bitten by strange animals – perhaps representing the torments of the damned. Lions' heads flank the door, which has a Norman rose window above.

Similar carved heads, human and animal, were found below cornices in the polygonal church the Templars built in Pilgrim's Castle in the Holy Land. The foundations of another round chapel can be seen in Bristol, below the ruins of a later church. (The Templars also constructed part of Bristol's city walls and a stone bridge there, near their Preceptory.) Northerly examples of round churches can be found on the Baltic island of Bornholm, perhaps testifying to the Templars' role in the 'Crusade' against the Pagan Estonians and Wends. St Bernard of Clairvaux had called for no truce with the Wends until 'either their religion or their nation shall be wiped out'. The Knights Templar, it seems, were established throughout Christendom, and militarily active on all its frontiers, but their focus always remained the Holy Land.

The Templars' Fleet

Maritime activity was always an important feature of both pilgrimage and Crusading. Often both pilgrims and Crusaders found themselves exploited by the Italian merchant republics that dominated shipping on the Mediterranian Sea, and who charged heavily for passage and assistance. As the Military Orders grew, they came to possess a substantial fleet of their own ships, freeing the Crusading movement, to a certain extent, from its reliance on Venice, Pisa and Genoa.

Medieval mariners navigated by astrological observation and by loadstone compass. In England the Templars had a number of ships at Bristol, Rye, Dover and Portsmouth, while in France they were concentrated in La Rochelle on the Atlantic coast, and Marseilles on the Mediterranean. From La Rochelle the Templars exported wine and victuals to their brethren in England. Cargoes of wool from Templar estates in England arrived in La Rochelle from Dover and Bristol. This appears to have been for use within the Order, rather than for re-sale. Treasure to fund Crusading enterprises also arrived in La Rochelle from England.

Marseilles was more significant as a connection between France and the ports of the Levant. In 1233 the Templars encountered opposition from local ship owners at the port, who were losing out in the market for providing passage to the Holy Land for pilgrims. The merchants managed to restrict the Templars to the taking of only two shiploads of pilgrims a year, one passage at Easter time, the other around August. Before that time the Templars apparently operated a far more substantial pilgrim fleet from the port.

The Templars also had sturdy warships, constructed at massive expense, that took part in several naval battles fought during the Crusades. The Order's largest vessels were called *busses*. These were transport ships, propelled by oars. Of Byzantine design, they featured a ramp at the stern for landing forces onto beaches. Besides their crews, they could carry in excess of forty horses and as many soldiers, as well as all the provisions needed by the force. Slightly smaller were the Order's battle galleys, armed with pointed metal rams at the prow to sink enemy ships. These were, again, propelled by oarsmen – mostly unfortunate Muslim prisoners, chained in rows below deck. The galleys also had holds for horses and cargo, and carried smaller, oared landing barges for ferrying these ashore. Additionally, the Templars, in their heyday, had various classes of smaller warships, reliant on sail. It is said that the Templars' marine battle flag was the skull and crossbones, while the sails of their ships displayed the red cross of the Order. These vessels would have been among the first European ships to be steered by a rudder as opposed to a side-mounted steering board, and the first to adopt the triangular lateen sail, developed by the Arabs, that made it easier to sail into the wind.

The Order contained expert shipwrights, overseeing the costly construction of these ships. In 1226 the Templar Brother Thomas, a trusted official, oversaw the outfitting of King John's navy, and the building of a new flagship at Portsmouth. He was later involved in the mustering of some two hundred warships. He was also responsible for many smaller boats, used by the Order, involved in trade, the fishing industry, and transporting pilgrims.

Banking

The gold and silver coins early pilgrims carried on their long journeys made them tempting targets for brigands. Realising this, the Templars introduced arrangements for looking after money. They invented coded receipts, for pilgrims to redeem their deposit, with a modest service fee. This probably meant the pilgrims, no longer carrying large bags or chests of money, were less appealing targets to the robbers who remained at large, so the Templars could increasingly concentrate their energies on fighting battles.

Templars, over time, thus became sophisticated international financiers, as well as warriors. Perhaps their most lasting achievement was economic. By helping to overthrow the Church's attitude towards usury, they contributed to the rise of capitalism. They were exempt from restrictions on charging interest, with their Crusader status. They offered unparalleled security, too, having fortified establishments to store treasure in and plenty of armed men to guard money while it was being moved. They also offered better rates than either the Jews or the Italians (the latter of whom would ultimately supplant them). They were soon entrusted with the treasuries of numerous princes; even certain Saracens did business with them.

The financial services the Templars offered to clients were numerous. There were current accounts, where money was regularly paid in by the holder, and could be withdrawn with their written consent. There were safe deposits for money, gold and jewellery. There were loans and credit, and there was the safe international transmission of money as cash or letters of credit. The Templars also acted as trustees for the payment of annuities and as tax collectors and receivers (on behalf of rulers and in their own right as landlords). Places such as the New Temple in London were also where private citizens could go to repay their debts to others, getting a Templar to bear witness to the payment. This was all possible because of the Order's near-universal reputation for trustworthiness in such matters.

Relations With Others

There were spells of peace during which relations between the Muslims and the longer-settled Franks in Palestine seemed quite cordial. Only newly arrived Europeans caused trouble. A Syrian dignitary named Usama ibn-Munqidh recalled in his memoirs such an incident, when the Templars came to his defence.

> When I used to enter the Al-Aqsa mosque, which was occupied by the Templars, who were my friends, the Templars would evacuate the little adjoining mosque, so that I might pray in it . . .[4]

One day the Muslim rolled out his prayer mat and began to make his observances in the usual Islamic way, when a Frankish man rushed on him and tried to turn him to face eastward, mocking his bows towards Mecca. When it happened again the Templars rebuked and threw out the man, apologising to Usama, saying:

> 'This is a stranger who has only just arrived from the land of the Franks, and he has never seen anyone praying except eastward.' Therefore I said to myself I have had enough prayer, so I went out and

have ever been surprised by this devil of a man, at the change in the colour of his face, his trembling and his sentiment at the sight of one praying towards Mecca.

The account of Usama ibn-Munqidh shows that a degree of religious tolerance prevailed among the Templars, despite their status as holy warriors. This sometimes alienated the less pragmatic, fresh Crusaders who arrived from Europe spoiling for a fight. The heedless keenness of such men to spill Saracen blood often did the cause of the Christians in the east little service.

In the west the Templars usually acted as ordinary landlords. The New Temple in London was a haven of peace, home to many retired veterans. The streets surrounding the establishment, however, could often get rough. In 1272 Simon le Waleys, servant of a papal nuncio staying at the Temple, was in a street brawl with Laurence the barber, and killed him. Simon fled and was declared an outlaw. In the same year a neighbour of the Templars, William Ashby, went to sell silks to Maud, the wife of Adam de Linton. The jealous husband and his servant sprang out on them while the business was being done. Adam came out from hiding and killed William. Maud and her maid were subsequently arrested (on charges appertaining to adultery) and died in Newgate prison. The Templars, in the meantime, seized Adam's property, and took him into the Temple where he claimed sanctuary and worked as a legal clerk for the brethren. He was eventually pardoned. There was also a notorious brothel near the Temple. There were no reports of Templars sneaking out to it, but the servants of the Bishop of Durham, who stayed at the Temple, were involved in another drunken brawl with local men, which took place outside the brothel.

The Templars were thought to be a very rich institution, from the proceeds of the regimented management of their estates, their business dealings and their tax exemptions, but there is little evidence that they ever lived luxuriously, and huge amounts of their revenue was swallowed up by their military expenses. Few appreciated this fully, or the fact that much of the money they handled and the treasure they guarded was not theirs. However, the Order's privileges seem to have earned the envy of much of the Church. In 1150 the Abbot of Cluny wrote to Pope Eugenius III that many of his monks saw the Templars only as knights, and not as monks. A symptom of resentment from other parts of the clergy was the fact that Templar priests were vetoed for promotion, and few became prelates.

William of Tyre complained that the Templars '. . . have also taken away tithes and first fruits from God's churches, have disturbed their possessions, and made themselves exceedingly troublesome'. This hostility from certain other parts of the Church establishment would not disappear, and may have been a factor in their downfall. The Templars suffered such criticism mostly between Crusades. By the 1160s the Military Orders were criticised for their sometimes internecine rivalry. They were also criticised for their excessive pride. The Military Orders were seldom accused of cowardice. Indeed, Walter Mapp, Archdeacon of Oxford in the 1180s, accused them of loving violence excessively.

In the course of their history, the Templars occasionally became involved in political struggles that distracted them from the greater purpose. Matthew Paris (1229–50), the English chronicler, described one such diversion, when the Order involved itself in the papacy's dispute with the German Emperor.[5]

On another occasion, one styled 'Prester John' wrote to the Pope and the Princes of Europe in 1165:

> There are Frenchmen among you, of your lineage and from your retinue, who hold with the Saracens. You confide in them and trust in them that they should and will help you, but they are false and treacherous . . . pray, do not forget to put to death those treacherous Templars.[6]

Around this time, the Templars were campaigning in Egypt, under King Amalric of Jerusalem. 'Prester John' claimed to rule a fantastical Christian Empire beyond the Islamic world, sometimes identified with 'India'. One theory, however, attributes the letter to the Emperor Harbay Zagwe of Ethiopia, who would be deposed by Lalibela, his brother, on Lalibela's return from Jerusalem, perhaps aided by the Templars.[7] Whoever 'Prester John' may have been, however, his warning was not heeded.

As for holding with the Saracens, the Templars did have Muslim contacts. They received tribute from a murderous Ismaili Muslim sect, the Assassins, who were terrorists in the purest sense. They were Shi'a mystics also, blindly loyal to their Grand Master, known as the 'Old Man of the Mountains' in the impregnable castle Alamut. They had developed an extensive system of murder in order to establish their reputation, somehow seeing their murders as a sacred duty. Chillingly, they did not expect to return from their missions, and would commit suicide unquestioningly to prove their loyalty.

Their name derived from the hashish they smoked to give themselves courage. The victims of the Assassins could be anyone – several Sunni Emirs had been slain outside their mosques. It is unclear what the Assassins' precise agenda was, though their effect was to destabilise the Islamic world, and provide a great bonus for the Franks. However, in the 1130s they also deprived the Franks of several castles. When these fanatics killed Raymond, son of the Count of Tripoli, in the Church of the Virgin in

Tortosa, the Templars set off to avenge him. It appears they defeated the Assassins, and compelled them to pay an annual tribute of 2,000 crowns to the Templar treasury.

In 1172 the Templars sabotaged a proposed *entente* between the Ishmaili Assassins' Imam Sinan Ben Suleiman of Syria and King Amalric of Jerusalem, by killing the Ismaili envoy. Templar relations with Amalric deteriorated. The King intended to ask Rome for the abolition of the Templars, but was prevented from carrying through with this by his death in 1174. William of Tyre blamed Templar greed for their action, thinking they feared to lose the annual tribute of gold if the Assassins bonded with the King. The Assassins, it seems, had proposed to convert to Christianity and support Amalric against Nur ed-Din, if he released them from this tribute obligation. It is equally possible, though, that the Templars sought to save Amalric from a misguided alliance.[8] At any rate, the main cause of contention arose after the Templars refused to hand over to King Amalric their brother knight, Walter de Mesnil, who had killed the envoy. The Grand Master insisted that his Order answered only to the Pope. Grand Master Odo cared more for the autonomy of the Temple than anything else, although he did put Mesnil in chains. He intended to send him to Rome for judgement, but later backed down and handed him over to the King. Mesnil's ultimate fate is unknown, but it seems unlikely that he acted unilaterally, given the importance his Order attached to obedience.

Before 1300 the Templars in Europe generally escaped the accusations of sodomy commonly made against other monks. Fraudulent acquisition of money and property more usually occasioned complaint. In 1238 Gregory IX wrote to the Order in western France, decrying the practice of summoning legal opponents to courts in distant places and fining them for not appearing by the appointed time. Such opponents grumbled that, though individually the Templars professed to owning nothing, collectively they wanted everything. There is also some evidence that secular Princes in Europe were growing concerned with the extent of the Order's independence. In 1223 relations grew strained between the Templars in England and King Henry III. Henry complained to the Pope about their abuses of privilege, their encroachments on royal rights and the impudent manner of the Grand Prior Alan Marcel. The Pope responded with the bull *De insolentia Templariorum reprimanda,* literally a rebuke of the insolence of the Templars. Two abbots were charged with investigating the matter. Relations must have recovered, however, for the following year Henry III sent Marcel to negotiate peace treaties with France and Germany on his behalf, and a marriage of Henry with an Austrian princess. By the 1240s Henry so favoured the Templars that he extended their church in London and intended to be buried there.

The Templars were frequently prepared to act as peace brokers in disputes between Christians, but were very reluctant, generally, to participate in fighting. Later, in 1263, when England saw an uprising against Henry III, by the King's brother-in-law Simon de Montfort (the younger), Earl of Leicester, the Templars remained militarily neutral.

Templar alms collectors often caused disputes, for it was sometimes difficult for the people to see where their taxes were going; increasingly little good news came from the Holy Land. Suspicions lingered that the Orders had somehow betrayed the Crusades. In 1270 the troubadour Daspol laments that:

> . . . their pride and greed made them do evil instead of good
> and unable or unwilling to defend the Holy Lands.[9]

NOTES

1 Lord, Evelyn, *The Knights Templar in Britain*, p. 59.
2 Read, Piers Paul, *The Templars*, p. 116.
3 Barber, Malcolm, *The Trial of the Templars*, pp. 8, 10.
4 Read, op. cit., pp. 130–1.
5 Paris, Matthew, *Chronicles.* Never had there been 'so intense a hatred as existed between the Lord Pope and Frederick'. The worldly Holy Roman Emperor Frederick II was anathema to Rome, with his interest in science and sorcery, his fraternisation with Muslim scholars and his reputed debauchery. The Templars refused to march with him during his Crusade. When Frederick negotiated the return of Jerusalem, the Muslims retained Temple Mount, and the Templars were never able to re-claim their old home. Yet they went only so far as non-cooperation, never allowing themselves to be used in combat against the Emperor. Paris could not hide his grudging admiration for Frederick, and distaste for the 'Lord Pope's' devious plots against him, such as attempted poisonings. Paris was sometimes untrusting of the Templars, whom he accused of disseminating false reports of success against the Saracens. He was critical, too, of the Crusades to Diametta in Egypt. 'Christians ought not to have crossed the sea with any intention other than to gain possession of Christ's inheritance.'
6 Hancock, Graham, *The Sign and the Seal*, p. 111.
7 Ibid., pp. 109–14.
8 Read, op. cit., pp. 143–61. The ruler of Aleppo, Nur ed-Din actively led the *Jihad.* He had spent much of his career reuniting Islam, after the fragmentation of the Seljuk Empire.
9 Partner, Peter, *The Murdered Magicians.* p. 100, citing Daspoil.

CHAPTER VI
The Loss of Jerusalem

One group who were equally, if not more deserving of criticism for pride and greed, were the nobles of Outremer. Feudal barons often came to power there through brutality and treachery, and through foisting themselves on rich widows in the various Crusader states. They frequently alienated their natural allies, the native Armenian and Syrian Christians, by plundering and oppressing them, and denying them freedom of religion. Steeped in martial culture, some of these Frankish lords sometimes seemed indifferent to who they fought, and were as happy making alliances with various Muslim Emirs against their Christian rivals as they were of acting for the greater good of their co-religionists. The same could easily be said of the quarrelsome and greedy Turkish Princes, whose fiefdoms neighboured the Crusader state. If this had not been so, the Franks in Palestine would have been unlikely to have lasted nearly as long as they did.

When he reached his twenties, Baldwin III found his mother Melisende reluctant to yield up power, and a state of virtual civil war ensued in Outremer. The local magnates became embroiled on opposing sides, the Templars favouring the Queen. The realm was divided, after which Baldwin invaded his mother's territory. Later the King and his mother were reconciled, and he allowed her a say in state affairs. Baldwin managed to thaw relations with Byzantium (despite the plundering of Cyprus, which was then a Byzantine colony, by a Frankish adventurer named Reynald de Chatillon), and married the young Greek Princess Theodora. However, her uncle, the Emperor Manuel, went behind the back of the Franks to negotiate a Byzantine alliance with Nur ed-din, against the Turks in Anatolia. Though this treaty resulted in the freeing of Christian captives, including Blanquefort, the Grand Master of the Knights Templar, it was seen as a betrayal by many Latins.

Baldwin died childless in 1162, and was succeeded by his obese brother, Amalric, who seems to have lacked his brother's charm and diplomacy. In the following years he led generally unsuccessful campaigns in Egypt, against Nur ed-Din's army, sent there under the Sultan's Kurdish general, Shirkuh. The Fatimid Caliphate in Cairo was in terminal decline, and both Amalric and Nur ed-din were interested in taking over the land. During these actions, King Amalric accused the Templars of surrendering an impregnable cave to the enemy. He later hanged twelve of the brethren. Meanwhile, in the King of Jerusalem's absence, Nur ed-Din attacked the principality of Antioch, trying to take the castle at Harenc. The Templars contributed to the force, under Prince Bohemond III of Antioch, that successfully repulsed them. The Muslims feigned retreat, thereafter, and ambushed the pursuing army. There followed a bloodbath from which only seven Templars escaped. After this costly disaster, the Templars seem to have resolved to put their own military judgement above that of secular Princes.[1]

In 1167 Philip de Nablus became the Grand Master of the Temple, the first to have been born in Palestine. Philip refused to accompany Amalric and the Hospitallers on the King's third raid into Egypt, which he saw as a needless breach of a peace treaty the Templars had helped to broker with the Visier in Cairo. Amalric saw this stance as a betrayal, and proceeded anyway. His army slaughtered the defenceless inhabitants of Belbeis, a city on the Nile delta. This city was given to the Order of the Hospital of St John, which had come of age as a Military Order. Its Master, Gilbert d'Assaily, was a confidant of Amalric, and had militarised the Order so it could go after the riches of Egypt. However, the Muslims took swift reprisals, driving Amalric back to Jerusalem. Belbeis was abandoned, and the Hospitallers fled. Amalric's hatred of the Templars festered. Though their decision not to involve themselves with the Egyptian adventure had been a prudent one, Amalric blamed them for his defeat. In 1170, perhaps to placate the situation, Philip de Naplous resigned as Grand Master. He was replaced by Odo de St Armand, a man, who, according to William of Tyre, feared neither God nor man before his eyes, certainly not Amalric. He had previously been a court official to Amalric (not to mention a prisoner of Sultan Nur ed-Din) and it may have been hoped that he would smooth relations with the sovereign. His clash of perogatives with the King, however, after the Assassin affair of 1173 (when a Templar killed an envoy of the Syrian Assassins to thwart their negotiations with Amalric), of course, only soured relations further.

The Fatimid Caliph, on hearing of Amalric's last invasion of Egypt, had sent the hair of his women to Nur ed-Din, a token of distress in Islamic custom. The Sultan sent a formidable force into Egypt, crossing Transjordan which was a nominal possession of the Crusaders, and engaging them in the vicinity of the Nile delta. This force was led by the formidable general Shirkuh, joined now by his young nephew Yousuf ben-Acoub-ben-Schadi, who had led a wayward life in Damascus, and was a reluctant warrior at first. But for Amalric's ill-advised expedition, the young Kurd might never have become Saladin, or *Salah-ed-Din* (integrity of religion), the great champion of Islam. With the deaths of the Fatimid Caliph and the Visier of Egypt, and then of Shirkuh, Saladin (1137–93) moved in to create a power base for himself, styling himself Sultan. He was now independent of Nur ed-Din. In 1172 he besieged the city of Gaza, which was governed by a detachment of Templars. The city, south of Ascalon, was Palestine's strategic key to Egypt. After fasting and praying, the Templars rode out in an unexpected sally against the camp of this enormous enemy. They fought with such valour that Saladin relinquished all hope of taking the city, and retreated to Egypt.

Saladin waited until the death of Nur ed-Din in 1174, and then embarked to make himself the master of Syria also. Having completed Nur ed-Din's unification of the Muslims, he prepared to accelerate the *Jihad*. He assembled an army of over 40,000 cavalry and foot soldiers, including Bedouins, Kurds, Arabs, Sudanese and Egyptians, the latter including an elite bodyguard of 1,000 Mamelukes, a caste who had been brought to Egypt from the Steppes as slave boys, and who had been indoctrinated and trained there to become fanatical, skilled and bloodthirsty warriors.[2] This army ravaged Palestine. Meanwhile Amalric died in the same year, leaving the throne to Baldwin IV, who was 9 years old, and as his tutor William of Tyre sadly observed, showed the early symptoms of leprosy. Raymond III of Tripoli was appointed regent, but another power struggle seemed unavoidable.[3]

Saladin, capitalising on divisions between the Christian leaders, took an army deep into their territory. He bypassed the Templar-garrisoned town of Gaza in 1177, and besieged Ascalon. The leprous King Baldwin IV took an army to save the city, only to be outflanked by Saladin who made for an undefended Jerusalem, after leaving a force to hold back the young King. Baldwin summoned the Templars from Gaza, and the Christian force caught up with Saladin at Montguisard. They took the Muslims off guard and won a surprising victory. At this battle, near Askalon, Odo and eighty Templars broke through Saladin's guard of Mamelukes, slaying their commander, and reaching the Sultan's tent. Once more Saladin was forced to flee (almost naked, as William of Tyre reports) on his fastest palfrey, whilst his army were scattered into the desert. Saladin retreated to Egypt. The next year, however, Saladin raised another mighty army, and was back at Damascus.

The Templars began building a castle to protect the frontier with Damascus, near Jacob's Ford on the Jordan river.[4] The location dominated the road from the coast to Damascus, and the fertile plains of Banyas. Saladin marched, failing to halt the castle's progress, but winning a crushing victory over an army led by Baldwin IV, Raymond of Tripoli and Odo de St Armand. After Saladin's mounted archers wheeled on the Crusaders' wings, the Franks scattered in chaotic confusion. Only the Templars and Hospitallers stood fast. The wounded Master of the Hospital swam the Jordan and fled to Castle Beaufort. When the Muslims attacked the castle in force, the Templar garrison were either burned alive within its walls, or drowned in the river after leaping from its flaming parapets, or were dashed to pieces on the rocks. Most of the Templar prisoners were sawn in half. The Grand Master was taken to Aleppo in chains. Saladin offered to ransom him for one of his nephews, whom the Crusaders held prisoner. The proud Odo replied that a Templar may offer nothing in ransom but his girdle and knife. He died in his prison the following year.

In the meantime, the Turkish warlords in Anatolia rallied against the Byzantines, and crushed Manuel's army at Myriocephalum. Byzantium was effectively cut off from Syria, and could no longer offer any assistance to the stricken Franks. Saladin continued to lay waste to much of Palestine, storming a succession of Crusader castles. After his sack of Nablus, however, the Franks managed to force him back to Damascus. Saladin found he had domestic intrigues to deal with, and he agreed to a treaty with the Christians in 1184. In exchange for a fortune in treasure, he promised to suspend the *Jihad* for four years.

A council in Jerusalem agreed to dispatch Patriarch Heraclius and the Grand Masters of the Military Orders to appeal for help from the west.[5] They invested their hopes especially in Henry II of England, who was the cousin of the King of Jerusalem and the new husband of Eleanor of Aquitaine. After the murder, in 1170, of Thomas à Becket, the Archbishop of Canterbury, by four knights who thought they were doing the King's will, Henry had been obliged to take the Cross, by way of penance. He was sworn to go on a Crusade. The murderers of the archbishop had already taken crusading vows, for their own absolution. The Pope had threatened Henry with eternal damnation if he did not keep his own vow to go and fight the Infidel.

The Templar Grand Master Arnold of Torroja died after falling ill in Verona, but his companions continued on to England. They were received at Reading by Henry in 1185, and fell at his feet begging for aid on behalf of the Holy Land. They gave him the keys to the Holy Sepulchre, papal letters, and the Royal Banner of the Latin Kingdom. Their reports of Saladin's advances and the danger Palestine was in were said to have brought tears to the eyes of the King of England and his courtiers. Henry promised to bring the matter before Parliament. The Patriarch, meanwhile, visited the London Temple, whilst there consecrating the new Temple Church to the Blessed Mary.

Parliament convened in the Hospitaller Commandery at Clerkenwell. There, the English nobles argued that Henry's coronation oath took priority over the penance the Pope had imposed on him – that his sacred duty was to remain, and to defend his own country from the French. They did, however, offer to raise 50,000 marks for troops, and to allow all nobles and prelates, who desired to undertake it, to go on the Crusade. Henry II therefore told Patriarch Heraclius that he was unable to leave his realm to be plundered by Frenchmen, but he would contribute financially to the Crusade. Heraclius replied that he sought a man, not money.[6]

In echoes of his conversations with Becket, the King walked along the shore with the Patriarch, trying to placate him. It was to little avail. In the end Heraclius supposedly cursed Henry. 'Hitherto thou hast reigned gloriously, but hereafter thou shalt be forsaken by him whom thou at this time forsakest.' Henry expressed his worry that his sons, with French backing, would rise against him in his absence, if he went on the Crusade. Heraclius said it was no wonder, for (at it seems it was widely said of the Plantagenet Princes) '. . . of the Devil they came and to the Devil shall they go'.[7]

Despite these arguments, Heraclius was still with Henry II when, months later, he went to Normandy, for a meeting with the King of France, Philip II Augustus, concerning a potential Crusade. The meeting was not a great success. Many predicted, pessimistically, that the True Cross, recovered from the Persians in olden times by the Patriarch Heraclius, would be lost under the pontificate, and by a Patriarch of the same name.

In the meantime, a powerful baron named Gerard de Ridefort secured for himself election as Grand Master of the Templars in the east. Ridefort, a knight of Anglo–Norman ancestry, was a militant Crusader, with a lust for glory and a proclivity for scheming and power-broking. He developed a grudge against Raymond III of Tripoli, under whom he had taken service on his arrival in the east, when Raymond reneged on a promise of land. This festering grudge would ultimately have dire consequences.

When the blind and disfigured Baldwin IV died of his leprosy in March 1185, his 7-year-old nephew was crowned Baldwin V, in the Church of the Resurrection. The child was the son of Baldwin IV's sister Sybilla by her first husband, William of Montferrat. The Templars provided security, and afterwards entertained the royal court in the Temple. Seven months later they escorted the boy's body back from Acre, where the child King had died, and buried him with his forebears in Jerusalem.

Rideford supported Sybilla, when she made herself Queen, to rule jointly with her second husband, Guy de Lusignan. Guy was a handsome parvenu knight from France, whom Sybilla had married against all good advice, having browbeaten her brother into sanctioning it. Guy's older brother was the constable of the realm, and a lover of Sybilla's mother, Queen Agnes. Guy's sovereignty was by no means universally respected; William of Tyre thought him unequal to the burden both in force and wisdom. Guy's own brother Geoffrey reputedly exclaimed 'since they have made *him* a king, surely they would have made *me* a god!'[8] The Templars had to surround the palace with troops, and close the city gates before the coronation. They also delivered the royal regalia to Patriarch Heraclius (reputedly another of Queen Agnes's former lovers), lately returned, who crowned the couple. In protest, many great barons withdrew from court, following Raymond of Tripoli, and refused to do homage at such a scandalous court. Factionalism tore the realm at a time when unity was most vital.

One of the more audacious barons of the Kingdom of Jerusalem, a friend of Ridefort and a supporter of Sybilla, was the volatile warlord Reynald de Chatillon. He had a ferocious reputation. He would, for example, throw his enemies from the walls of his fortress at Kerak with their heads encased in wooden boxes, so that they would be conscious when their bodies were broken on the rocks below. Like Guy, he had arrived from France with little, and owed his position to advantageous marriages, which brought him mastery of Antioch and Kerak. He had previously taken it upon himself to ravage the friendly island of Cyprus, where he had murdered, raped and pillaged the Greek inhabitants and cut the noses off nuns. When the previous Patriarch had refused to fund de Chatillon's 'punitive expedition', de Chatillon had seized him and taken him to the citadel where the wretched priest was stripped, smeared with honey and left for the flies in the blazing sun. De Chatillon had also survived sixteen years as a prisoner of Nur ed-Din. Later, in 1183, he had moved against the Muslim world by building a fleet on the Red Sea to harass their shipping and molest pilgrims on their way to Mecca, making the *hajj*. He had then launched a raid against Mecca itself, which he hoped to profane and destroy. His pirates had been caught and beheaded, but de Chatillon himself had escaped. Now, in the late months of 1186, he broke the truce with Saladin, brokered by Raymond III of Tripoli, and attacked a rich Muslim caravan that was crossing his territory. Saladin requested the return of de Chatillon's booty and prisoners. King Guy entreated de Chatillon to comply, but in vain.[9]

Saladin declared war, mobilising the armies of northern Syria, Aleppo, Damascus and Egypt for *Jihad*. In May 1187 Malek el Afdul, one of the sons of Saladin, led a force of 7,000 men over the Jordan. They cut to pieces the Christian force of 150 that met them at Kishon, hastily mustered by the Templar Grand Master. The Knight Templar Jacquelin de Mailly fought with such valour that he was singled out for praise even by the enemy, falling finally above a pile of his slain foes. In fact, the Muslim soldiers were returning from a reconnissance in force, at the time (an incursion permitted by Raymond III, who was still endeavouring to preserve his truce with Saladin). The Christian charge was unnecessary. Mailly had advised Ridefort against attacking them, when the odds were so unfavourable. The irascible Grand Master had accused him of cowardice, saying; 'Do you then love your blond head so much that you are so anxious to keep it?'[10] The charge was brave but doomed. The Muslim army saw the charge coming, and opened up, allowing the Christian riders into their midst, and then closed in on them, overwhelmingly. Roger de Molines, the Hospitaller Grand Master, and all his brethren were killed. Only Ridefort and two others survived of the Templars. The Muslim victors marched to Tiberias, with the severed heads of the warrior monks attached to their lances. They went on to take and kill all the Christian garrison of Nazareth.

After this blow, King Guy had barely 700 knights in the kingdom, insufficient to engage Saladin's empire in open battle. His best strategy was to adopt a defensive stance. Saladin had already moved, however, and was besieging Tiberias, on Lake Galilee. The city was in the fief of Raymond III of Tripoli, its defence left to his wife, the Countess Eschiva. Despite this, Raymond advised Guy against going to her aid, arguing that they could not reach the enemy without running out of water, and it would be better to hold off and wait for Saladin to attack, so that they could fight him under more favourable conditions. However, Raymond's ambitious rivals, including Reynald de Chatillon and Gerard of Ridefort, the Templar Grand Master, accused Raymond of treachery and cowardice, slurs which would reflect on King Guy if he followed his council. Guy had already been much criticised and mocked for not fighting Saladin before now. The hawks eventually goaded him to action. They played straight into Saladin's hands. The result was the battle of Hattin, fought near Tiberias, in July 1187.

The Christian armies, all the warriors the Latin Kingdom could muster, assembled at Acre. They marched out behind their sacred totem, the 'True Cross', carried in a golden reliquary by the Patriarch Heraclius and guarded by the Templars and Hospitallers, as if they were the new Levites and their relic a new Ark of the Covenant. The Temple had, by now, been badly depleated – two thirds of its brethren were dead, and Ridefort had been hastily forced to recruit mercenaries. The whole combined Christian force comprised at most 3,000 cavalry and 30,000 infantry, of whom many were inexperienced civilian pilgrims.[11] With better leadership and greater unity, they might have stood a chance. Tragically, Guy de Lusignan was at best indecisive, while Ridefort and de Chatillon refused to co-operate with Raymond.

Mounted Muslim archers harried the Christians throughout their dusty march to meet Saladin's main force. The Templars bore the brunt of the punishment. The army rested for the night below a twin peaked mountain known as the Horns of Hattin. The only well in the vicinity was dry, the only stream diverted by Saladin. As Raymond had predicted, they were trapped for a day without water, sweltering in their armour, in sight of the glistening lake, with Saladin's army of 80,000 men massed between them and it. Arab writers compared the Muslim hordes to mountains on the move, or the vast waves of an agitated sea. Moving up from their well watered position, the Islamic armies surrounded the Crusaders.

When the Templars advanced in battle formation, the sound was 'like the loud humming of bees'. They were 'horrible in arms, having their whole bodies covered with triple mail'. An Islamic witness remembered that he had never seen a bolder army, nor one more feared by believers in the true faith.[12] As the Christians charged, Saladin lit the dry grass between the forces, and the prevailing wind drove the choking smoke into the faces and the parched throats of his enemies. His archers let off a barrage of arrows into the knights advancing as if into Hell.

As Saladin instructed them to, the Saracen archers first targetted the Crusaders' horses. When the few knights remaining in the saddle reached the enemy, the Muslims repeated their tactic of parting before them, in order to close back in from all sides, with devastating effects. As 'desolation and destruction overtook the miserable sons of Baptism', Heraclius abdicated the honour of carrying the 'True Cross' before the army, to the Bishops of Ptolemais and Lydda. Soon afterwards Raymond of Tripoli (who may have been in Saladin's pay after all) and his knights withdrew, their horses trampling their own foot soldiers as they fled over them. This also enabled the Saracens to surround the warrior monks.

The Bishop of Ptolemais was killed, and Guy's army was pushed back up the slopes of Hattin. They made a determined last stand and twice beat the Muslims back. Saladin turned pale at the sight of the resurging Christians (as his son witnessed), but there was nothing to fear. Inevitably the Muslims, with such numerical superiority, overwhelmed their opponents.

The much maligned King Guy was captured, though he had fought courageously and was among the last to surrender. Also captured was the 'True Cross'. A Muslim witness saw:

> . . . the mountains and the plains, the hills and the valleys around covered with their dead. I saw the fallen banners sullied with dust and blood. I saw their heads broken and battered, their limbs scattered abroad, their blackened corpses piled one upon another like the stones of a building. I remembered the words of the Koran, *The infidel shall say 'What am I but dust?'* Their king and their cross were captured. The cross . . . which they bear aloft and worship with their

> eyes; they say it is the identical wood to which the god whom they adore was fastened. They have adorned it with fine gold and brilliant stones; they carried it before their armies . . . it was their first duty to defend it, and he who should desert it would never enjoy peace of mind. The capture of this cross was more grievous to them than the capture of the king. Nothing can compensate them for the loss of it.[13]

The surviving Christians were stripped and tied up, thirty or forty men sometimes, so it was said, bound with one cord. The Muslims claimed that there was not enough rope to tie up all their captives and that, in one place, 200 defeated and wretched knights were guarded by one Muslim horseman. The price of a Christian captive in the slave markets of Damascus soon dropped to three dinars. One Frank, it seems, as a sign of his new status, was sold for a single shoe.

The Grand Master of the Hospitallers escaped the carnage, to die of his wounds in Ascalon. The most important prisoners, including Gerard de Ridefort, King Guy and the noble Reynald de Chatillon (whose raid on Mecca had not been forgotten), were escorted into Saladin's tent. The Sultan offered a bowl of sherbert (some sources say wine, or iced water), symbolic of hospitality and protection, to the wretched King and the Grand Master. According to Bohadin, a secretary of Saladin, this symbolic courtesy was not offered to de Chatillon, whom Saladin rebuked for his treacheries, and demanded from him acknowledgement of Islam and its Prophet. De Chatillon refused, with a sullen hauteur. Saladin instantly beheaded him. Two days later, the Sultan offered a similar choice to the three hundred or more captured Hospitallers and Templars. To a man, common serving brothers as well as knights, they chose death over the Koran. Accordingly, the captives were led out onto a promontory above the lake. It was given to the Sultan's Sufis, Muslim scholars and holy men, to have the honour of beheading these warrior monks, whilst Saladin smiled and his soldiers applauded. It was said that the pious Templars eagerly embraced martyrdom, striving to be the first to die. Guilt and despair could have had as much to do with it. Only the Grand Master, Ridefort, was spared the massacre, for he would be kept for ransom.

Ridefort's deputy, Brother Terric, the Preceptor of Jerusalem, wrote to the west, imploring instant aid. To the London Master he wrote that after Hattin:

> The pagans, drunk with the blood of our Christians, then marched . . . against the city of Acre, and took it by storm. The city of Tyre is at present fiercely besieged and neither by night or day do the infidels discontinue their furious assault . . . They cover like ants the whole face of the country, from Tyre to Jerusalem, and even unto Gaza. The Holy City of Jerusalem, Ascalon, Tyre and Beyrout are alone left to us

> . . . and the garrisons and chief inhabitants of these places, having perished at the battle of Tiberias, we have no hope of retaining them without succour from Heaven, and instant assistance from yourselves.[14]

Saladin took Ascalon on 4 September 1187, though the small garrison resisted fiercely, even after the captured King and the Grand Master of the Templars were paraded before the walls by the Muslims. Saladin captured more than thirty Crusader castles, deprived of defenders after the disaster at Hattin. On 20 September the armies of Saladin surrounded the Holy City, and commenced a siege.

A barefoot procession led by the Queen, her ladies, priests and monks went to the Holy Sepulchre to pray for salvation. Women cut their hair and cast it to the wind to show their humility and distress. Young noblewomen did penance by standing naked in vats of cold water on Mount Calvary, but:

> Our Lord Jesus Christ would not listen to any prayer that they made, for the filth, the luxury and the adultery which prevailed in the city did not suffer prayer or supplication to ascend before God.[15]

Only two Knights Templar and a handful of Serving Brothers remained of the Order by then. Balin of Ibelin, a secular knight who had fled Hattin with Raymond of Tripoli, took command of the defence, though he was reduced to knighting young boys and commoners and spending the last of Henry II's penitential treasure on mercenaries to make up numbers. When the assault came, one witness, himself with an arrow tip stuck in his face, recalled that:

> . . . Arrows fell like raindrops . . . There were so many wounded that all the hospitals and physicians in the city were hard put to it just to extract the missiles from their bodies.[16]

The Frankish citizens of Jerusalem, a city filled with peasant refugees, widows and orphans, offered stubborn resistance to the attackers. In the end the Patriarch persuaded Balin to negotiate with Saladin, rather than see the survivors annihilated.

Saladin tried to put the wind up Balin by telling him that he intended to massacre the Franks as the first Crusaders had massacred Muslims in the Holy City. Balin responded that, if this was the case, then he would have the Dome of the Rock destroyed and his Muslim prisoners killed. Moreover, he said that his men would kill their own families, then come out to sell their own lives dearly in battle. Bluff or not, it caused the Sultan to relent, and to negotiate the ransom for the people.[17]

Jerusalem surrendered on 2/3 October (27 of Regeb by the Islamic calendar, the very anniversary of Mohammad's mystical night-flight from the Temple, through the seven Heavens to the throne of Allah). Islam took back the Temple, and the Dome of the Rock mosque, hauling down the cross that the Christians had put there, and dragging it through the streets. Saladin reconsecrated the mosque, purifying it with rose water, and installing a *nimbar* (preaching stage). This *nimbar* had been constructed specially for the mosque on the orders of Nur ed-Din, in anticipation of the recovery of Jerusalem. The Al-Aqsa mosque was similarly purged of Christian trappings. The Templar buildings were pulled down, to make a prayer court. Altars, statues, images and stalls were removed as abominations, and the place became a centre for Muslim pilgrimage once more.

Saladin was deliberately generous with the lives of the captives, and when they pleaded poverty, he dramatically reduced the price he asked for their ransom. Those who could pay the ransom were allowed to leave for Tyre. Several thousand were even set free unconditionally. Patriarch Heraclius, meanwhile, paid the ten dinars ransom for his own liberty, then quickly made away with his horde of gold, leaving his poorer flock, who could not pay, and who missed the amnesty, to be marched off to slavery. Some of the victorious Arabs took a particular delight in subjecting the captured Frankish women to rape and humiliation. Templars and Hospitallers paid to save some of them, but were somewhat parsimonious, needing to preserve whatever funds they retained for future campaigns, and naturally lothe to surrender money to the enemy. The Sultan, meanwhile, gave the Holy Sepulchre to the custody of the Syrian Christians, though some of Saladin's advisers would have preferred to see it demolished. Ten Hospitaller monks were permitted to remain for one year, to tend the sick.

The Templars re-established themselves far north in Antioch, where the Queen, the Patriarch and various barons also found safety. The remaining Hospitallers and Templars continued to resist the Muslims from various castles and territories. Saladin was delayed by the Hospitallers who made a tenacious stand at Belvoir Castle, in the Jordan valley. The Military Orders also contributed ships to a small fleet under Lord Conrad of Montferrat, which engaged Saladin's galleys.

Conrad was the brother of Sibylla's first husband, and had arrived in Outremer on pilgrimage, without realising that the Kingdom of Jerusalem was on its knees. He had sailed into Acre from Constantinople, little expecting to find the port full of Muslim warships. He captured eleven galleys and nine admirals before the remaining Muslim fleet escaped and was scuppered on Saladin's orders. Conrad's arrival at Tyre was a great morale boost for the beleaguered defenders, who at once withdrew from negotiations with their besiegers. Saladin paraded Montferrat's father (captured at the battle of Hattin), below the walls of the city, threatening to expose him to certain death in the front line if Conrad refused to surrender. Conrad's reply was that he would sooner shoot his father *himself* than yield the city. The people of Tyre repulsed numerous attacks, and by winter Saladin was forced to retire.

The Sultan gained eleven cities, however, including Ascalon, Gaza and Jaffa, as the ransom for King Guy and for Gerard de Ridefort, the Templar Grand Master. Given their record of strategic blunders, it is a wonder the Franks accepted them back. Conrad, at least, would have nothing to do with Guy, whom he refused entry into Tyre. Humiliated and with a meagre following, Guy moved north to besiege Acre. He was somehow able to establish a fortified camp there, severing the city from the mainland, which Saladin's relief forces failed, in repeated attempts, to dislodge.

Back in Europe, Pope Urban III died of grief on hearing from the Templars of the fall of Jerusalem. His short-lived successor, Gregory VIII, called for a new Crusade. The disaster had been God's punishment for the sins of all Christians, and it was time for atonement. Joscius, Archbishop of Tyre, met with Henry II of England and Philip II Augustus of France, who had been fighting one another over Normandy. The archbishop appealed for a truce between them, so that they might both take the Cross. The Templars, meanwhile, hired a fleet of ships from the Italian republics, and brought 300 Crusaders to the relief of Tyre, along with more money forwarded from Henry II. The Templars were at odds with Conrad of Montferrat, however, disputing his claim to the throne of Jerusalem. They refused to pay him any of the money.

In 1198 Gerard de Ridefort resumed command of the Christian forces. The inexperienced Crusaders, who had joined the Franks besieging Acre, attacked Saladin's camp. Believing themselves victorious, they began to pillage the camp. However, Saladin soon rallied his men, and launched a devastating counter-attack, during which Ridefort was shot through with arrows (or captured and beheaded, as other sources have it).

The next Templar leader was one Brother Walter, who in turn fell at the siege, along with the Patriarch Heraclius. The war continued, centred on the siege of Acre, where as many as 100,000 Christians perished in three years. Reinforcements arrived sporadically, from Italy, France, the British Isles and Germany. Acre was besieged by these Crusaders, who were, in turn, harried by Saladin's army. Saladin, meanwhile, proved himself an inspiring leader to his men. Even though afflicted with disease, he never rested and always led from the front, sharing all the risks faced by his men.

NOTES

1 Read, Piers Paul, *The Templars*, p. 146.
2 Brega, Isabella, *Egypt, Past and Present*, pp. 42–3. The Mamelukes were of Turko–Circasian origin. They were an early example of the Muslims converting the children of their slaves from Christainity or paganism to Islam and using them as troops.
3 Read, op.cit., p. 149.
4 Ibid., p. 152. Jacob's Ford was reputedly the place where Jacob had wrestled with an angel, as recorded in Genesis.
5 Ibid., p. 153. The Patriarch Heraclius allegedly owed his position to the fact of having been the lover of the King's mother, Queen Agnes. As Patriarch, he was notorious for keeping a concubine called Paschia de Riveri, who had reputedly poisoned her husband, a draper from Naplous. Heraclius seemed to do his best to rouse support for the cause of the Holy Land during his visits to western Europe, but went on to abandon his duty at the battle of Hattin.
6 Addison, Charles G, *The History of the Knights Templars*, p. 117.
7 Ibid., p. 118. Lord, Evelyn, *The Knights Templar in Britain*, p. 152. Lord attributes the line 'Of the devil they came . . .' to Bernard of Clairvaux. According to a legend, the Plantagenet Counts of Anjou were descended from a witch or vampire called Melusine, who flew out of the window of her earthly castle, never to be seen again.
8 Addison, op. cit,. p. 119. Addison cites the *Chronicles* of Bernard the treasurer.
9 Oldenbourg, Zoé, *The Crusades*, pp. 408, 518. Some say Saladin's sister was among those taken prisoner following de Chatillon's raid. When evaluating who was to blame for the disaster that soon befel the Latin kingdom, Oldenbourg says of de Chatillon: 'His behaviour was a real masterpiece, not even of clumsiness, but of diabolical brilliance in exacerbating the enemy just at the very moment when it was most important not to provoke him.'
10 Ibid., p. 409. Mailly's reported response to the Grand Master's taunt was: 'I shall die like a knight and you will be the one to flee.' Oldenbourg cites the *Estorie d'Eracles*, a French translation of William of Tyre, continued by a later chronicler.
11 Ibid., p. 410.
12 Addison, op.cit., p. 120.
13 Ibid., p. 125, quoting Saladin's Secretary, Omad ed-Din Kateb abu Hammad Momammad bin Hammad.
14 Ibid., p. 129.
15 Ibid., p. 130, quoting a Syrian Christian in Jerusalem.
16 Billings, Malcolm. *The Cross and the Crescent*, p. 104.
17 Oldenbourg, op. cit., p. 429.

CHAPTER VII
The Third Crusade and its Aftermath

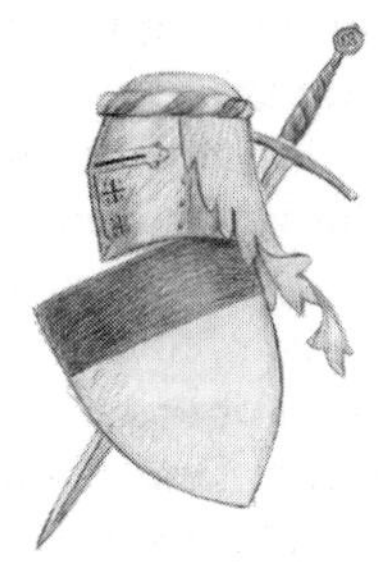

Europe had neglected the cause of the Holy Land for some time, but this changed after it became aware of the shocking loss of Jerusalem in 1185. Many ordinary people felt duty bound to sell whatever property and land they had to enable them to undertake the expedition to recover Jerusalem. Knights, meanwhile, came to identify 'Crusade', a newly popular term, with nobility, adventure and the chivalric ideals they aspired to. It offered not only salvation but the ultimate test of courage and virtue.

The German Emperor, Frederick I Hohenstaufen, was the first great prince of Christendom to heed the call of the Third Crusade. Frederick Barbarossa, as he was known, was a veteran of the Second Crusade.[1] He led a formidable army down through the Balkans, under his banner of a black eagle, having written to Saladin with warnings that he should return what he had taken or discover the consequences.

The Byzantine Emperor, Isaac Angelus, mistrusted westerners, what with the Italian Normans encroaching into Macedonia, and other Catholics supporting the rebellions in Byzantium's Balkan provinces.[2] Isaac had grown quite close to Saladin, and only under duress did he agree to transport the German Crusaders across the Dardanelles. The Teutons preserved their discipline and survived the harsh journey through Anatolia. They defeated a Turkish army under Saladin's son Malik, and progressed through the Taurus mountains. Then, one day, after a long hot trek, Barbarossa fell from his mount while crossing the surging Calycadnus river, and was drowned. Deprived of their leader, the disciplined Germans fell apart, and many were so demoralised they immediately started home again. Some carried on, but they suffered terrible losses. Many of those who made it to Syria did so only to die of the plague there.

In France and England, a tax called the 'Saladin Tithe' was levied to finance the new Crusade, demanding a tenth of everyone's income. Parishioners had to pay the money to a committee which included the local priest, a Templar and a Hospitaller. The Crusade was delayed, however, by new troubles between Henry II and Philip II Augustus, the latter having formed an alliance with Henry's son, Richard the Lionheart. Richard (whose mother, Eleanor of Aquitaine, had accompanied her first husband, Louis VII, on the Second Crusade) forced his father to a truce under humiliating terms. Eleanor, whom Henry had kept in prison, had raised Henry's sons to hate him. Henry died within days of his humiliation, on 6 July 1189.

King Richard the Lionheart arrived in the Levant in 1191, some time behind his ally, Philip Augustus of France. Richard, on his way through the Mediterranean, had fought King Tancred of Sicily, from whom Richard rescued his sister. Later storms broke up Richard's fleet, and some of his men were washed up on Cyprus, and imprisoned by the Byzantine despot of the island, the self-styled Emperor of Cyprus, Isaac Ducas Comnenus. Isaac, who had been governor of Cicilia, also trapped Richard's bethrothed, the Princess Berengaria of Navarre, and his mother Eleanor of Aquitaine, when the ladies and their company also found themselves shipwrecked in Cyprus. Richard arrived and forced Isaac to make restitution. Isaac reneged on his agreement and Richard, joined by Guy de Lusignan, went to war. Soon Cyprus was conquered, and Isaac was in chains.

Richard's partnership with Philip Augustus had become somewhat strained on the eventful journey. (Philip was affronted by Richard's marriage to Berengaria. Richard had rejected Philip's sister, Alaise, because, so Richard claimed, she had been deflowered by his father, Henry II). The siege of Acre had dragged on for two years, supervised by Guy, and consolidated by Philip and the French army. By the time Richard's main force arrived, thousands of Crusaders were already dug in around the landward part of the city, including a significant Italian contingent, Templars and Hospitallers, and a new German Military Order, founded along Templar lines – the Teutonic Knights.[3]

The Templars fought under their new Grand Master, Robert de Sable, who had earlier commanded a division of the impressive English fleet of over 200 ships. The besiegers had built formidable siege engines, including ballistas, and a massive trebuchet, wittily named the 'bad neighbour', with which they pounded the land wall with huge boulders. However, no great offensive could be launched because Saladin's force remained at large, effectively besieging the besiegers. If this was not bad enough, there was much dissent and suspicion among the Christians. Fever also took a considerable toll all the while, and morale was low.

The Muslims from Acre launched a devastating sally against their besiegers, causing the French King to fall into such melancholia that he would not even mount a horse. Richard was different. Like Saladin, he would lead his men from the front, sharing their risks and calling out encouragement, even though at times he became so ill that he had to be carried about on a litter. With the city now blockaded as well as besieged, meanwhile, the defenders could no longer receive supplies by sea. In July 1191 Acre's Muslim garrison finally negotiated surrender. The Templars had taken a coastal part of the city after a marine assault, and proceeded to make their new headquarters there. They built a stronghold that, a century later, would become the last part of the Latin kingdom to fall to Islam.

The King of England had conquered Cyprus, which he now sold to the Templars for 3,000 *livres d'or*. The Templars were not popular rulers among the Greek Orthodox islanders, however. The high taxes the Order imposed led to riots. Some of the islanders plotted to move against the Templars (who were few in number) and to kill them all, on Easter day, 1192. The Templars became aware of the plot, and retired to their citadel in Nicosia, which the rebellious Cypriots then attacked. It seems the Templars offered to quit the island if their lives would be spared, but the Cypriots refused these terms, probably fearing future reprisals. The Templars rode out at dawn, launching a surprise attack on the Cypriots, killing many and crushing the rebellion. They later conceded that they had not the resources to retain the island, however, and sold it back to Richard.

In Outremer, Queen Sybilla of Jerusalem and her two daughters by Guy had died in the epidemics. The heiress to the kingdom was now Isabella, Sybilla's half sister, who had married Humphrey of Toron, son of Reynald de Chatillon. (The union had taken place in the castle of Kerak, then besieged by Saladin. The child bride might not have survived the wedding night, had not the hostess sent some cake out to the Sultan, who in turn enquired which tower the newly-weds would sleep in, so that he could tell his army to try to avoid it in their bombardment.)[4] The Latin nobles wanted to have Isabella's marriage to Humphrey annulled, so that they could marry her to Conrad, and make him titular King of Jerusalem. The poor Princess was therefore abducted from her tent and forced into this second memorable wedding. Louis favoured this, being a cousin of Conrad, whilst Richard continued to support Guy de Lusignan, who was his friend and vassal. A compromise was eventually reached. Guy could keep the crown for his lifetime, which would afterwards pass to Conrad and his descendants. Conrad was given large territories to compensate. Later a settlement was agreed between Guy, Richard and the Templars, whereby Guy surrendered his claim to Jerusalem altogether in exchange for becoming 'Emperor' of Cyprus.

Richard, while in Acre, stayed with the Templars, whilst Philip Augustus lodged in the city's citadel. It was at this time that Richard's men tore down the Duke of Austria's ensign, which had been raised to an equal position with the Plantagenet leopards and the fleur de lys standard of the King of France. It was Templar diplomacy that helped to preserve unity after this affront. Philip, meanwhile, a reluctant Crusader anyway, soon took his leave of the expedition and sailed home, though much of the French army stayed behind under the Duke of Burgundy.[5] Richard was eager to move south, planning to recapture the coast before striking inland towards Jerusalem. He had his men slaughter his 2,700 Muslim prisoners of war when Saladin refused any ransom and prevaricated in his negotiations.

The Crusade marched out for Jaffa in August, along the shore, with the Templars and Hospitallers taking the van and rearguard of Richard's army. The fleet kept pace with them, and the baggage train went between the army and the sea. A column of foot soldiers and English archers made a protective screen on the left flank of the cavalry, against the shadowing Muslim army. They marched towards Jaffa. They were clearly hardy men. One of their enemy recalled that some Crusaders marched on with ten or more darts stuck in their bodies.[6] They moved all day, harried all the time by Saladin's mounted archers, and went foraging by night.

The constant assault at last became too much for the proud Crusaders to bear and, without Richard's orders, the Hospitallers, then the Templars, then the rest, counter-charged at the Muslims. Taking a savage vengeance, they left the sand strewn with the bodies of horses, camels and decapitated men. Richard resumed the lead, cutting his foes down like a reaper. He decisively repulsed Saladin at this, the battle of Arsuf.

However, the Third Crusade lost momentum on the path to Jerusalem. After taking Jaffa and Gaza, the Military Orders advised Richard against attempting to take the Holy City, tantalising though that option was. They believed their force too small to hold it, and that the wiser strategy lay in taking measures against Egypt. Whilst Ayyubid Egypt remained powerful, Outremer remained vulnerable.[7]

After negotiating a treaty with al Adil, the brother of Saladin, safeguarding pilgrims, and securing Tyre, Acre and Jaffa in Crusader hands, Richard abandoned his quest for Jerusalem. He refused even to look upon the city. He had come within twelve miles of it. A council was held with the local barons, who rejected Guy outright as King. However, before they could crown their candidate Conrad of Monferrat, Conrad was slain by some Assassins – sent by their sheik, Rasid al-Din Sinan, disguised as monks. Speculation as to their motive for the murder was rife. Some averred that Richard had put them up to it. As for the Templars, their links to the Assassins remain mysterious, but they were no particular friends of Conrad. The barons' next choice for King (be it in name only) of Jerusalem was Count Henry of Champagne, whom they married to Isabella, who was still only 21, a mere week after Conrad's death.

Richard received troubling news concerning Prince John's usurpation of power in England, and Philip's treacherous encroachments on Normandy. He made a last attempt for the Holy City, this time getting even closer.[8] By now, however, King Richard had grown seriously ill, and his men were exhausted, broke and homesick. Saladin's men were also worn out from years in the field, far more time than Muslims customarily owed for military duty. Desertion was an increasing problem for the Sultan. In a final treaty, Saladin permitted the Christians to keep all their coastal cities, and to have free access to the holy places. However, he obliged them to demolish Ascalon (which they had only just rebuilt), a thorn in Saladin's side on the route to Egypt. Balin of Ibelin, Henry of Champagne and the Grand Masters of the Military Orders signed a five-year peace treaty.

Most of the Crusaders departed for home by sea. Richard himself opted to travel by land. The Templar Grand Master Robert de Sable helped him by providing the ship for the first part of his journey, and four Templar guards, with whom he would travel disguised as another member of the Order. After more adventures, however, Richard was discovered, and made a prisoner by Leopold, Duke of Austria, in collusion with the German Emperor Henry VI, Philip Augustus and Prince John, until a massive ransom was extorted from Richard's loyal subjects, to the ruination of England. None could have predicted Saladin's imminent death, in 1193, by which time the Third Crusade had disintegrated.

Gilbert Horal, who became Grand Master of the Templars in 1195, launched the building of the massive fortress called Pilgrims' Castle, commanding the road between Acre and Jerusalem. At Acre the Templars built two towers, 100 feet high, seventy-four feet wide, and other fortifications with formidable walls. Their complex contained a Grand Master's palace, chapels, houses, halls and offices, pastures, vineyards and orchards, all enclosed in a fortress above the sea.

The Fourth Crusade was preached in 1198 by the lawyer-Pope Innocent III. Innocent taxed the clergy to raise money, and threatened nobles with dreadful judgement if they neglected to take the Cross. Count Tibald of Champagne sent delegates to negotiate transport arrangements with the maritime republic of Venice. They agreed to pay the city 85,000 marks, and to split any booty. Thibald of Champagne was sickly, however, and command passed to Marquis Boniface of Montferrat.

Falling in debt to Venice, the Crusade became highjacked and diverted. The Venetians had profitable trading relations with Alexandria, and would have gained little from a Crusade against the Muslims. They did hate their economic rivals, the Byzantines, however. The Venetian president, or Doge, Enrico Donaldo, who joined the Crusaders, had been blinded in Constantinople during a riot against resident Latins that flared up in 1182. Venice now used the Fourth Crusade for its own ends – profit and vengeance. In 1202 it attacked the Christian city of Zara, which Venice had lost to the Hungarians. The citizens were robbed and dispossessed. Innocent III excommunicated the entire army, but later rescinded, rather than see his Crusade crumble. The Crusade fizzled out anyway after the invasion, plunder and perfidious rape of Constantinople in 1204.

Emperor Isaac Angelus had been deposed and blinded by his brother, Alexius III. The son of Isaac Angelus, another Alexius (later Alexius IV), approached the Crusaders, promising them treasure galore, trading privileges, Church reunification and military help in the Crusade if they would restore him and his father to power. When the Crusader fleet arrived at Constantinople, the mercenaries of Alexius III offered little resistance. Prince Alexius and his father were crowned. During the winter, however, relations deteriorated. The Byzantines rebelled against the westerners. Another palace coup deprived the Crusaders of their puppet rulers, and they responded by taking the glorious city for themselves. The French Crusaders and the Venetians, from their galleys, attacked the ancient walls, defended by the Greeks and their English and Danish mercenaries. The Crusaders scaled the walls and took the city in a night. Three days of plunder, rape and murder followed. They gleefully despoiled the unimaginable treasures of its palaces and churches. There was a scramble for holy relics also, during which the Crusaders made off with several pieces of the True Cross, two nails from the Crucifixion, the Holy Spear (a different one from that found at Antioch), vials of Christ's blood, the Crown of Thorns, and a 'head of St John'. The Crusaders then burst into St Sophia's Cathedral, where they drank stolen wine from the bejewelled liturgical chalices and seated a prostitute on the Patriarch's throne, where they had her sing profane songs. Later, under the same great dome, they crowned Count Baldwin of Flanders as Latin Emperor of Constantinople.[9]

The Knights Templar, under Philip de Plessiez, who became Master in 1201, to their credit, played no part in these outrages. They had their own fleet, and like many other Crusaders went to the Holy Land by other routes, perhaps wiser to how Venice might manipulate them. They did, however, play a minor role in the government of the Latin kingdoms, that the Crusaders subsequently established in the former Byzantine Empire (having divided it among their chiefs), and in the conquest of central Greece. These colonies in no way helped the cause of the Holy Land, rather they diverted vital resources and settlers away from Palestine, and secured the eternal enmity of the Greeks. Venice was filled with looted riches, meanwhile. Though in 1261 the Greeks would reclaim

Constantinople, the Byzantine Empire would never again be as it was. The Fourth Crusade was a wonderful gift to the Muslim cause.

In 1204, in the Holy Land, Aimery, the titular King of Jerusalem, made a six-year peace treaty with Sultan al-Adil. Aimery had realised that few of the so-called Crusaders would be tempted from the rich pickings of Constantinople. After the Fourth Crusade, the Pope would escalate 'Crusades' within Europe, to suppress the Cathar or Albigensian heresy in southern France, and other groups who decried the worldliness of the Church or opposed it politically. There was also an on-going 'Crusade' against the pagan Livs. Pope Innocent III granted the same spiritual indulgences to warriors who fought (for a term of forty days) in the Albigensian and Baltic 'Crusades' as had hitherto been given to knights who fought for the Holy Sepulchre. Full Crusader indulgences were also offered to those who fought the Moors in Spain. In 1212 the Templars made up a contingent of the army under Alfonso III of Castille, which routed the Muslims at Navas de Tolosa.

Pope Innocent III had also instigated a French invasion of England, after a dispute between King John and the clergy. King John often stayed at the London Temple. He issued the order for his fleet to assemble at Portsmouth to resist the French from there. During his disputes with the Pope, the Templars often acted as mediators. Finally browbeaten, John surrendered his kingdom to '. . . God and the holy apostle of Peter and Paul'. He made himself a vassal of the Pope.

The reign of Innocent III (1198–1216) also saw the foundation of the Dominican Order, from which the Inquisition arose. Domingo de Guzman, a Castillian monk, was sent to preach against the Dualist message of the Cathars. He soon founded a zealous Mendicant Order that concerned itself with the rooting out of heresy in the Languedoc (south-western France). Dominican Inquisitors created a climate of fear and denunciation, enforcing dogmatic conformity in a region already wasted and soaked in blood by the armies of Catholic 'Crusaders' from the north.

The 'Crusaders' attacked the lands of Count Raymond VI of Toulouse, a descendant of the Raymond who led the First Crusade. Count Raymond VI now refused to persecute his own people, as the Pope demanded. On Ste Mary Magdelene's day (22 July) 1209 the 'Crusaders' massacred the people of Béziers and burned up to 7,000 in her church there, whilst others were run through in the streets. Arnold Amaury, the Cistercian abbot of Cîteaux, oversaw the massacre, and told his troops, when they asked how to distinguish between believers and heretics: 'Kill them all, God will know his own.' Similar massacres occurred in Carcassonne and Albi.[10]

The 'Crusade' dragged on for two decades, led by Simon de Montfort (the father of Simon de Montfort, Earl of Leicester, more famous in England for his revolt against Henry III). Simon de Montfort the elder was a ruthless but devout knight, who had abandoned the Fourth Crusade in disgust after the debacle at Zara. Now hundreds of Cathars were burnt at the stake and others were mutilated. Most of those who resisted the forces of Simon de Montfort, however, were not Cathars at all. Pedro II of Aragon, known as Pedro the Catholic, a hero of Navas de Tolosa, was killed fighting de Montfort's 'Crusaders' the following year. In the end, the Count of Toulouse was brought down, his line extinguished and the region subjected to the Capetian dynasty.

The Military Orders had many establishments in the locality, but seem not to have played any belligerent part in the Albigensian Crusade. The Counts of Toulouse had been generous patrons to them in better times, and therefore the Orders tried to preserve their neutrality. This conflict was less of a Crusade than a feudal civil war, stirred up by a partisan Pope. The Templars had fought alongside Pedro the Catholic against the Moors, but at the same time could not escape their duty to Rome. In 1215 de Montfort stayed in a Templar Preceptory whilst attacking Montpellier. Other Templars accompanied Louis VIII on his attacks on Marmande in 1219, but do not seem to have participated in the ensuing slaughter. Still, it seems it was accepted that the Templars' primary commitment was to the Holy Land, and they were not obliged, and showed no particular desire, to take part in the papally sanctioned campaigns against other Christians.

The Inquisition

The medieval Catholic priesthood were the preservers of learning and literacy in western Europe, and generally a civilising influence. However, they were also a totalitarian body, intolerant of religious dissenters. They denounced any diversion from their dogma as heresy – the holding of beliefs which could imperil the soul. The Inquisition was the weapon the Church created with which to persecute heretics. It would force people to say and do things that they did not believe, rob, imprison and mutilate them, make them accuse others, and often roast them to death, 'for the salvation of their souls'.

In 1188 Pope Lucius III had authorised his bishops to arrest and question people in regions infected with heresy. Anyone found to hold non-Catholic beliefs was to be 'handed to the secular arm' for punishment. In 1199 Innocent III proclaimed that all property of heretics should be seized. The proceeds were shared with local potentates who supported the Inquisition. Always there was the presumption of guilt. The Dominican friars rose up in the Languedoc to counter the heretical message of the Cathars. Soon it became clear that preaching alone would not wipe out the alternative creed.

In 1233 Gregory IX affirmed the Dominicans' responsibility for investigating heresy, forbidding even bishops to interfere with their work. In 1252 torture was officially sanctioned by Innocent IV.[11] This, allied to a presumption of guilt and the rewarding of informants with a share of seized property, secured easy convictions. Methods of torture included thumbscrews, toe-screws, foot-crushing boots, and the strappado and rack (described later). The mouth pear was a vice-like device which was employed to pry the heretic's jaw open to an agonising degree.

The Inquisitors would visit a town, and preach against heresy. They would then call for heretics to come forward voluntarily to receive penances, and also call for informants. These informants could give names anonymously. Torture and false promises often extracted a list of other heretics from each victim, so there was usually a satisfactory number of convicts for the Inquisitors to hand over to the secular arm. Any official who refused to execute these heretics would himself be charged with abetting heresy. Execution took the form of a public burning, often over slow fires. Terror of torture produced confessions which confirmed the prejudices of the Inquisitors. People said whatever they thought their tormentors wanted to hear, and responded to their leading questions. By the 1300s, the Inquisition was a victim of its own success, and was running out of heretics to pursue. It asked the Pope to extend its mandate. Thereafter, the emphasis would shift towards workers of black magic and those perceived to be in league with the Devil, in secret plots against the Church.

NOTES

1 Read, Piers Paul, *The Templars*, p. 167. 'Barbarossa' meant 'red beard'.
2 Oldenbourg, Zoé, *The Crusades*, p. 441. Isaac Angelus had risen to power amid a period of upheaval that had seen the massacring of Italians living in Constantinople, and the elimination of the Comneni dynasty.
3 Read, op. cit., p. 169. The Order of Teutonic Knights was founded by Crusaders from Lubeck and Bremen to tend their sick and wounded comrades. Like the Knights of St John, they ran a hospital, but adopted the Rule and white habit of the Templars, though with a black cross. They were dedicated to Sainte Mary of the Germans. In 1196 Pope Celestine III approved them as a Military Order.
4 Ibid. Not that there would have been much activity that night in the bridal tower, the bride being but a child at the time, and the groom being as effeminate and gentle as his father was bellicose and brutal. Isabella's marriage to Humphrey when she was below the age of consent was used as an excuse for its annulment by the barons. The hapless young bride actually loved Humphrey well enough, and found herself torn from him to serve the political ambitions of other men.
5 Ibid., p. 171. Philip Augustus had it in mind to break the 'Truce of God' and invade Richard's realms in western France, while he was still away. Philip came home acting the conquering hero, when many knew him to be a

turncoat. He spent the intervening years badmouthing Richard to anyone who would listen, and plotting against him.

6 Addison, Charles G, *The History of the Knights Templars*, p. 144, quoting Bohadin.

7 Read, op. cit., pp. 173, 216. The Ayyubids were Sultans and Emirs of Saladin's blood. Ayyub was Saladin's father. Saladin set up several relatives as rulers in Egypt and Syria. These were deposed eventually by the Mamelukes.

8 Ibid., p. 174. There was also the famous skirmish at Jaffa, which Saladin invaded and which Richard and a few ships came to relieve. Saladin, impressed by Richard's courage, sent him fresh horses when Richard's horse was killed under him, making it clear that Richard was to know who had sent them.

9 Ibid., pp. 188–9; Jones, Terry and Ereira, Alan, *Crusades*, pp. 155–68; Billings, Malcolm, *The Cross and the Crescent*, pp. 125–8, and Haldon, John, *Byzantium: A History*, pp. 46–7. The Venetians, trading profitably with the Ayyubid Sultan of Cairo, had no desire to let the Fourth Crusade attack the Nile. Ensnaring them with debt, Venice first used the Crusaders to attack the Christian city of Zara. After the Fourth Crusade, Byzantium suffered more at Christian hands than it ever had at Muslim ones. The Doge of Venice, Enrico Donaldo, had all the revenge he could wish for. There had been bad blood between the Catholic and Greek Orthodox Churches for generations. The Byzantines had been alienated by the Franks, whom they saw as Barbarians. The Catholics saw the Greeks as schismatic heretics, from whom they had no qualms about 'rescuing' sacred relics along with anything else they fancied. Hordes of fabulous treasures were stolen and taken to Venice. Meanwhile, the victors divided up the Byzantine Empire into Latin kingdoms. These diverted much needed manpower and resources that could have gone to the Holy Land. The Italian maritime republics put their commercial interests above matters of spiritual fidelity. Genoese and Venetian merchants would sell arms, slaves and timber to the Mamelukes.

10 O'Shea, Stephen, *The Perfect Heresy*, pp. 5, 88–103, 137.

11 Ibid., p. 229. The Pope permitted the use of torture by the Inquisition, in the bull *Ad expiranda*. However, he advised that the victim should not lose a limb, too much blood, or their life. A heretic was to be in relatively good health when they burnt him. Heretics would always be sentenced to burn '. . . the unbelieving and the abominable . . . and sorcerers and idolaters shall have their part in a lake which burneth with fire and brimstone' (Revelation, 21:8).

CHAPTER VIII

The Fate of the Holy Land

In AD 1212 thousands of children across Europe spontaneously ran away from home and set off on a quest to liberate the Holy Sepulchre. It was believed by certain preachers that the sinfulness of the adult Crusaders had brought about the loss of Jerusalem and the favour of the Lord, but that the innocence of children might yet restore it. It seems some hundreds of these children were taken on board by Genoese sailors, who delivered them to Egypt, where they sold them into slavery.

The Holy Land, meanwhile, witnessed more bloodshed. Guillaume de Chatres became Master of the Temple there in 1217. His reports to the Pope praised Saphadin, the Ayyubid Sultan of Egypt, as a reasonable ruler, reluctant to molest Christians. A great number of pilgrims visited the Holy City, including the King of Hungary, the Duke of Austria, and various German Princes, without trouble from the Muslims. This did not suit the Pope, to whom the concept of compromising with the Infidel was anathema. A plan was launched, therefore, to attack the town of Damietta in Egypt, then to march on Jerusalem. Indulgences (certificates of divine forgiveness) were sold by the clergy to raise money, and the Pope tried to suspend the European 'Crusades' the Church had brought about, to free up men for the east. This Fifth Crusade began with a few skirmishes in Palestine, led by King Andrew of Hungary, who soon returned home, having collected the head of St Stephen. Other knights remained in the east for the advance on Egypt. Reinforcements arrived, and the Crusaders attacked the strongly defended Damietta. Subsequently, the Sultan offered a thirty-year truce, and the return of all the territory of the Kingdom of Jerusalem, but for two fortresses in the Transjordan linking the Ayyubid domains of Egypt and Syria. King John 'of Jerusalem' was eager to accept, but was over-ruled by the Papal Legate, Cardinal Pelagius, who expected the arrival of the German Emperor, Frederick II. Damietta fell to the Crusaders and the Christians waited for Frederick, rebuffing generous peace overtures from the Sultan. Twenty months went by and Frederick did not come. The army moved out for Cairo (a city identified by the Crusaders with Babylon).

The expedition ended in disaster for the Christians, and in 1218 Guillaume de Chatres was killed leading his knights. He was succeeded as Grand Master by Peter de Montaigne, erstwhile Grand Preceptor of Spain. Peter had this to write to Alan Marcel, the Grand Preceptor of England:

> Hitherto we have had favourable information to communicate unto you touching our exertions in the cause of Jesus Christ: now, alas, such have been our reverses and disasters which our sins have brought unto us in the land of Egypt that we have nothing but ill news to announce. After the capture of Damietta, our army remained for some time in a state of inaction which brought upon us frequent complaints from the Eastern and the Western Christians. At length . . . the legate of the Holy Pontiff and our Soldiers of the Cross put themselves in march by land and by the Nile, and arrived in good order at the spot where the Sultan was encamped, at the head of an immense number of enemies of the Cross. The river Taphneos, an arm of the great Nile, flowed between the camp of the Sultan and our forces. Being unable to ford this river, we pitched our tents on its banks, and prepared bridges to enable us to cross. In the mean time, the annual inundation rapidly increased, and the Sultan, passing his armed galleys through the ancient canal, floated them into the Nile below our position and cut off our communications with Damietta.
>
> Nothing was to be done to retrace our steps. The Sultans of Aleppo and Damascus, two brothers of the Sultan . . . with an immense multitude of infidels had come to their assistance, attempting to cut off our retreat. At night we commenced our march, but the infidels cut through the embankment of the Nile, the water rushed along several unknown passages and ancient channels, and encompassed us on all sides. We lost our provisions, many of our men were swept into the stream, and the further progress of our Christian warriors was arrested. The waves continued to increase upon us, and in this terrible inundation we lost all our saddles . . . and everything we had. We could neither advance nor retreat, and knew not whither to turn. We could not attack the Egyptians on account of the great lake which extended itself between them and us. We were without food, and caught . . . like fish in a net. There was nothing left for us but to treat with the Sultan . . .[1]

1a. Knight slaying an Albigension heretic.

1b. Islamic portrait of a Sultan, probably Saladin.

1c. Saint Bernard of Claviraux.

1d. 'Agnus Dei'. The lamb of God, a device used by the Templars, surviving in the arms of the Middle Temple.

1e. Richard the Lion-Heart.

2a. Covento de Christo, Tomar, Portugal, HQ of Templars and their successors, the knights of Christ.

2b. Group of Templars from the tomb of the Infante Filipe, Villasorga, Spain. 13th Century.

3a. Gate under which Templars would have been led from jail at Lincoln Castle to trial in the cathedral.

3b. The tower called 'Cobb Hall' at Lincoln Castle, wherein the Templars were imprisoned.

3c. The Jew's House, Lincoln – formerly a Templar property.

4a. Crucifix carved in Cobb Hall, Lincoln Castle, by a medieval prisoner, probably a Templar. *(top left)*

4b. Graffiti in Cobb Hall Tower, Lincoln Castle, carved by medieval prisoners, probably Templars. These are similar in style to carvings in Royston cave near Baldock, Herts. *(top right)*

4c. Cross carved by a medieval prisoner at Lincoln Castle. *(left)*

5a. Gnostic grave stela showing severed heads.

5b. Templar Grand Master with rod of office.

5c. The head painted on a board found at Temple Combe.

5e. Grave of Templar, showing sword and elongated chalice. *(right)*

5d. The seal of the Templars showing two knights on the same horse. *(left)*

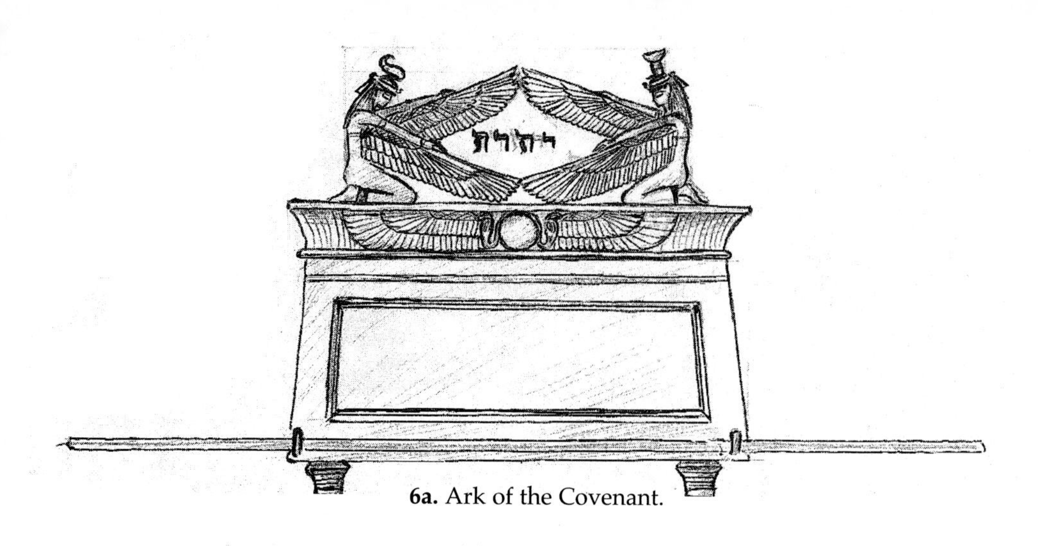

6a. Ark of the Covenant.

6b. Battle of Hattin (copied from the chronicle of Matthew Paris).

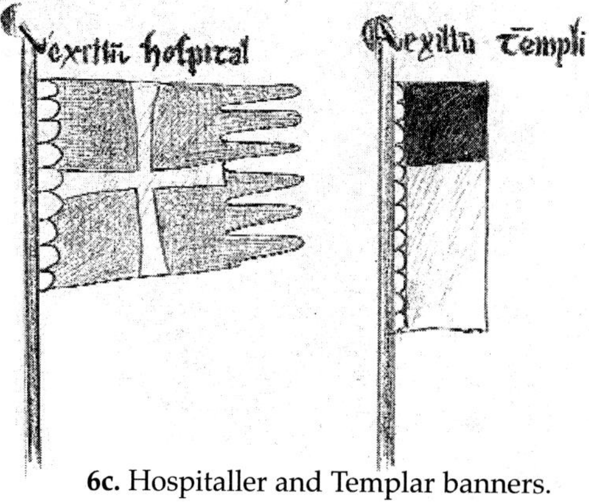

6c. Hospitaller and Templar banners.

6d. Two Templars on a horse (copied from the chronicle of Matthew Paris).

7a. Temple Church, London.

7b. Baphomet illustration by Elepha's Lévi in "Transcendental Magic: Its Doctrine & Ritual".

8a. Tomb of King Philip the Fair, in St Denis's Abbey. *(left)*

8b. Tomb of Knight Hospitaller Bernard de Faix, Gerona, Spain c1382. *(right)*

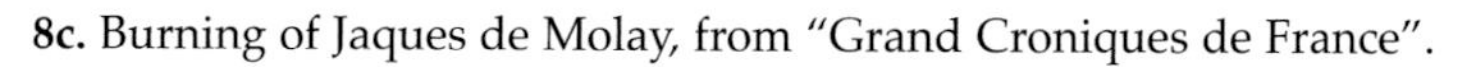

8c. Burning of Jaques de Molay, from "Grand Croniques de France".

The Crusaders were forced to agree to evacuate Damietta, and to free their Muslim prisoners in Tyre and Acre. In return, the Sultan conceded to the return of Christian prisoners. Many Crusaders in Damietta were discontented with these terms, but there were neither men nor money to defend the city. A less favourable truce was agreed. The year was 1221, and the Sultan took back Damietta in triumph.

In 1227 Frederick II Hohenstaufen, Emperor of Germany and Sicily, married Princess Yolande, heiress to the Kingdom of Jerusalem and had himself crowned King. Then, whilst he seduced her cousin, he banished his 14-year-old bride to his harem on Palermo, where she died a week after giving the Emperor a son. In 1228, without papal approval, Frederick II invaded the Holy Land, which he presumed to rule as regent for his infant.[2]

Frederick's diplomatic dealings with Sultan al-Kamil recovered Bethlehem, Nazareth and (supposedly for a ten-year term) Jerusalem. The Muslims retained Temple Mount, and Jerusalem remained an open city, unfortified and connected to the coast only by a narrow corridor of Christian territory. The Muslims also agreed to return the 'True Cross' (though in the end they apparently could not find the relic). In return Frederick promised to protect the Sultan's interests against all enemies. Frederick was also required to give no aid to the Templars and Hospitallers. This probably little bothered the Emperor. The Templars had refused to march with him, as he had been excommunicated, and was embroiled in a notorious power struggle with the Pope. Though the Emperor employed a Templar as his chancellor, as a whole the Order were no friends of Frederick. He was loyally supported, however, by the Teutonic Knights. Frederick crowned himself in the Holy Sepulchre, causing the Pope to lay Jerusalem under interdict, forbidding all church services there. Frederick left the Holy Land in 1229, having learned that his territories in the Italian peninsula had been invaded by papal armies. The autocratic Emperor left the Christians in the east so malcontented that, as he departed from Acre, he was reputedly pelted with scraps of rotten meat.

Armand de Perigord became Grand Master of the Templars in 1236. Groups of Crusaders under Tibald of Champagne and then Richard of Cornwall, the brother of Henry III of England, arrived in the Holy Land and strengthened the position of the Latins. Treaties with Damascus and Egypt secured the return of much of the Judean hinterland to the Christians.

In a letter to the Templar Master of England, Perigord reported that the Christians had compelled the Sultan to restore to them all the territory west of the Jordan. Jerusalem was in Catholic hands again:

> . . . all the Saracens being driven out . . . To all the sacred places there is again free access to the faithful of Christ, nor is it to be doubted but

> that in this happy and prosperous condition we might long remain, if our Eastern Christians would from henceforth live in greater concord and unanimity . . .[3]

Perigord could, alas, report no such spirit of co-operation. The barons and prelates were once again at one another's throats, inspired by envy and hatred, and the defence of the kingdom rested on the Temple, virtually alone. Perigord planned to build a great castle to defend Jerusalem, but doubted whether the Templars could stand long against the Sultan of Egypt, whom he considered a most powerful and talented man, unless Christ and his faithful extended an efficacious support.

Eight hundred and fifty workmen and 400 slaves were put to work on the rebuilding of Castle Saphet, but it was to no avail. Before it was complete, Jerusalem was lost to another savage warrior tribe, the Khorezmians, and the Crusaders were decimated.

Matthew Paris (though not an eye-witness) recorded an impression that faith began to waver among the Crusaders in the east.

> Many people . . . began to give way to desperation and blasphemy as well as hunger . . . They said to one another 'Why has Christ, for whom and with whom we have been fighting, abandoned us? . . . Christ's enemies triumphantly glory in our blood and booty taken from us. First at the city of Damietta, when surrounded by the waters of the Nile, we were forced to give up that city, won at the cost of so much blood. Again, not far from Antioch, the distinguished Knights of the Temple, their standard-bearer decapitated, were defeated in confusion. Again, a few years later, we were defeated by the Saracens at Gaza, after having been redeemed by the Englishman Earl Richard. Afterwards, almost the entire Christian community in the Holy Land was cut to pieces by the Khorezmians who polluted and destroyed all the places that are called holy . . . What benefit to us is our devotion, the prayers of the monks, the alms of our friends? Is not the law of Mahomet better than the law of Christ?' And thus delirious words resounded from the tottering faith and the lenten days seemed more a time of punishment than penance.[4]

The Khorezmians were a race of nomadic Turks, recently camped near Edessa. They had fled from their homeland in the wake of the invading Mongols, and offered a foretaste of the savagery to come. As mercenaries for Egypt, the Khorezmian war bands, comprising perhaps ten thousand horsemen, bypassed Damascus, and ravaged Crusader Galilee. They took Jerusalem in 1244, from the small garrison Frederick II had left. The city fell after three days. Only around three hundred out of a population of six thousand escaped the ensuing massacre. Then the Khorezmians violated the Holy Sepulchre, slew the priests there and set fire to that church and the other churches of the city.

The Khorezmians met up with the Egyptian army, under the Mameluke general Rukn ad-Din Baybars, at Gaza. At the battle of La Forbie/Herbiya, they defeated a flimsy alliance of Crusaders and Damascenes, under Philip de Montfort. The Crusaders' side attacked first, but were held off until the Khorezmian cavalry bore down on their flanks. The Damascenes fled before the Khorezmian onslaught, leaving them to kill five thousand Christians and take eight thousand prisoners, including the Templar Grand Master, Armand de Perigord. It was the worst defeat the Franks had suffered since Hattin. Only eighteen out of the three hundred strong Templar contingent survived.[5] The Grand Master of the Hospitallers also died.

The vice-master of the Temple wrote to the Pope, describing the slaughter of the children, women and old men who sought sanctuary in the Holy Sepulchre, and the decapitation of the priests as they knelt in prayer. 'Alas, the sins of our Christian people have just now raised up for . . . [the Holy Land's] destruction an unknown people, an avenging sword from afar.' Altogether the situation precisely resembled the desolation and the abandonment by a wrathful God described in Psalm 79.

Pope Gregory IX, however, was preoccupied with another 'Crusade', this one against the twice excommunicated Frederick II, whose forces in Italy were thought to threaten Rome itself. The Pope's hatred of Frederick was such that his agents had several times tried to poison the Emperor. Henry III of England took the Cross in 1250, probably with a view to saving the Holy Land. In 1254, however, the Pope converted Henry's vow to one where Henry would conquer Naples and Sicily. The Pope collected tithes and sent an army there, but Frederick's forces defeated it. In 1258 the Pope sent the bill for the failed expedition's expenses to England, amounting to three times the realm's annual revenue. The Pope ordered Henry to pay up and, moreover, to conquer Naples for the Holy See within the year – or face excommunication. Henry appealed to his barons for help, and soon met an assembly of them, under the Earl of Leicester, Simon de Montfort, at the New Temple in London. There the barons demanded that government should be passed to a council of twenty-four nobles, and that Henry should dismiss his foreign councillors. If he agreed, they pledged help with paying the Pope's extortionate demand.

By 1263 the barons, however, were in full revolt. Henry III eventually sought refuge in the London Temple, where Prince Edward, on his return from fortifying Dover, found him alone and destitute. Edward and some of his knights broke into the Templars' store, seizing £1,000 in gold. Perhaps he acted with the Order's tacit approval. By allowing an apparent robbery, the Templars were able to support the Royal cause, though preserving the outward appearance of neutrality. The Templars did not participate in the revolt on either side under arms, but their Master was among the senior churchmen invited to the parliament convened by the Earl of Leicester.

In France and England, protests were growing against the Pope's political 'Crusades', which debased the whole concept and led to bloodshed between Christians. People were starting to wonder whether there was any spiritual virtue in dying for the Bishop of Rome's political objectives. The Capetian dynasty of France involved itself in the Pope's struggle more to gain power at the expense of the German Emperor than to show piety. In the 1260s Charles of Anjou, the brother of the King of France, would take Sicily from Frederick's heirs, and soon the last Hohenstaufen male would be executed. In ridding itself of its old ememy, however, the papacy would fall under a new shadow, equally dark.

The Latin kingdom in the Holy Land, meanwhile, never recovered from the defeat at La Forbie. Little remained to the Christians in the east, besides a few castles defended with great difficulty by the over-stretched Military Orders, and Acre, a city filled with filth, sorrrow and death. Pope Innocent IV called for a new Crusade at the Council of Lyons, but the response was feeble. The papacy had offered Europe's chivalry the same spiritual rewards for killing their Christian neighbours as for killing faraway Muslims, and had diverted huge amounts of Crusade funds away from the east. This expedient policy had demeaned the notion of the great, soul-saving pilgrimage, and engendered more than a little cynicism. European Princes were increasingly more interested in arguing with each other.

The resilient Knights Templar held a chapter in Pilgrim's Castle, and elected William de Sonnac their new Grand Master in 1245. Meanwhile, the Pope sent envoys to Cairo, talking the language of peace, and preaching about Jesus. The Sultan listened, but replied that he could not agree to peace with the Pope whilst strife and warfare existed between the Pope and Frederick II, who was actually on good terms with his kindred spirit the Sultan. As for the Papal messenger's evangelical endeavours, the Sultan told the Pope:

> . . . We have put faith in his words concerning Christ, upon whom be salvation and praise. But we know more concerning this same Christ than ye know, we magnify him more than ye magnify him . . .

In 1277 the Templars and Hospitallers were reinforced from Europe. They won a victory over the Khorezmians, but the danger from Egypt remained. Peace with the Sultan was not to be. The Templars faced fresh annihilation following the pious King Louis IX of France down the Nile.[6]

Louis had taken the Cross in 1244. In 1248 he left France to the care of his mother, Blanche of Castille, and took his army (and his wife, Queen Marguerite) on a campaign to knock out Egypt.

Louis' splendid chivalry, and a significant contingent of Templars and Hospitallers, achieved initial success at Damietta, winning a battle and recapturing the city, along with the Egyptian army's supplies. They cut the chain across the Nile that the city defended. Some Crusaders wanted next to attack Alexandria, which they thought could be used to bargain for the return of Jerusalem. The prevailing view, however, was that the Nile valley ought to be conquered, thus stamping out the greatest Muslim power for good. It was said that if you want to kill the serpent you must first crush the head. The Seventh Crusade moved south, just as the knights of the Fifth Crusade had, this time intent on attacking the Sultan's stronghold at Mansurah. As before, the Templars fought at the van, under their newest Grand Master, William de Sonnac.

The Lord de Joinville, a noble close to the King of France, reported in his account of the Crusade how, on the march, Louis had ordered that none should break ranks in the face of enemy harassment:

> One of the Turks gave a Knight Templar in the first rank so heavy a blow with his battle-axe that it felled him under the feet of the Lord Reginald de Vichiers' horse, who was the marshal of the Temple. The marshal, seeing his man fall, cried out to his brethren, 'At them in the name of God, for I cannot longer stand this!' He instantly stuck spurs to horse, followed by all his brethren, and as their horses were fresh, not a Saracen escaped.[7]

The Templars killed the Sultan Fahr al-Din (the son of Frederick II's old friend) in battle. His heir was in turn eventually murdered by Baybars and his elite Mameluke warriors, who then effectively seized power.

During the fierce fighting, the Mamelukes lured the Christian leader, the Count of Artois, into Mansurah, with the advanced guard of Louis' army, who had made it across the river. Throwing caution to the wind, the Templars charged in too, not wanting to miss out on any glory. Then the trap was sprung – the waiting Mamelukes attacked in force from the side streets. Only two out of 282 Templars escaped the carnage. William de Sonnac, the Grand Master, had withdrawn after losing an eye.

This was the first disaster of many. The remaining Crusaders rebuffed waves of attack against their camp. The Lord de Joinville recorded that the Templars made a rampart from captured Saracen siege engines:

> . . . but when the Saracens marched up to the assault they threw Greek fire upon it . . . It caught fire immediately, and the Saracens, perceiving that the brethren of the Temple were few, dashed through

> the burning timber, and vigorously attacked them. In the preceding battle of Shrove Tuesday, brother William, the Master of the Temple, lost one of his eyes, and in this battle the said lord lost his other eye, and was slain. God have mercy upon his soul! And know that immediately behind the place where the batallion of the Templars stood, there was a good acre of ground, so covered with darts, missiles and arrows that you could not see the earth beneath them, such showers of these had been discharged against the Templars by the Saracens.[8]

De Sonnac was succeeded as Grand Master by Reginald de Vichiers. The Mamelukes cut the Crusader supply lines, by transporting a fleet of ships north on camelback. Sickness and hunger were rife in the Crusader camp. Louis, formerly such a heroic figure, was now more dead than alive from terrible dysentery. He was finally captured, having refused to flee by boat.

On the Nile, Baybars and his Mamelukes brutally murdered the new Sultan whom the captive King tried to negotiate with. The soldier-slaves now became the masters of Egypt. Many of the Christians who had remained in Damietta thought the King dead, especially after the Egyptian army tried a ruse to gain entrance into the city, wearing the armour and holding the banners of the fallen French. Queen Marguerite managed to bribe the Italian contingent not to desert Damietta. The city bought her husband's liberty. The Mamelukes demanded an additional 800,000 gold beasants for the King's life. Louis could not pay and it fell to the Templars to make up the difference with a loan. Meanwhile, a great many were unable to escape, and the Mamelukes beheaded the poor Christians left behind in Damietta.

Outremer was mortally weakened by the fiasco in Egypt, as was the Order of the Temple. Matthew Paris has only three Templars escaping, and lists a number of famous knights killed or captured by the Egyptians, who cut the heads, hands and feet from the slain. Arriving back in Acre still in his prison rags, King Louis learned that he was needed in France. He was so desperate for some success that he sent overtures to the Mongols, the horsemen who had swept through Asia destroying all in their path. The reply from Mongka Kahn at Karakorum, a year's travel away, to Louis' proposed alliance was less than encouraging. The Khan demanded of Louis tribute and submission to Mongol overlordship, or death. So, meanwhile, did the still powerful Assassin sect.

Louis, before he departed from the Holy Land, could only re-fortify the coastal cities, and oversee the transfer of all the remaining inland castles to the Military Orders. News of the King's failures, meanwhile, touched his religiously minded subjects in a strange way. This time a popular Crusade sprang up, led by visionary shepherds, who thought that their own simple piety might save the cause of the Cross. The preachings of their leader, dubbed the Master of Hungary, drew great crowds. However, this phenomenon achieved no more than the children's Crusade had. Rather it lead to mass anticlerical riots and attacks, before it finally dispersed without passing far beyond France.

The Mongol hordes, with their speed and discipline, seemed as invincible as the onset of night. Their tactic was to advance swiftly in two waves – the first only killed, the second harvested the plunder, to share it later. Everything between China and Poland fell easily to the riders, who were known to the Christians as Tartars. The sons of Genghis Khan had added much of Russia, Persia, Asia Minor, and even eastern Europe to their father's great Asian empire. In 1256 the Mongols commenced their invasion of the Middle East, under Hulagu. Their army wiped out the Assassins at Almut, then took Baghdad itself in 1258. The Mongols butchered 80,000 there, including the Caliph himself. By 1259 the Mongol horsemen were at the gates of Aleppo, where they soon massacred the Muslim population. The Christian rulers of Cicilia and Antioch rode out – to pay homage.

Only the Mamelukes had sufficient forces to meet the Mongols in battle. They had decapitated the Khan's envoy who came to Cairo to demand their homage, and now made an arrangement with the Franks, who had finally come to realise that the Mongols presented a greater threat. The Franks (themselves divided in a dispute that had started between the Venetian and Genoese merchants and had escalated to embroil the barons and the Military Orders) allowed the Mameluke army to cross their territory to meet the common foe. Meanwhile, the Great Kahn died in 1259. When news of it reached Hulagu, the warlord withdrew to Mongolia, with most of his army, to be present while the succession was being determined. So, in 1260, at the Ain Jalut, the Pools of Goliath, the remaining Mongols met an Egyptian army under the Mameluke Sultan Qutuz and General Baybars. The Mamelukes outmanoeuvred their enemy, hiding half their force and leading the Mongols into an ambush. They tore the Mongols apart, and saved Islam. Soon after the victory, Baybars murdered his Sultan. He took power, and turned his army loose against the Crusaders.

The Mameluke army now rampaged through the Christian lands, leaving a trail of destruction and slaughter in their wake, and undoing all of Louis' work. Baybars sacked Caesaria, Halfia and Arsuf in 1265. The Templar castle Saphet offered stubborn resistence, and held him up until the following year. When Baybars finally overwhelmed it, he ringed it with the heads of its defenders. Homs, Belfort, Bagras and Sidon, Laodicea, Gabala, Tripoli, Beirout and Jaffa subsequently fell to the unrelenting Mameluke war machine. The Mamelukes raided the country around Acre in 1267, killing and destroying. Next came the Templar castle of Beaufort. Those knights of its garrison who survived were enslaved. Baybars then utterly demolished the great city of Antioch, in 1268, slaughtering some 17,000 people, and taking 100,000 into slavery.

Louis poured money into the cause of the Latin kingdom, and dreamed of redeeming the Holy Land. The Pope gathered great armies of Crusaders and unleashed their might against the German Emperor's supporters in Italy. The Byzantines capitalised on these preoccupations to take back Constantinople, although Charles of Anjou (brother of King Louis) as he established himself in Sicily, also extended Capetian influence into much of Greece. Louis IX embarked on Crusade again in 1267, but could persuade no more than 10,000 men to accompany him. For some reason they sailed to Tunis, in north Africa, it seems hoping to convert the local Emir to their faith. Disease decimated the French among the ruins of Carthage, and claimed the lives of Louis and most of his nobles.

Prince Edward, later Edward I of England, brought as many knights as he could (which was only about 1,000) to reinforce Acre. The situation seemed hopeless, not least because the business-minded Venetians were openly selling the Mamelukes wood and steel for weapons and the Genoese were supplying them with slaves. The competition between the Italian merchants often spilled over into violence on the streets of Acre. Control over the trade in oriental silks and spices was also at stake, and the local barons and Military Orders became partisan in this corrupting squabbling. The trade between the two worlds was highly lucrative for merchants; the Crusading frenzy often something that just got in the way.

Prince Edward somehow induced the Mamelukes to return to Egypt and negotiated a ten-year peace treaty. The Prince made his will in Acre in 1272, with Grand Master Berard of the Templars as witness. The next year Guillaume de Beaujeu succeeded as Grand Master. Beaujeu, a relative of the Capetian dynasty, was somewhat resented in the east for being a supporter of the claims of Charles of Anjou to the title King of Jerusalem. He acted as Charles' agent in *Outremer*, for example in the sale of grain. Beaujeu travelled west and came to England to raise support for Acre. He was also present at a Church Council in Lyons where it became manifest that he would leave empty handed. The Grand Master returned to the Holy Land and tried to broker new treaties to enable the Christians to hang on to their remaining territory. Some in Acre would accuse him of cowardice and treachery, when he took to them the offer of the Mameluke Qalawun, who succeeded Baybars in Egypt, proposing peace in exchange for a Venetian penny from every citizen.[9]

Sensing the impending doom, the merchants, the barons and the settlers of European descent gradually withdrew from the Holy Land, many making for Cyprus. Qalawun resumed the Mameluke rampage and the

Crusader state lost castle after castle. Another ancient city was wiped off the map when Tripoli shared the terible fate of Antioch. Few Europeans, besides the Military Orders, remained in the Holy Land, and these could only write of their plight, and implore succour, though their calls went unanswered. The Pope lamented:

> By the deaths of so many knights of both Orders, the noble college of the Hospitallers and the illustrious Chivalry of the Temple are almost destroyed, and I know not how we shall be able, after this, to find gentlemen and persons of quality sufficient to supply the places such as have perished.[10]

Soon few places besides Acre remained in Christian hands. The boundary of the Latin Kingdom had receded almost to the great land walls of the city. The wall had a number of resonantly named towers, such as the Accursed Tower, the English Tower, the Gate of Evil Step, Bloodgate and the Tower of the Flies – which stood in the bay guarding the chain that could close off the harbour. Pope Nicolas IV's calls for a Crusade achieved only the mustering of a small band from Europe. This ill-disciplined mob arrived in Acre in 1290, and lynched a number of Muslim merchants in the city – giving the Mamelukes all the excuse they needed to attack. They destroyed Sidon and Beirout, and drove the Templars out of their last two castles, Atlit and Tortosa. Qalawun died before he could finish his business, however. In 1291 his son, al Ashraf, took his forces against the last Crusaders in the Holy Land.

Sultan al-Ashraf came with an immense army:

> . . . thirsting for Christian blood, the earth trembled beneath their footsteps, and the air was rent with the sound of their trumpets and cymbals . . . The points of their spears shone like the innumerable stars of heaven . . . They wandered round about the walls, spying on their weaknesses and defects, some barked like dogs, some roared like lions, some threw darts, some cast stones, some shot arrows and bolts from crossbows.[11]

Al Ashraf besieged Acre with some 160,000 infantry, 60,000 cavalry, and an awesome array of artillery, including 1,000 mangonels – devices which hurled big stones from a long beam either counter-weighted or pulled back between twisted ropes. The Cypriot contingent and their King fled in their ships, at the sight of the Mamelukes. The remaining defenders could muster at most 14,000 foot and 800 horse. Different sections of wall were defended by Templars, Hospitallers, Teutonic Knights, Italians and Franks. (The Knights of Lazarus also prepared to fight, with the suicidal fury of a Military Order drawn entirely from men dying of leprosy.)

For many days and nights this out-numbered force foiled every attempt the Mamelukes made to take the city, sabotaging siege works and sallying out against the enemy. Then the Mamelukes broke in through a thinly defended position, reaching the centre of the city. The Templars and Hospitallers drove them back and threw them from the walls.

The Templar Grand Master, Guillaume de Beaujeu, was slain after the sixth week of siege, during which more and more Muslims had arrived to reinforce al-Ashraf, and the attack had been relentless. The towers fell, undermined and bombarded with missiles and 'Greek Fire'. So many siege engines had never been assembled in one place, including ballistas (more advanced catapults) that could hurl quarter-ton missiles. The Mamelukes filled the moat with earth, wood and dead bodies, and surged in over them, goaded by 300 drummers on camels. The Templars and Hospitallers again drove them back out. The women, children and elderly of the town were taken towards the few ships available. Piratical captains grew rich taking money from those desperate to escape; other sailors, however, evacuated people for nothing, then returned to save more. Some women refused to leave, not wishing to abandon their men. Before many could embark, however, the Mamelukes began their main assault, and butchered them.

The Templar Master, Theobold Gaudin, also sent the Templar treasury and 'holy relics' away by boat. After days of struggle, al-Ashraf offered terms. The Christian leader, one Friar Pierre, accepted. A Mameluke delegation were admitted to receive the Christians' surrender, and their crescent flag was hoisted. Then some of the Mameluke contingent started to rape the remaining women and boys. The outraged Templars slew the Mamelukes, tore down the crescent and hoisted *Beauseant* again. Only the Templar stronghold remained. A few women and children made it to the 'Fortified Temple by the sea', where the Templars gave up their own fleet to save them. The knights, even the wounded, remained. 'When they set sail,' a witness reported, 'everyone of the Temple who remained raised a great cheer, and thus they departed.'[12]

The Templars repulsed wave after wave of Muslim assault. The knights fought until the undermined walls toppled around them. Inevitably, the Mamelukes prevailed. Acre was reduced. Afterwards the Mamelukes left not a well unpoisoned and not a tree or building standing all along the coast for the Crusaders to use if ever they returned.

NOTES

1 Addison, Charles G, *The History of the Knights Templars*, p. 243. Addison quotes from a letter from Peter de Montague, humble Master of the Soldiers of Christ, to his beloved brother in Christ, Alan Marcel, Preceptor of England.

2 Read, Piers Paul, *The Templars*, pp. 198–203; Jones, Terry and Ereira, Alan, *Crusades*, p. 179. Frederick II was excommunicated by Gregory IX for turning back from his Crusade in 1227, because of sickness. Frederick embarked later without being redeemed, having begun to negotiate an arrangement with al Kamil, whereby Jerusalem would be returned in exchange for an alliance against the Sultan's brother. Frederick II was called *Stupor Mundi,* or the 'Wonder of the World'. He was a tyrant who composed music, spoke six languages and had read the Koran. Many labelled him an atheist. He was also an exponent of experimental philosophy, often using human subjects in his grotesque experiments. On one occasion, he had a man imprisoned in a wine barrel, to see if the soul could be seen leaving the body as the subject died. On another occasion, he had newborn children taken and raised in complete silence, to discover what language they would develop naturally.
3 Addison, op. cit., p. 165, quoting a letter from Armand de Perigord to Robert de Sandford, Master of England.
4 Paris, Matthew, *Chronicle* (trans. Richard Vaughan), pp. 136–7.
5 Billings, Malcolm, *The Cross and the Crescent*, p. 152.
6 Ibid., pp. 220–43. Louis IX of France was famously pious. Matthew Paris records how Louis bought the Crown of Thorns from Baldwin, the Latin Emperor of Constantinople, in 1249. Louis carried it barefoot to Ste Chapelle, the exquisite shrine he built for it in Paris.
7 Addison, op. cit., p. 180, quoting Lord de Joinville.
8 Ibid., p. 181.
9 Barber, Malcom, *The Trial of the Templars*, p. 13.
10 Addison, op. cit., p. 183.
11 Ibid., p. 186.
12 Seward, Desmond. *The Monks of War*, p. 85.

Part Two

Baphomet

CHAPTER IX
The Aftermath of Acre

The defeat of the Christians in Acre meant the loss of the last remnant of the Christian possessions in the Holy Land. This may have seemed calamitous for the west – but (to borrow an apt line from the poem 'Lepanto' by G K Chesterton) dead was all the innocence of anger and surprise. Events in the Holy Land no longer moved the knighthood of western Christendom (an entity gradually losing its cohesion as a spirit of nationalism arose in different states) enough for them to take arms in the cause of religion, nor did the Mameluke rampage galvanise Catholic society to respond with action. Europe still used the rhetoric of the Crusades, lied to itself that it had not given up on the dream of Jerusalem, but the truth was that, long before 1291, all but a few romantics had abandoned all serious hope of the religious war ever succeeding. Subsequently to the loss of Acre, the remains of the Knights Templar based themselves on Cyprus, the island given to the de Lusignan dynasty, as compensation for the crown of Jerusalem.[1]

By the beginning of the fourteenth century, Crusading zeal, especially among ordinary society, but among the nobility too, was dying. To mitigate defeat, some scapegoat was needed. The theological and personal alternative was unthinkable. Following the fall of Acre, Pope Nicolas IV called Church councils in every province. In 1292 the Archbishop of Canterbury reported the 'common assertion' in England. The lands granted to the Military Orders by earlier generations should have provided sufficient income to recover/defend the Holy Land '. . . so long as Christ's warriors hold themselves humbly and devoutly towards God'.[2] Clearly, the apathetic Archbishop reflected a feeling that this was not the case, and the same seems to have been true throughout western Christendom. The Military Orders had either squandered their resources, or failed to live up to their religious vocations, thus incurring divine displeasure. Either way, they quickly became scapegoats for defeat, for societies and Princes no longer prepared, themselves, to make the sacrifices a Crusade demanded. As the most famous of the Military Orders, the Templars probably attracted the most suspicion and hostility.

The returning Crusader Orders retained their privileges and honours, but had manifestly failed in their mission, and had therefore lost their justification for being. Anti-clericalism and disillusionment were also becoming widespread. With regard to the loss of the Holy Land, the Templars, perhaps, bore the immediate brunt of these sentiments. The irony is that the only men who had not abandoned the original focus of the Crusade were the Templars. Popes had subverted Crusading by turning the movement against other Christians, for suspiciously worldly reasons. When the Church preached to secular knights that killing Cathars or Byzantines was of the same religious value as fighting to free Jerualem then it should have been no wonder that, consequently, the higher and harder quest lost popularity. The other Military Orders had found new theatres of operation, meanwhile. The Hospitallers had taken over some of the Greek islands, and continued to launch raiding 'caravans', this time by sea, as their galleys sought out Muslim shipping to harass. The Teutonic Knights, the German Order founded during the Third Crusade, moved first to Venice, then to Marienberg, the Order's fortress in Prussia, from where it struck out brutally against the pagan inhabitants of Prussia and the Baltic lands. Like the Hospitallers soon would at Rhodes, the Teutonic Order in Prussia carved out a little independent state of its own.

The Templars, however, continued to try to win back Palestine. Jerusalem and the Temple of Solomon remained the centre of their world and they lacked the shrewdness or the stomach to find another focus. Cyprus, somewhat reluctantly, played host to the rump of the Templars in the east. King Henry II of Cyprus resented the privileges of the Order, which maintained several forts and towers on his island, and which had supported Charles of Anjou's claim to the crown of Jerusalem over his own. In the 1280s the Cypriot King had seized their Preceptory in Limassol, only returning it at the behest of the Pope. In 1298 Henry complained to Rome about the conduct of the Templars.

In 1293 the Templars in Cyprus had elected Jacques de Molay (1243–1314) as their Grand Master. From there, in 1302, de Molay launched a hopeless raid, to try to win back a toe-hold in the Holy Land. He lost 120 knights trying to land on the Syrian mainland, from the island of Raud.

The situation in the Levant, in these years, was less than stable. Bands of pirates and brigands came to dominate the sea and the islands. One group of gaiours (as the Turks would call these freebooting infidels) was captained by a former Templar sailor called Roger de Flor. Roger had been expelled from the Order of the Temple for demanding huge bribes from the women of Acre before taking them to safety on his ship. He went on to command a sizeable fleet of Catalan pirates, with which he raided the Turks in Anatolia, on behalf of the Byzantine Emperor – in exchange for treasure and the hand of the Emperor's daughter. (The Emperor was probably not particularly happy with this arrangement, indicative of the degraded state of Byzantium as it was, and must have feared that if he did not give the adventurer what he demanded then it would not be Byzantium's enemies whom the pirates would attack). De Flor was later killed by his own gang, who then seized power in Athens, to rule it for the next seventy years.[3]

In 1306 King Henry II of Cyprus was forced to abdicate by local barons favouring his brother Amaury de Lusignan. The Templars actively supported this rebellion. The event may have caused a stir among other monarchs, worried about rebellion from their own barons. The Templars were a network spread across Europe. If they dared to depose a King in Cyprus, as European monarchs may have asked themselves, what would stop these arrogant knights turning on other Kings in the west? As early as the reign of Henry III of England, such a threat had been felt. Henry III, in the 1260s, threatened to confiscate some of the Order's land and treasure because of the outrageous hautiness of the knights. The Master of the London Temple had retorted: 'Far be it that thy mouth should say so disagreeable and silly a word. So long as thou does exercise justice thou wilt reign, but if thou infringe it, thou wilt cease to be King.'[4] This may have been taken as a veiled warning that the Templars were prepared to play king-makers in Europe as well as in the Levant. Henry had to combat just such a baronial revolt, lead by the Earl of Leicester, Simon de Montfort, though the Templars had stayed neutral then.

According to Genoese cartographer Giovanni da Carignano, 1306 was also the year in which a unique embassy of thirty envoys from Ethiopia travelled to Avignon seeking an audience with Pope Clement V, stopping at Genoa during their return voyage. Carignano's lost chronicle was summarised briefly by the fifteenth-century writer Jacopo Foresti. 'It is said that their Emperor is most Christian, to whom 74 kings and almost innumerable princes pay allegiance . . .'[5] Because of the timing of this contact, the embassy's purpose may have related to the Templars – the Ethiopian Emperor Wemed Ara'ad may also have had occasion to resent the Templars and to call for their destruction. The Ethiopian embassy, it is true, never seems to have been brought up at the trials after the arrest of the Knights Templar, and may have had nothing to do with the Order. It was not the Pope, moreover, who inaugurated the attack on the Templars.

That was done by the King of France, Philip the Fair. The timing of the embassy, however, is of interest, and it is not impossible that what the mysterious Africans told the Pope (supposing they achieved the audience they desired) added to any suspicions held against the Knights Templar.

Soon the Pope in Bordeaux summoned the Grand Masters of the Military Orders from Cyprus for a conference regarding strategy in the east:

> We order you to come hither without delay, with as much secrecy as possible, and with a very little retinue, since you will find on this side of the sea a sufficient number of your knights to attend upon you.

The Grand Master of the Hospitallers declined to leave, and sent his excuses. De Molay obeyed the Pope's summons, seemingly oblivious to the impending fate of himself and his beloved Order. Seemingly oblivious, that is to say, to the fact that the Temple was doomed.

NOTES

1 Read, Piers Paul, *The Templars*, pp. 247–8; Barber, Malcolm, *The Trial of the Templars*, pp. 14–15. Pope Nicolas IV did plan a new Crusade, but the response was feeble. Some, meanwhile, still clung to the vain hope that the Mongols might be converted to Christianity, and might help restore the Latin kingdom in the Holy Land. At the Council of Lyons, in 1274, one of the Templar delegates had likened the Crusades to 'a little dog barking at a great one, who takes no heed of him'.
2 Addison, Charles G, *The History of the Knights Templars*, p. 200. Also Read, op. cit., p. 249.
3 Read, op. cit, p. 249.
4 Addison, op. cit,. p. 217.
5 Hancock, Graham, *The Sign and the Seal*, pp. 161–2. Hancock quotes Giovanni da Carignano, in Facopo Fillipo Foresti's abstract from the lost earlier work. How these supposed Ethiopians made it from the African heartland of Prester John past the territory of the Mamelukes is not recorded, but it is possible that some pilgrimage traffic continued through Egyptian territory.

CHAPTER X
The Sleep of Reason

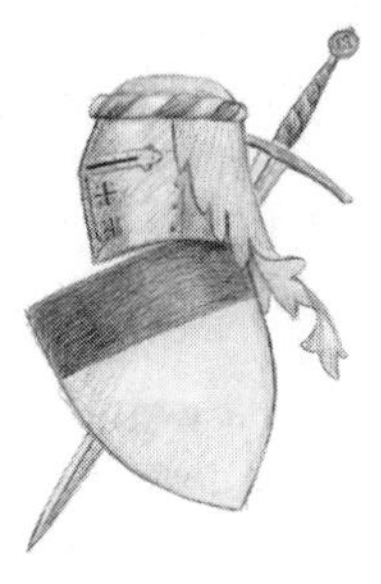

King Philip IV, known as Philip the Fair, had come to the throne of France in October 1285. As a result of the wars his predecessors had fought against the English and the Albigensians, Philip's Capetian dynasty had gained authority over much of the land that constitutes modern France.[1] Philip II Augustus, though a failure as a Crusader in contrast to Richard the Lionheart, had achieved far greater success domestically. Before his death in 1223, he had defeated John Lackland's forces in Normandy and Anjou, and benefited from the reduction of the power of the Counts of Toulouse. He had expanded and reformed the civil service, and appointed paid royal officials to do his work in the provinces. These were known in the north as *baillis*, and in the south as *senechaux*. This was the set-up inherited by Philip the Fair.[2]

The Church had come to support the principal of the Divine Right of Kings, the doctrine that monarchs were chosen to rule by God. Philip IV, clothing himself in the mantle of his grandfather, the sainted Louis IX, presented himself as a champion of Christendom, and as the spiritual guardian of his subjects.

On Friday 13 October 1307 Philip the Fair's *baillis* and *seneschaux* arrested the French Templars *en masse*, following dawn swoops, meticulously planned with the tightest secrecy over the previous few months. When they came to stand trial, the majority of the Templars, including their Grand Master, would confess terrible things.

Philip's previous actions as King may provide clues to his seemingly inscrutable character and to his motives concerning the Knights Templar.

Like his contemporary, Edward I of England, Philip had long striven to increase the power and standing of the monarchy. In their early reigns, the two Kings had fought each other over Gascony, which Edward I had taken, though Philip had prevented him from conquering any other area of France, and gained prestige in the process. Philip had taxed the clergy to finance this war. His relationship with the Pope, Boniface VIII, collapsed after 1296, largely as a result of this taxation policy. Boniface put under interdict anyone who exacted from the Church without papal consent.[3] The King and the Pope had also long been rival claimants to spiritual supremacy. Philip soon welcomed into France the Colonnas, members of a powerful Roman family opposed to Boniface. They hatched a scheme to be rid of the Pope. With the ending of his costly wars, meanwhile, Philip sent his daughter Isabella to marry Prince Edward. She became Queen of England when, in 1307, the Prince became Edward II.

Pope Boniface VIII had staged a grand pageant in Rome for the Holy Year of 1300. There he had declared himself Caesar, the last Pope sufficiently strong to seriously claim universal sovereignty. Boniface died shortly after he was attacked at Anagni, in 1303, by Philip's agents. The plot was to arrest the Pope for witchcraft and heresy. Guillaume de Nogaret, the Keeper of the Seals (an important minister in Philip's government) directed the botched abduction, along with Scirra, a key member of the Colonna faction, who had wanted to execute Pope Boniface there and then. Nogaret, on the other hand, had wanted to take Boniface to face trial in France and be deposed. The plotters argued about what to do for some time, and it was only this dispute which gave the Pope's supporters time to rescue him. Boniface never recovered, however. He had been struck by Colonna, and had suffered a heart attack shortly afterwards. Benedict XI was elected in 1303, and under great pressure from the French, absolved all but Nogaret from blame for the attack on his predecessor. Benedict himself died in strange circumstances the following year.

Though an excommunicate, Nogaret prospered under Philip's patronage. He represented a class of educated, secular lawyers and officials who were rising to prominence in the emerging nation states of Europe. Such men of the law owed little to the Church or the aristocracy, and while they aided their various sovereigns to subdue these old rivals, they subtly helped themselves to a share of the power the men of the cloth and the sword were losing. As King Philip's closest adviser, Nogaret became a driving force in anti-Templarism. Nogaret would try to imply connections between the Templars and the Cathar heresy. In fact, Nogaret himself came from Cathar stock; his parents had, by some accounts, been executed as heretics in Toulouse. Nogaret, indeed, remained under interdict throughout the Templars' trials. His real, personal agenda may have been to be avenged on the Roman Church, but his rhetoric was naturally all about defending orthodoxy and crushing heresy wherever it appeared.

Meanwhile, years after Boniface's death, Philip IV's regime obstinately pursued legal action to get the late Pontiff posthumously condemned. This was much to the detriment of the papacy's standing, and Nogaret was principally responsible for pursuing this policy.

When Benedict XI died suddenly on 7 July 1304, the path became clear for Philip's nominee, Bertrand de Got, Archbishop of Bordeaux. He was crowned Pope Clement V at Lyons in November 1305, in King Philip's presence.[4] The papacy, as we have seen, had previously grown close to the Capetian dynasty, seeking to use the French Kings to counter the power of the German Emperors. By now they were uncomfortably close. Philip kept the Pope within or near France through coercion, and his soldiers were always near at hand when important decisions were taken. Clement was a sickly man, probably cancerous, and often afflicted with debilitating attacks of the gripes and dysentery. He was prematurely old, without the moral will or the resources to challenge the manipulative King.[5]

When Clement V summoned the Grand Master of the Templars from Cyprus in 1306, Jacques de Molay arrived with proposals for a new Crusade. The Pope first desired to discuss the merger of the two principal Military Orders. Traditionalists both, however, the Grand Masters resisted the idea. Philip IV, for his part, favoured the amalgamation, keen to see one of his sons heading the new Order, so that his dynasty might use it to achieve dominance in Christendom.[6] Philip may have had megalomaniacal tendancies, he may even have believed in his own righteousness, but he was no Crusader. True, he had taken the Cross amid great pomp and display of piety. However, in the two decades since then, he had squandered a fortune of 'Crusade' funds, without budging a step, or lifting a finger to aid the Holy Land. He, like his fellow Princes, had been preoccupied with other matters. Besides, both his grandfather (Louis IX) and father (Philip III) had died while waging futile Crusades, and it was clearly not a tradition Philip the Fair was eager to maintain.

Philip IV had also already seized the wealth of the mercantile Jews and Lombards, and evicted them from France. The Templars, in their holy hubris, had similarly shunned and stood apart from mainstream society. The knights were drawn from the powerful petty nobility, but, in an odd way, they rejected rather than reflected the values of their class. They turned their backs on family ties, for example, choosing their spiritual brotherhood over their natural bloodlines, and having no wives or children. The Templars had many debtors, besides the King, who would be glad to be rid of them. Few would rush to defend the Order; men like Nogaret could bank on that. Many nobles, in fact, were clearly growing more interested in the prospect of taking back lands granted to the Templars by their ancestors. The Templars surely did not deserve to keep their lands and revenues, these nobles reasoned, for they had failed to use them successfully for the defence of the Holy Land. Bishops, meanwhile, had long tended to resent the Templars, for their independence and their competition for tithes.

In 1306 Philip's currency devaluation had caused riots, and he had been compelled to seek refuge from his irate subjects in the Paris Temple. There he surely gained an impression of the Templars' wealth (perhaps an inflated impression, given that the Templars guarded much treasure that was not their property, on behalf of various clients). Jacques de Molay was in Paris by June 1307, and presided over a Chapter meeting at the Temple there. De Molay's arrival in France gave the King the opportunity, perhaps, to resort to a more audacious financial expedient.

Once he had decided to act, King Philip did not compromise. He attacked the Templars vigorously, urged other monarchs to do likewise, and used intimidation and coercion when he needed to secure ecclesiastical co-operation. It was something of a gamble, but Philip had managed to install his people in many key positions in the clergy; men who could be relied upon to support his policies. Many French bishops were royal nominees, while others were simply afraid of the King. The French Inquisition, in the meantime, had become more an instrument of royal power than an enforcer of papal policy. Guillaume Imbert de Paris, the Grand Inquisitor, was Philip's personal confessor. Though a Dominican Friar, he was much closer to the King than to the Pope and his position had been created by the King.[7]

If any cleric in the France of Philip IV had shown too great a propensity for free thought, he had been brought down amid accusations of heretical depravity and black magic. Such had been the fate of Bernard, Bishop of Pamiers, a some-time critic of the King, who was burnt in 1301, having been condemned for sorcery, heresy, simony, treason and fornication. Guichard, Bishop of Troyes, was likewise executed, following charges of using witchcraft to murder Philip IV's wife, Joan of Navarre, after her death in 1305.

Philip usually tried to appear to operate constitutionally. The King's agents arrested the Templars in the Inquisition's name, with the active support of the Grand Inquisitor. The Inquisition, indeed, would offer the King invaluable help branding the Templars as heretics. However, though Philip had previously raised certain issues with the Pope, he never consulted Clement V prior to the arrests. There was no permission from Clement and any claim to be acting on papal instruction was false.[8]

NOTES

1 Barber, Malcolm,*The Trial of the Templars*, p. 27.
2 Ibid., p. 28.
3 Ibid., p. 23.

4 Ibid., p.16. Lyons was then still officially part of the Holy Roman Empire, but was well within Philip's sphere of influence.
5 Ibid., p 17.
6 Cohn, Norman, *Europe's Inner Demons*, pp. 82–3.
7 Ibid., p. 90. Guillaume de Paris was well disposed to help Philip secure the suppression of the Templars, for the sinister heresies the King accused them of, and to use the Inquisition to legitimise their destruction. It may have been the case that with the near destruction of the Cathars, the Inquisition was looking around for another group to persecute, to justify its continuing existence. To maintain their base of power, the Dominicans were prepared to turn against fellow monks and members of the Church. As hunters of heresy, the Dominicans were defined by their opposition to anti-Christian or at least anti-Catholic forces. Therefore, though pledged to the wiping out of Satanic groups, the Inquistors were in fact dependent on them, much as rat-catchers need rats. If there were no heretics, the Inquisition had to create them, using the mechanisms of torture and terror originally meant to destroy them. This was a fact, even if the Inquisitors were unwilling or unable to admit it to themselves.
8 Barber, op. cit., p. 45.

CHAPTER XI
The Downfall

This seems to have been a time of apocalyptic speculation and high unease, when old certainties were starting to break down, arguably to as great an extent as Christendom had witnessed at any time before the Protestant Reformation. The failure of the Crusades was a significant factor. People still believed in God and the Devil, angels and demons, but it was no longer beyond question that God was always with the Pope and his churchmen, any more than he had always been with the Pope's Crusaders. It was a time when the King and those close to him could take advantage of popular paranoia and superstition to justify the persecution of political opponents. Pope Boniface suffered as a result of this shift in attitude, and so would the Knights Templar; for in this jumpy new climate it was believed possible that the Devil's agents could and had infiltrated the heart of the Christian establishment.

On 14 September 1307 Philip IV had informed his agents that:

> A bitter thing, a lamentable thing, a thing which is horrible to contemplate, terrible to hear of, a detestable crime, an execrable evil, an abominable work . . . a thing almost inhuman, indeed set apart from all humanity has, thanks to the report of several trustworthy persons, reached our ears . . . causing us to tremble with violent horror . . . [The Templars] surpass unreasoning beasts in their astonishing bestiality, they expose themselves to all the supremely abominable crimes which even the sensuality of unreasoning beasts abhors and avoids. Not only by their acts and their detestable deeds, but even by their hasty words, they defile the earth with their filth,

> they undo the benefits of the dew, they corrupt the purity of the air and bring about the confusion of our faith.[1]

The formal drafting of the articles of accusation that were listed in the royal missal may be attributed to Nogaret. They included the charge that the Order refuted Christ's divinity. When the Templars admitted a new member they made him renounce Jesus three times. They made initiates spit on a crucifix or holy image, before taking part in rituals involving three profane kisses, on the mouth, navel and 'base of the spine'. The Templars adored as idols severed heads, cats and graven figures, during secret midnight chapters, in well guarded Temples.[2] The Order's statutes also allegedly insisted that brethren be ready to practise sodomy, while, as an institution, they flouted the laws of the land and corrupted the services of the Church. Now fragmentary trial records survive, containing Templar confessions to some or all of these crimes, and of more besides. However, the Inquisitors used torture, or the threat thereof, in order to extract these confessions.

A convicted criminal and supposed ex-Templar, Esquin de Floyran, had taken the first allegations of Templar scandal to Philip IV, as early as 1305. He expected to be rewarded for doing so.[3] Previously he had tried to alert James II of Aragon, but found the Aragonese court strangely sceptical. Philip the Fair was more receptive to such stories. He sent spies into the Order,[4] and collected reports from malcontent Templars, of whom several were found. Etienne de Troyes, for example, a serving brother, claimed to have been forced at sword-point to deny Christ and the apostles, to spit at the Cross, to strip naked, give and receive obscene kisses, and to take the cord that he was given to wear and to touch it against an idol – an idol in the form of a disembodied head. Jean de Folliaco objected only to the austerity of the Order, and had feared being sent east. Only later did he subscribe to the denying of Christ allegation.

Many contemporaries, including the Florentine poet Dante, doubted the Templars' guilt, suspecting that Philip and his associates, coveting the Templars' wealth, had opportunistically invented the charges. They wished to exploit the papacy's weakness to plunder the Order of the Temple. However, the fact that the Templars observed secrecy was seldom disputed. Even those Templars who adamantly denied heresy admitted that the Order's ceremonies were generally held behind closed doors, with no outsiders in attendance. All accounts of the initiation ritual referred to taking vows to keep the Order's secrets, and to the wearing of the cord, which the articles of accusation stated the Templars wore after touching their idols with it. It might have been supposed that these cords kept them in thrall to the idol, by means of some strange, occult power.[5]

In one account (which influenced the description in the official chronicles), the idol took the form of a head 'covered in old skin, with two carbunkles for eyes, as bright as the brightness of heaven, and it is certain that all the hopes of the Templars were placed in it. It was their sovereign God, they trusted it with all their hearts.'[6] The Templars were further accused of feeding young brethren the ashes of the dead in their food and drink, of burning sacrificed infants, anointing their idol with the fat, and of sometimes abusing young virgins in their abominable and mysterious rites.

The air of strangeness and horror around the proceedings was thickened by contemporary superstition, some of it deliberately encouraged by Philip the Fair's sordid propaganda. Later myth contributed to the Order's supernatural reputation, but many genuine mysteries remain. The secrecy of the Templars is difficult to account for without there bring something worth hiding. The graffiti left by Templars in castle dungeons, paintings in a number of Preceptories, and the carvings in Royston Cave contain peculiar symbolism, and there were a number of aspects of the Order that seemed to have heterodox origins. It is possible to attribute many of the accusations against them to the well-established propaganda apparatus used to blacken the reputations of earlier heretics. The religious establishment would later make frequent use of such ghastly concepts to demonise suspected witches. In centuries to come, many would be tortured into confessing to having attended Satanic Sabbaths, where abuse of the Cross supposedly preceded similar ritualised sacrilege, Devil-worship, unclean kisses, cannibalism, infanticide and promiscuous, unnatural copulation. There is little evidence that such things were ever practised by any real cult or heretical group in the periods in question. Instead, these activities stem predominantly from the dark imaginings of Inquisitors, officials and theologians who inverted the practices and values of the Christian institution and society they aspired to defend. All this fails, however, to explain the bizarre and anomalous concept of worshipping a head. Meanwhile, the fate of the Templars' mysterious treasure has provoked endless speculation and fruitless searches, for hundreds of years.[7]

NOTES

1 Cohn, Norman, *Europe's Inner Demons*, p. 85.
2 Barber, Malcolm, *The Trial of the Templars*, pp. 248–52. The accusations are given in full in Barber's Appendix A.
3 Cohn, op. cit., p. 84. According to Cohn, Esquin de Floyran was by 1313, 'comfortably in possession of a piece of land which had belonged to the temple'. He was also supposed to have taken an active part in the torturing of a number of Templars.
4 Ibid. It does not seem that the alleged spying operation was successful, for no spies were called to testify at the ensuing trials.

5 Ibid., p. 87.
6 Barber, op. cit, p. 182.
7 Lord, Evelyn, *The Knights Templar in Britain*, p. 58. Rumours of lost treasure had early origins. It seems rumours of underground passages led Edward III to send an expedition to dig in Temple Dinsley, in search of the buried fortune of the Templars, reputed to be lying there in secret vaults. Modern myths associate the Templar treasure with sites as dispersed as southern France, Scotland, and even the New World.

CHAPTER XII
The Destruction of the Temple

The Arrest

Philip IV instructed his agents that the idol the Templars held sacred was:

> . . . a man's head with a large beard, which they kiss and worship at all their provincial chapters, but not all the brothers know this, save only the Grand Master and the senior ones.[1]

Philip became determined to act on his 'vehement suspicion'. He sent his lieutenants sealed instructions, describing Templar iniquities, and giving instructions for their seizure. As a precursor to the operation, he had Templar properties surveyed, suspicion being averted by the extension of the survey to all religious estates, on the pretext that a new tax was planned.

On 13 October 1307 as many as 15,000 Templars, and individuals associated with the Order, were arrested in France, and thrown into royal prisons or into their own dungeons. Most of those seized and subsequently questioned could hardly be called senior. The majority were retainers and farmers; a mere 500 were full brethren, i.e. chaplains, sergeants and knights. No more than 138 full knights would be heard by the Grand Inquisitor. The remainder were servants and tenants and husbandmen from the estates, including humble shepherds.[2]

The next day the accusations were published in a royal manifesto. On 15 October the King's officers publicly explained the charges to the citizenry and university philosophers of Paris; then, on 16 October, the King sent out letters to foreign Princes, seeking to justify his shocking actions and encouraging them to take similar measures.

The operation to arrest the Templars was achieved with great success. Virtually all of the important leaders of the Order were arrested, along with the vast majority of the rank and file, all of whom seem to have been taken by surprise. Jacques de Molay had been given the honour of acting as a pall-bearer at the funeral of the King's sister on the very day before the arrest. (This fact must cast grave doubt on Philip's sincerity. If he had honestly suspected that this man Jacques de Molay was the leader of a pack of Satan-worshipping sodomites, guilty of 'supremely abominable crimes', he could hardly, with any propriety or honour, have allowed it, even to mask his intents.)

Philip directly took all the Temple's land and property into royal custody. However, his agents never found the records of the Order, leading some to suspect that the leaders had been tipped off, and had burned or hidden their documents. Little of their legendary treasure was found either. Jean de Chalons was one of the Templar prisoners soon questioned at an ecclesiastical court. According to de Chalons, Gerard de Villiers, the Grand Preceptor of France, had caught wind of the planned arrest. Fifty Knights Templar, de Chalons said, had escaped to their port at La Rochelle with the Visitor of the Order's treasure. They set sail with it, on eighteen of the Order's ships. They were never heard of again.

Inquisitorial Hearings

For most of the brethren there was to be no escape. The Templar prisoners in France were first terrorised by their captors, imprisoned in irons, deprived of sleep, and kept on bread and water. They were asked leading questions appertaining to severed heads and obscene kisses, and invited to confess. They were then subjected to varying degrees of torture, to extract these confessions. Guillaume de Paris wrote to his Inquisitors about the crimes of the Templars. The Templars' crimes were a 'burning shame to heaven', and the Inquisitors were to show them no mercy. Incidentally, Philip's minions would quickly forget that it was only supposed to be a select cabal of Templars who took part in the heretical rites; the interrogaters extracted grisly and highly unlikely confessions even from humble serving brothers.

The rack and the strappado were the tools favoured by the Inquisition for torturing heresy suspects. The rack stretched the torture victim over a table, and dislocated his joints. The strappado victim had his hands bound behind him with a rope, that ran up over a pulley. The jailor hauled on the rope, hoisting the prisoner aloft, and allowing him to fall rapidly, almost to the floor. Sometimes weights were attached to the prisoner's feet or genitals. The elderly Templar Gerard de Pasigo claimed to have endured this at the hands of the royal *bailli* of Macon.[3]

According to an anonymous tract defending the Templars (written to the Paris University theologians in 1308) even after torture they (the prisoners) were always:

> . . . held in dark prison cells, with only the bread of sorrow and the water of affliction, in winter time, with the pressing cold, lying with sighs and grief on the ground without straw or coverings. In the middle of the night, to increase their terror, now one, now another, are taken from cell to cell. Those whom they [i.e. the Dominican/Jacobin friars who acted as Inquisitors] have killed in torture, they secretly bury in the stable or in the garden; for fear that such savage deeds should reach the royal ears, since they have been told to tell that the aforesaid brothers did not confess their crimes by violence but of their own accord . . .
>
> . . . The human tongue cannot express the punishment, afflictions, miseries, taunts, and dire kinds of torture suffered by the said innocents in the space of three months, since the day of their arrest, since by day and night constant sobs and sighs have not ceased in their cells, nor have cries and gnashing of teeth ceased in their tortures . . . Truth kills them, and lies liberate them from death.

Some Templars had their legs held in iron frames, and grease smeared on the soles of their feet. Their tormentors then brought flames towards the soles of the prisoners, with a movable screen to vary the intensity of agony inflicted. One victim, the Templar priest Bernard de Vado, suffered this until the blackened bones dropped out from his heels – bones which he later presented to the commissary of police, when he revoked his confession. Another Templar revoked a confession made after having four of his teeth pulled out by his torturers.

The Dominicans produced a confession signed by the Grand Master, who apparently had suffered the flaying of his limbs and testicles.[4] The interrogating friars and royal officials promised the Templars pardon and freedom if they confessed. There was every incentive for the Templars to give in, but dozens perished, swearing that they were innocent. The majority of Templars eventually capitulated. Of the 138 questioned in Paris, 134 confessed. Most of the hearings were presided over by bishops and Inquisitors, handpicked by Philip, many of whom had themselves overseen the torture. Other French monks, loyal to the King, toured the kingdom preaching against the Templars.

Clement V, who established the papal curia at Avignon, grew indignant at Philip for taking it upon himself to hunt heresy (historically a matter for the Pope), for attacking a religious Order under the protection of the Pope, and for pretending to do so *on behalf* of the Pope. It amounted to a grandiose violation of ecclesiastical jurisdiction which no stronger Pontiff would have tolerated. In February 1308 Clement V determined to recover control of the situation. After meeting in secret with his cardinals, he ordered the suspension of the Inquisitorial hearings. He reassured the Templars in his entourage that he would protect them.[5]

By now, though, the Inquisition had successfully extracted confessions from the bulk of the Templars in France, including their leaders, the Grand Master, the Preceptor of Normandy and the Visitor, Hugues de Pairaud. The Templars had repeated their confessions at tribunals presided over by two canons, two Dominicans, and two Franciscans. Philip sent certain Templars to repeat their confessions to the Pope, which caused Clement to think again. In November 1307 Clement had sent the bull *Pastoralis praeeminentatiae* to the other monarchs of Europe, with orders to arrest all the Templars in their kingdoms, and to hold them in the name of the Pope.

Hugues de Pairaud had previously been closely in league with Philip IV, and had supported his action against Boniface. It did nothing to save him. He seems to have earned little love meanwhile, from his subordinate Templars. Many of those who confessed blamed their alleged wrong-doings on him, by confessing their unwilling participation. Clement sent two cardinals to investigate the goings on in Paris. Pairaud and the Grand Master withdrew their confessions in their presence.

In the face of Clement's objections and complaints, Philip IV moved to have the legality of his action supported by the Paris University theologians. In March 1308, with a few token provisos, the scholars provided favourable answers, strengthening Philip's legal grounds. Then, at Tours, the King convened the Estates-General, a parliament attended by representatives of every town in France. Philip used the Estates-General to drum anti-Templar propaganda into his subjects; while casting himself as the pious grandson of Saint Louis – engaged in a comparably heroic defence of the Catholic Faith. Nogaret issued a proclamation, summoning delegates from the provinces. The proclamation declared the Templars' guilt, saying: 'Oh Grief! The abominable error of the Templars, so bitter so lamentable, is not hidden from you . . .' The crimes of the Templars were, as Philip's propaganda had it, sufficient to agitate Heaven and earth, and to disturb the elements. Philip called for unity against such a crime and reminded his people where their loyalties lay.[6]

The King then visited Clement at Poitiers, with a great retinue. Philip stage-managed a great consistory of clergy, where a royal minister, Guillaume de Plaisians, made two thunderous speeches listing Templar iniquities before the Pope. 'They hold their chapters and meetings at night which is the custom of heretics, he who does evil flees the light.' Plaisians presented Templar confessions as evidence of their guilt. After such speeches, anyone who defended the Order might almost themselves appear to be a conspirator with these dark forces against the faith and the Church. Implicitly, if the Pope now protected the heretical depravity of the Templars, King Philip would be forced to defend Catholicism further by removing Clement too![7] Meanwhile Philip's royal publicist, Pierre Dubois, disseminated pamplets and orations with the purpose of convincing the public that the Templars were a great evil and a threat to their way of life. If the Pope failed to act, the people of France would have to take the law into their own hands.

Harangued and intimidated, the Pope must have found it easier to contemplate the possibility that the accusations against the Templars were true. Philip's agents had all but openly threatened his life. The unhappy demises of Boniface VIII and Benedict XI surely entered Clement V's considerations as well. Clement ordered a Commission of Cardinals to convene to investigate the Order of the Temple. The path was also clear to re-open the proceedings against the Templars as individuals.

Heresies and Crimes

The list of accusations, as finalised by Nogaret in August 1308, ran to 127 items, boiling down to seven criminal errors. The prosecution suggested that a past Grand Master had been taken prisoner by a Muslim Sultan, and was released only on the proviso that he introduce these practices:

> Although the Order had been solemnly established and approved by the Apostolic See, nevertheless at the reception of the brothers of the said Order . . . there were preserved and performed by the brothers these things which follow . . .[8]

Denial of Christ

According to the accusations, initiates into the Order of the Poor Knights of Christ and the Temple of Solomon were forced on pain of death to renounce all the things they had been brought up to hold sacred:

> Each in his reception . . . denied Christ . . . sometimes Christ Crucified, sometimes Jesus, and sometimes God, and sometimes the Holy Virgin . . . led and advised by those who received him . . . The receptors taught that Christ . . . is not the true God . . . They made those whom they received spit on a cross.

The novice Templars allegedly had to call Christ a false prophet, crucified not to redeem mankind but 'on account of his sins'. They had to spit or trample on a Cross, and otherwise abuse it. Many Templars, after being interrogated by the Inquisition, confessed to doing so, but not from their hearts, and spitting at or near the crucifix, against their will.

Could a Templar ever have spat at Jesus on the Cross? The Knights Templar, whilst fighting *for* the Cross, could have encountered alternative teachings which repudiated it as a symbol. For example, Gnostics and Cathars had loved Christ, but hated the Cross, seeing it as a murder weapon. Equally, though Jesus is greatly esteemed in Islam, the Muslims had ridiculed the veneration of the 'True Cross'. Saladin's men, after recovering the Dome of the Rock, had dragged the Cross, that the Crusaders had put on it, through the dirt.

However, the clear implication of the accusation is of a complete rejection of Jesus, and of all the apostles and saints. Templar statutes supposedly considered Jesus' claim to be God and King of the Jews to be '. . . in contempt of him who is the true God in Heaven'. By 1265 many Templars may already have found their faith in Jesus sorely tested. Arsuf and Caesaria were lost. Heartbroken Crusader troubadour Ricault Bonomel contemplated '. . . suicide, or laying down the Cross I once assumed to honour he who was laid upon the Cross, for neither the Cross nor His name protect us against the accursed Turk. Indeed . . . God is supporting them in our spite.' Mohammad 'put forth his power' from beyond the grave to support the Sultan, while the prayers of the Christians had all gone unanswered. After the fall of Acre especially, this sort of crisis of faith, this level of disillusionment, could account for apostacy and the practice of Cross-spitting, some have supposed. Conversely, it might have been a test of faith.

Logically, one would be unlikely to scorn and spurn the Cross as idolatrous, only to worship a severed head in the next minute. Cross-spitting was denied by many Templars, whilst many others revoked their confessions of guilt. Geoffroi de Gonneville had been the Preceptor of Aquitaine. He told his interrogators that at his reception as a Templar, the Master presiding had demanded that he renounce Christ. Gonneville claimed that he had refused to do this, and that the Master had let him off (supposedly because Gonneville was the nephew of an important royal minister in England). However, Gonneville said that his receptor had required him to swear on the Gospels that he would not reveal to any Templar that he had been so excused. This account sounds unconvincing, for it would be contradictory for anyone in one instance to require a repudiation of the Son of God, and then to request an oath on the Christian Gospels in the next. Gonneville's explanation for how the custom of denying Christ was introduced into the Order (i.e. that an evil Grand Master had been captured by the Infidel and was only released on condition that he compel every subsequent initiate into the Knights Templar do this thing) also seems highly implausible. It seems more likely that Gonneville was trying to give satisfaction to his Inquisitors while avoiding self-incrimination.

Disbelieving Sacraments

This was the second chronological accusation in the list:

> That they did not believe the sacraments of the Altar . . . nor in the other sacraments of the Church . . . That the priests of the Order by whom the body of Christ is consecrated did not speak the words in the canon of the mass.

The accusation that the Templars disregarded the sacraments (including transubstantiation) and omitted key words from the rite, was significant. By doing so, as Barber argues, they would implicitly have been defrauding those patrons who paid them to pray for their souls and for the souls of the dead, in their monastic capacity. The inclusion of this charge would alienate any noble who might otherwise have defended the Order. It also implied another Cathar trait. The Cathars seem to have regarded masses, chantry rituals and all such as little more than empty ceremony.

Severed Heads and Black Cats

According to the accusations:

> . . . in each province they had idols namely heads of which some had three faces some one, and some a human skull . . . Item, that they adored these idols, and especially in their great chapters and assemblies.

The teratological head was allegedly brought from a shrine with doors and worshipped as a font of fertility, power, riches and wisdom. It made the trees flower and the land germinate. Hugues de Pairaud, as a number of Templars in France testified, often carried the demonic idol to an altar, threatening inferiors with death if they ever revealed the 'true nature' of the Order. The idol, sometimes named as *Baphomet,* was described variously. One guise of the head was gold and silver. Another appeared to be a real embalmed head, with long hair and a black beard, and, encasing the neck, a bejewelled reliquary with three or four legs. One witness, Etienne de Troyes, testified that after the relic was placed on an altar, during a midnight ritual, Pairaud told the brethren to '. . . adore it and make homage to it, which helps us and does not abandon us'. Some had claimed that it was the head of Hugues de Payens. Etienne was among a number of Templars who were made by Philip to repeat their confessions before Clement V at Poitiers, after the Pope suspended the Inquisitorial proceedings. Etienne claimed that on return from the east, where he had been molested by another brother, he had left the Order.

However, the Templars had seized him back, and had not released him until he was 'redeemed by his mother for 200 livres'. Etienne testified that sodomy and the rituals of the initiation were part of a secret rule kept from the junior members of the Order.

The head mentioned in other confessions had three faces. Another was gold and wood, with two faces, and four legs. Another was horned – some said it was a devil's head, horrible and frightening. Another version was half black, half white. Another still was a representation painted on a beam. In 1951 a similar, 'Jesus-like' head, long-haired and bearded, and situated inside a diamond quatrefoil, was discovered by accident in Templecombe, in the west country of England, when a wall in a cottage was pulled down. The painting would seem to date from the Templar period.[9]

The only head the Episcopal Court's agents actually claimed to have discovered, after a search of the Paris Temple, was labelled 'Caput LVIIIm'. It was female, and encased in a beautiful silver reliquary.[10]

A notary, who had been associated with the Knights Templar in *Outremer*, Antonio Sicci di Vercelli, testified before the papal commission in March 1311. He had heard a macabre story at Sidon (a town near Tyre), involving one Templar who was made wretched by his unrequited love for an Armenian lady named Yse:

> He had never known her carnally whilst she was alive, but at length secretly had intercourse with her when she was dead in her tomb, on the night she was buried. When he had done this, he heard a certain voice saying to him: 'Return when it is time for birth, because you will find a head, offspring of yours.' And I have heard that when the time was passed, this same knight returned to the tomb, and found a human head between the legs of the buried woman. Again he heard the voice saying to him: 'Guard this head, because all good things will come to you from it.'[11]

Apparently the Templar Matthew le Sarmage was then Preceptor of Sidon, and had made himself blood-brother to the Sultan of Egypt. A similar yarn was spun by Hugues de Faure, a Templar from Limoges. This time 'a certain noble' cut off the dead damsel's head, '. . . and a certain voice rang out that he should take good care of the said head, since whoever saw the head would be totally destroyed and routed'. De Faure supposedly heard this story in Cyprus from the *bailli* of Limassol. This time the protagonist of the tale used the head to bring down the castles of his Greek enemies. On a voyage to Constantinople, his nurse had opened the box containing the head and instantly a storm caused the ship to sink.

This was a widespread myth, hitherto not especially linked to the

Templars. In the more common variant of the legend, the head was found by the necrophile's later wife, a Greek Princess, who threw it into the Gulf of Satalia, where great storms and a treacherous whirlpool marked the place. Some identify this tale as a muddling of the classical myth of Perseus and the Gorgon, surviving in oral folklore. The myth featured in the literature of Ovid, translated in France by Chrétien de Troyes. It may also have been inspired by a mixed up version of the Isis and Osiris legend from Egyptian mythology.

The Paris trials produced little evidence of idol worship. Only nine Templars had seen heads. Raoul de Gizy described a demonic head, held by the Visitor. When it was unveiled all the Templars prostrated themselves before it.

Pierre d'Arbley's confession referred to an idol with two faces and four legs. Some dubiously identify the Turin Shroud (principally because the relic later emerged in the possession of the family of the Templar Preceptor of Normandy). Folded, it might show only a head, whereas unfolded the front and back of a crucified man may be seen, therefore displaying two heads and four legs.[12] Yet the idol d'Arbley described had two faces, four legs, and was of gold leaf and wood. The Ark of the Covenant suggests itself as readily. Two winged cherubim faced each other above the lid. Jewish representations of the Ark usually show four legs as well as carrying poles. Scripture attributes to the Ark similar powers as the accusations do to the Templars' idol. The Ark was not a heretical object of veneration, unless perhaps it was regarded as a conduit to God, bypassing the priesthood. Conceivably the Templars were interested in it, but there is no evidence besides that they possessed this relic.

The name *Baphomet* could, as some have speculated, simply be a corruption of the name of Mohammad, although this seems unlikely. In 1300s Europe, many still supposedly believed that Muslims worshipped idols of the Prophet.[13] However, surely the educated elite understood more about Islam than to accept such things (Christians intellectuals and merchants alike having interacted with Muslims for centuries, especially in Spain, there being chairs of Arabic at some of the universities, and there even being a Latin translation of the Koran).

A Templar of Carcassonne confessed that after the obscene kisses, a bronze idol of a man in a dalmatic robe was produced from a chest. The Preceptor allegedly said to the gathering: 'Here is a friend of God, who speaks with God . . . and to whom you must give thanks . . .' The brethren were supposedly told to genuflect to the idol and to spit on a Cross.

The name *Baphomet* also, supposedly, denoted a cockerel or donkey-headed idol – associated by some with the Gnostics. In black magic, *Baphomet* became the Goat of Mendes, the Creator of Evil, spuriously given Ancient Egyptian origins. The nineteenth-century occultist, Elephas Levi, envisaged *Baphomet* as a demonic composite idol of lust, generation and wisdom. The winged, goat-headed figure Levi drew had the breasts of a woman and a caduceus (the rod of Hermes) rising from its groin. Levi claimed to have based this composite idol on a gargoyle from a Templar preceptory. It wore a pentagram on its forehead. Pentagrams, five-pointed stars, appear, it seems, on Templar graves from Tomar. This symbol, now associated with the occult, is often linked with Sophia, the Gnostic embodiment of wisdom. Other explanations of *Baphomet* include a translation of the Greek *Baphe Metis* (Βαπηε Μετισ) or *Absorption into Wisdom*, or the Arabic *abufihamet*, or *Father/Source of Wisdom*. Andrew Sinclair is not alone in believing that Gnostic thought influenced the Knights of the Temple of Solomon, and that they worshipped the principle of sacred knowledge.[14]

After describing how the Order assembled on Good Fridays to trample and urinate on the Cross, in contempt of Christ and the Orthodox faith, the accusations state that: 'They adored a certain cat, sometimes appearing to them in their assembly.' Folklore linked cats with heresy, witchcraft and Satan. The Cathars were accused by Alain de Lille, in the late twelfth century, of worshipping a cat, absurd as the idea may seem. He said that Satan appeared to them in this form, and that they kissed him below the tail. The Inquisitorial tribunals never clarified whether the Templars' cat was real, demonic or a statue. The materialisation of a demonic cat could be counted as one of the 'traditional stock of defamatory clichés', as Cohn put it, which became the hallmarks of the imaginary Satanist conspiracy the Church dreaded. However, originally, little was made of the other usual elements. The Templars, for example, were never formally accused of practising magic, or of ritual murder or sacrifice, unlike the Jews, Gnostics, Cathars and Waldensians before them were, and 'witches' later would be. Moreover, none of these other victims of persecution would be denounced for worshipping a holy or a diabolical head.

Cords

> Item, that they surrounded or touched each head of the aforesaid idols with small cords, which they wore around themselves next to the shirt or the flesh.

The Templars, even Templars outside France, admitted wearing these cord belts around them, whilst denying touching any idols with them. Some maintained that the cord was a sign of purity, but most seemed ignorant of its function. The Templars were told never to remove these cords.

The cord was, according to Inquisitorial records, the sign that one had received initiation into the Cathar priesthood also, and this common practice may have been included in the accusations against the Templars to suggest taint with the Cathar heresy. By other accounts, the cord was nothing sinister, but a sign of purity.

Lay Absolution of Sin

> They believed . . . that the Grand Master could absolve them of sin . . . (and also the Visitor and Preceptors, of whom many were laymen) . . . They enjoined them not to confess to anyone except a brother of their Order.

It was said that non-ordained Templar Preceptors frequently heard confession and gave absolution. This seems to have been a confused area, with certain Masters absolving brethren for breaches of specific Templar rules. However, the implication was that Templars enforced internal confession, so no member could betray their terrible secrets.

It seems there was wide confusion between the confession of sins in a spiritual context, requiring absolution, and the simple confession of lesser faults which the Rule enjoined should be made to the Master of the Temple:

> If any brother, speaking or soldiering, or in any way commits a slight sin, he himself should willingly make known the fault to the Master, to make amends with a pure heart. And if he does not usually fail in this way, let him be given a light penance, but if the fault is very serious, let him go apart from the company of the brothers so that he does not eat or drink at any table with them, but all alone; and he should submit to the mercy and judgement of the Master and brothers, that he may be saved on the day of judgement.

This clause might easily be taken as internal absolution.

Indecent Kisses and Homosexual Activity

> Item, that in the reception of the brothers of the said Order . . . sometimes the receptor and sometimes the received, were kissed on the mouth, on the navel, on the bare stomach, and on the buttocks or the base of the spine . . . sometimes the penis . . .

> Item, that they told the brothers whom they received that they could have carnal relations together . . . that they ought to do and submit to this mutually.

With women anathematised and unavailable to them, it was alleged that Templars practised homosexuality. Only three confessions of sodomy arose from the Paris trials. The serving brother Guillaume de Giaco, one of those who admitted it, said that whilst he was in Cyprus he had carnal relations thrice in a night with the Grand Master. Another, Pierre de Safed, said he had been abused by a Spanish brother called Martin Martin, and had not resisted due to the precepts imparted at his reception.

Many, under pressure, testified to communal sleeping, and said that carnal activities were permitted. Yet there were clauses in the well-known Templar Rule outlining harsh penalties for Templars who might be caught having forbidden relations with their brethren, including beatings or expulsion, at the Master's discretion. This accusation, moreover, seems most to have offended senior Templars. Jacques de Molay, who apparently confessed relatively quickly to the denial of Christ, vehemently refuted the allegation that the Templars were sodomites. However, the Visitor was implicated by many of the Templars he invested, for forcing obscene kisses on them, and ordering that they submit.

Kisses were part of regular Church ritual; a chaste kiss on the mouth over the consecrated chalice signified the 'kiss of peace'. Likewise, the ritual affirmation of the bond between lord and vassal involved a ceremonial kiss. However, the Templars were accused of kissing one another on various parts of their bodies, including navels and the 'base of the spine'. The act would later be held to feature in occult sabbaths, where witches kissed the Devil below his tail.[15]

Crusaders trained by praying and fasting as well as by jousting. Appeasing God was a tactical necessity, with defeat taken as divine punishment for sins. Many therefore blamed vice in the Templars for the loss of the Holy Land. If they were not dealt with soon, perhaps God's wrath would follow them back to France! It must be said, however, that pride and avarice were the stereotypical vices of the later Templars, not sodomy, a vice which people more often suspected of friars and other monks. Clearly the charge of sodomy was deemed the most repugnant, insulting and shameful by the Templars heard in Paris. While 123 of the 138 Templars tried there admitted to spitting on the Cross, only three confessed to committing sodomy with other brethren. Sodomy was thought so offensive a deed among the Templars that it seems the Master and a group of worthy men of the house decided that it should not be brought to Chapter.[16] Could this mean it was hushed up to avoid scandal?

Unlawful Seeking of Gain

> Item, that they did not reckon it sinful in the said Order to acquire property belonging to another by legal or illegal means.

It was long said that the Templars were enjoined to procure wealth and land for their Order, by fair means or foul. A real, much documented grievance was being included here. Several acts of parliament and papal bulls had been written to curb the abuses of their powers by the Templars. The Order was commonly rumoured to have defrauded individuals, and made treacherous deals with the infidel for its enrichment. Power corrupts, as many have observed, and corruption, sometimes, empowers.

The fact that King Philip was the Temple's debtor may have had something to do with this charge also. He had borrowed 5,200 *livres tournoise* from the Paris Temple in 1297. The King, in the twenty-two years of his reign before 1307, had used every expedient to raise revenue. He had plundered the Lombards and Jews, taxed the clergy and appropriated Crusade funds – so if anyone was guilty of this charge it was arguably Philip's own government. It cannot be argued that the Templars were any greedier or more self-interested than any other land-owning institution of the day. It was relatively common for monasteries to enter into bitter land disputes with tenants and neighbours, and it is probably to the Templars' credit that they were more inclined to settle their own disputes about such matters through the courts rather than by resorting to force.

Secret Night Chapters

The heretical misdeeds of the Templars were done, it was alleged:

> . . . secretly, that because in this way they shut themselves up when a chapter was held, as all the doors of the house and the church in which they were holding the chapter they fortified so firmly that no one might nor could gain access to them or near them, nor could anyone see or hear what they were doing or saying.

In his speech against the Templars, before the Pope at Poitiers, Plaisians emphasised the accusation that the Brotherhood met at night, and therefore must be corrupt, as all evil things shun the light. Even those who defended the Order's innocence from the above crimes, acknowledged that they took grave oaths of secrecy. One has to wonder why there was this concern with covertness, if the Order was entirely orthodox in its Catholic faith. Military necessity aside, many supposed there was something within the Order that the leading Templars desired to keep from the rest of Christendom.

There is some evidence of secrecy within the Order of the Temple from the very start. The accusations clearly alleged that the 'depraved habits and errors' had existed for such a time that the Order could have been renewed in personnel once, twice or more from the time of their introduction, and that the entire brotherhood had kept this a secret from the Holy Mother Church.

NOTES

1 Barber, Malcolm,*The Trial of the Templars*, p. 54.
2 Cohn, Norman, *Europe's Inner Demons*, p. 91.
3 Barber, op. cit., p. 56.
4 Lord, Evelyn , *The Knights Templar in Britain*, p. 190.
5 Cohn, op. cit., p. 92.
6 Ibid., p. 93.
7 Barber, *op. cit.*, pp. 89–97. Plaisians' speech was probably written by Nogaret, who could not deliver it himself, as his standing with the Pope had been forever tarnished by his role in the attack on Boniface. Duhmus, Joseph, *The Middle Ages*, pp. 278–80. Nogaret's parents were executed for heresy (Catharism) and therefore he delighted in helping Philip IV harass and browbeat the papacy.
8 Barber, op. cit., p. 248. Barber's Appendix A gives in full the Articles of Accusation of 12 August 1308.
9 Ibid., p. 185. The painted head is now kept in the church at Templescombe.
10 Ibid.
11 Ibid., pp. 185–6.
12 Currer-Briggs, Noel, *The Shroud and the Grail* (general premise of book). The Shroud was possibly taken from Constantinople. It has been carbon-dated to AD 1216, but it has since been revealed that the part of the shroud tested may have been a repaired patch. The Bouchelon palace's loot also yielded a 'head of John the Baptist'. At least three of his other heads were already drawing pilgrims to various shrines in Europe. In 1389 the Shroud emerged in possession of the de Charney family, relatives of the last Grand Preceptor of Normandy, who accompanied Jacques de Molay to his death.
13 Barber, op. cit., p. 273, n. 8. If anybody should have been able to put people right about their misconceptions of Islam it was the Templars, having occupied a former mosque as their headquarters, and having such close contact with Muslims – as enemies in battle, as captors, as prisoners and as emissaries of peace. In Spain and Syria they were also landlords to a not inconsiderable number of Muslims.
14 Sinclair, Andrew, *The Discovery of the Grail*, p. 264. Sinclair makes an interesting observation concerning heads. 'Temple' refers not only to a building erected to house a god, but to the part of the human skull housing the seat of knowledge – the intellect which could be identified with the divine spark.
15 Maxwell-Stuart, P G, *Witchcraft: A History*, p. 50.
16 Read, Piers Paul, *The Templars*, p. 308.

CHAPTER XIII
Possible Non-Catholic Influences on the Templars

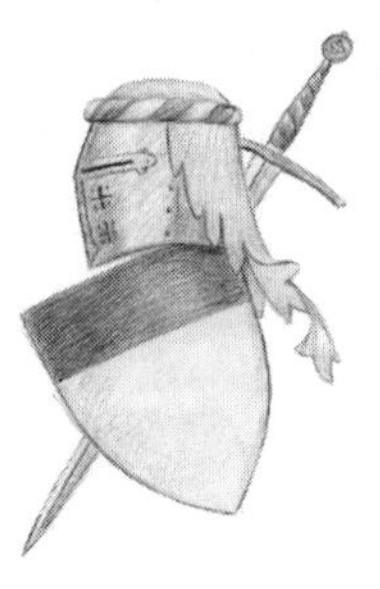

The medieval Church did not curtail the semi-idolatrous cult of relics because it often found it highly profitable and, perhaps, because it prevented the people falling back on more blatantly pagan magic for miraculous cures and such like. As we have seen, many saintly heads were preserved separately from their other parts, and credited with supernatural power. One contender for the skull of John the Baptist was housed in a golden, bearded, head-shaped reliquary in Ste Chapelle, alongside the Crown of Thorns, parts of the True Cross, and vials of Christ's blood – sacred loot from Byzantium. This Gothic shrine had been built to house these relics by Louis IX, Philip the Fair's beatified grandfather, who had bought them from the hard-up Latin Emperor of Constantinople. Cologne Cathedral, meanwhile, curiously, claimed to preserve the skull of 'John the Baptist' from when he was 'twelve years of age'.[1]

Many saints had been deprived of their heads. Many hundreds of Templars, likewise, were decapitated – the Muslims made quite a custom of it – yet these heads are not specifically linked to the alleged cult of *Baphomet*. There are several vague references to the Templars having Holy Relics, the things they salvaged from Jerusalem and Acre. The Hospitallers were also known to preserve a number of relics, including the arm of John the Baptist, encrusted with precious stones and wearing a brilliant ring (which was eventually stolen by Napoleon after his seizure of Malta in 1788). The puzzle is that no Templar explained convincingly what their head relic was. None tried to show that they merely held the bones of some beloved saint or martyr in veneration, a practice perfectly acceptable within Catholicism by the standards of the day. It was a secret, sacred head, and it had power. It was their god, according to the accusations. Its nature and meaning, its fate, even whether it ever existed at all, remain tantalising mysteries.

Celts

The Druids, the priests of the Celtic tribes of Europe, advised chiefs and officiated at sacrificial rites, before their suppression by the Roman Empire. Theirs was one of the first religions outside Egypt to teach the transmigration of the soul, which inspired their warriors to have no fear of death in battle. According to Ancient Greek writers such as Posidonius, certain ancient Celtic tribes revered severed heads. They believed that powers could be derived from dead enemies, and in the wisdom that came down from ancestral relics. The classical author Strabo, in his *Geography*, reported that the Celtic tribes:

> . . . when they depart from battle . . . hang the heads of their enemies from the necks of their horses, and when they have brought them home nail the spectacle to the entrances of their houses.[2]

According to Diodorus Siculus:

> The heads of their most illustrious enemies they embalm in cedar oil and preserve in a chest . . . Some of them, we are told, boast that they have refused its weight in gold . . . for not to sell the proof of one's valour is a noble thing.[3]

When the Celts slew the Roman general Postumius in 216 BC, they cut off his head and gilded his skull. This they used as a vessel in their rituals, believing it a source of power. At Entremount and Roquertuse, Gaulish shrines have been found with niches in standing stones, where carvings of severed heads or real skulls were placed. The tradition survived. The talking head of King Bran the Blessed was revered as a talisman of power, mentioned in the *Mabinogion*, a medieval volume of Welsh legends of Ancient British origin. In *Peredur*, another Welsh romance, a precursor of the Holy Grail appears as a bearded head on a bejewelled platter, with similar supernatural properties to the head supposedly revered by the Templars.

The nature god Cernunnos was sometimes shown as a horned, cloven-hoofed man, sitting cross-legged; for example on the Gundelstrup cauldron, where he also holds a snake.[4] This image has similarities with the goat-headed guise of *Baphomet* (envisaged by Elephas Levi).

Cernunnos also sometimes appeared as a three-faced, triple deity. A three-faced (tricephalic) stone head survives from Corleck, County Cavan, in Ireland. Another three-faced figure, featuring on a Romano–Gallic altar to Cernunnos, also exists, flanked by a male (Mercury) figure and a representation of the god in his horned, cloven-hoofed persona. Here we may have the extra-biblical origin of the Christian Devil as he appeared in medieval iconography. Thus the Templars' head was sometimes described as having horns. Horned, tricephalic heads survived to feature in medieval imagery. At San Pietro in Tosania, Viterbo, carved examples are to be found. The outer two mouths disgorge vegetation (rather like the so-called 'Green Man' heads, which may be related). The carvings date from the twelfth century. There are such heads above and below a Romanesque window, the lower of which has a torso and holds a snake.[5] A similar carving, a horned Green Man head, with foliage growing from his mouth, is to be found within the Templar church, at Garway, Herefordshire. This carving supports one side of the chancel arch.

Strangely, in much Christian art, the prophet Moses was shown with horns, due to an interpretation of an obscure passage from the Bible describing his altered state on his second descent from Mount Sinai with the Ten Commandments. The Templars were thought to revere Moses, the originator of the Ark and the law it contained, without which there would have been no Temple of Solomon. Coincidence it may be, but Moses was also associated with a serpent/staff (see Exodus 7: 9–14). It may be significant that a snake is among the devices carved at Temple Garway, the serpent having been a symbol also of immortality and wisdom, linked both to the horned god Cernunnos and to Moses.

Geographical correlation and certain symbols aside, it is difficult to link the Templars directly to the Celtic traditions. Common symbolism would not in itself constitute proof of links, as, at least according to the theory of Carl Jung, people from every society were predisposed to produce 'archetypal images', symbols that recur in mythology and religion. Arising from the collective subconscious, these do not necessarily imply contact. This said, however, the Celtic traditions undeniably survived as an undercurrent in medieval culture, and informed the authors of the Grail romances.

The Holy Grail

Celtic Arthurian myths containing magic heads and miraculous cauldrons (associated with death and regeneration) survived as an oral tradition well beyond the Dark Ages, and became a source of inspiration for poets and troubadors. By the Middle Ages a Christianised conception of the Grail had emerged. The magic cauldron had become the Holy Grail, the Cup of Christ, as used at the Last Supper. The same cup in which the legendary Joseph of Arimathea caught some of the blood of the crucified Christ, later to bring it from Palestine to Glastonbury in England, as one version of the myth had it. The Grail was magnified into an object that could bring about healing, higher consciousness and even immortality. It entered the Christianised stories of King Arthur as a holy relic that only the most worthy knight could obtain. The courtly Grail romances were principal among the cultural fashions of the Crusading era. They reflected its values of chivalry, piety, valour and sacrifice. There appears to be a subtext, however, of heterodox mysticism, involving a goddess and severed-head motifs that recur at various stages. A number of Grail romance writers shared patrons with the Templars and moved in the same cultural circles.

Count Henry of Champagne, known as Henry the Liberal, was another Templar patron. In 1180 he made a pilgrimage to Jerusalem, and also took part in skirmishes with the Muslims. Henry's wife, Countess Mary, daughter of Louis VII and Eleanor of Aquitaine, patronised Chrétien de Troyes (1135–82) the author of *Conte de Graal,* a Christianisation of the crude pagan myths. Chrétien was a learned man, who had earlier translated Ovid's *Metamorphoses*. In Chrétien's unfinished Grail epic, the Welsh knight Perceval embarks as an innocent and unsophisticated youth. After various adventures, and a poignant romantic encounter, he comes across the visionary Grail procession at a mysterious castle called Caerbanec, the home of the maimed Fisher King, whose wound from the Holy Lance keeps his realm a wilderness, and where the court of knights and ladies seem alive but are really dead. There, Perceval witnesses a procession where he sees the Holy Spear dripping blood, a silver platter and a celestial maiden carrying the Grail – so radiant the candles lost their brilliance. Perceval fails to ask the meaning of it all, and somehow, because of this, an opportunity to heal the land is lost. The knight joins King Arthur's court, and afterwards embarks with the other knights to rediscover the Grail castle, which exists in a realm between reality and Heaven, and can only be achieved by the purest and best of knights.

Templar-esque knights, called 'Templeisen', would enter the mysterious quest, featuring as Grail guardians, in Wolfram von Essenbach's German epic poem, *Parzival*. Wolfram (c1170–1220) was probably a knight himself, born into the lesser Bavarian nobility. In his version, written between 1195 and 1210, the Grail manifests not as a chalice, but as a stone. Andrew Sinclair proposes that this may allude to the Shetiyya foundation rock from the Temple of Solomon. Eventually Perceval/Parzival discovers his destiny as the next lord of the Grail castle, and his true descent from a mysterious 'Grail family'.

The poet Wolfram appears to have been interested in the reconciliation of the peoples of the three monotheistic religions. Like other Grail Romancers, he apparently sought inspiration from some exotic sources.

Along with Celtic and Christian elements, some researchers find traces of Gnostic, Cabbalistic, Neoplatonic and Islamic mysticism within the Grail stories. The motifs occurring in the stories are read allegorically – the maiden who holds the Grail is an allusion to the Gnostic Sophia, the absence of priests and altars an indication that the sacred light of salvation and eternal life can be found without them. Later in the thirteenth century, less pagan versions of the story were compiled in the *Queste del Saint Graal*, by Cistercian monks, and in these the blood of Christ became more significant as the object of the quest, inspired by Saint Bernard's meditations on its mystical significance. These writings were contemporary with the time when the Templars and Hospitallers brought the vial of sacred blood from the Holy Land to Westminster.

Perhaps the Templars liked to see themselves as the spiritual successors to the Knights of the Round Table, and the romancers based their Grail knights on them in admiration, or through flattery. Some suppose that Grail literature encodes concepts that could not have been expressed openly. Unorthodox ideas about symbolic objects that could function as keys to divine revelation and bring about a spiritual state of enlightenment. Through the protagonist's own trials, in the stories, they seek to attain salvation without reference to the Church's mediation. In this light, the Grail can be seen as a mystic metaphor for something else, the Virgin Mary with Christ in her womb, or possibly the Ark of the Covenant with the stones from Heaven – also identified with the Madonna as a container of holiness.[6]

The Grail knights come across some perplexing things during their convoluted quests – the Ship of Solomon, the maimed Fisher King, the Grail Castle and family, visions of Christ as a child within the Grail . . . but any interpretation can only be guesswork, and, at the end of the day, these are only stories. It is equally possible, it might be added, that the Templars' accusers appropriated the idea of worshipping heads from the Celtic Grail literature, as it is that the Grail myths hid within them the truth about the Templars. Moreover, the Templars featured far more directly in several other medieval romances, although these have proved far less enduring than the Grail legends.

Assassins

Templar castles in Palestine were vast and formidable. Atlit, built in 1218 by the fourteenth Grand Master, Guillaume de Chatres, was the greatest Templar fortress of all. Other Templar castles, facing the 'Assassin state' in Syria, included Tortosa and Castel Blanc. The mountain fortresses of the Assassins, however, were mightier castles still. Rashid al-Din Sinan, Syrian Grand Master of the Assassins (1162–93), known as 'the old man of the mountains', denounced all who did not adhere to the Assassin doctrine. He was regarded as a messiah by his acolytes. Fanatical young men, called Fedayeen, were indoctrinated to murder their master's enemies, usually at the price of their own lives. They supported the Shi'a faction of Islam, and therefore shared with the Crusaders an interest in subverting and dividing their Sunni Muslim neighbours. No ruler, however, be he Christian or Muslim, was safe from these hashish-intoxicated killers, except, it seems, for the Grand Masters of the Military Orders. Supposedly the Assassins knew that the Templars and Hospitallers could always replace their fallen leaders.

The Assassin mystics mirrored the Templars in several striking ways. They both lived as warriors, following similarly austere and aesthetic spiritual credos. They both emphasised religious purpose, courage, obedience and military duties; and both recruited from a middling, manorial class of men.[7] The hierarchical structures of the two brotherhoods were also parallel:

Templar	**Assassin equivalent**
Lay brother	lasiq(layman)
Sergeant	fida'i (agent)
Knight	rafiq (companion)
Prior	da'i
Grand Prior	da'i kabir
Grand Master	(Sheik) Grand Master

Like the Templars, the Assassin rafiqs were said to wear white mantles, adorned with red. Because Ismaili teachings were heretical, the Assassins were taught their complex doctrine in esoteric stages, with degrees of initiation and vows of secrecy. There was an Islamic mystical concept called *ras el-fahmat* (head of knowledge) concerned with mystical union with Allah. The Assassin Imams promised their followers revelations of the deeper truth of Islam, but perhaps this was just a snare to guarantee obedience and make them susceptible to brainwashing.

The Assassins were a larger organisation than the Knights Templar were in the Holy Land, and it is strange that they could have ever been compelled to pay the Templars an annual 'tribute' of gold. If, moreover, the Templars derived dress, organisational structure and architectural knowledge from the Ismaili Muslim Assassins, it is possible that some theological exchange also occurred. Little detail of Assassin doctrine survives, however, following the sect's destruction by the Mongols in 1256.

The English Templars' seal also depicted a star and crescent (taken from Islam) and a lion *passant guardant* (a symbol of Solomon, as well as of the English royal house). The Templars were accused of renouncing Jesus at their ceremonies and crying 'Yallah! Yallah!' Their contact with the

Assassins alone, however, would never make the Templars suddenly start repudiating Christ and the Crucifixion, let alone start worshipping grisly idols or relics, surely something anathema to any truly Muslim group. The deeply unorthodox Assassins may just have been the exception. According to one story, their sinister leader once convinced his company that he possessed a disembodied head that could give divine revelations. It turned out to be a young man with his body hidden below a table, and with his head sticking up through a hole. Afterwards the Assassin sheik had the youth's head properly severed.

Essenes and Jewish Mystics

The early Cistercian monks employed Jewish scholars for help in understanding Hebrew scriptures, at a time just before the Templars appeared.[8] Stephen Harding, the Saxon Abbot of Cîteaux and mentor of St Bernard, sought the help of learned rabbis as translators of scripture, in order to better understand the Word of God in its original form. There is some suggestion that this interest in Jewish texts might also relate to a belief in treasure or secret knowledge lying hidden in Jerusalem, beneath Temple Mount.

Mainstream historians tend to reject the possibility of any covert project having existed. They seem to see it as coincidental that Temple Mount, for thousands of years the centre of the world to Jews, suddenly became the headquarters of the Knights Templar. Indeed there is no strong evidence that the Templars learned of a treasure buried under the Temple from Jewish sources (such as the Talmud) and subsequently excavated the site in search of the treasure. However, in the light of the Jewish link to the Cistercians, a Templar excavation for Biblical treasures does not seem *so* unlikely.

Whilst the Templars' trials revealed no obviously Semitic practices, the Order's interest in Solomon's Temple was an interest in something distinctly Old Testament. The Temple was built to house the Ark of the Covenant, containing the law and somehow the essence of God. The Ark, according to scripture, miraculously won battles for God's chosen people and brought plagues to their enemies. It devoured in deadly jets of fire Nadab and Abiku, sons of the Priest Aaron, for violating the Tabernacle; offering '. . . strange fire before the Lord, which he commanded them not' (Leviticus 10:1–2). Demons held sway when the cloud appeared above the Ark, and its power brought down the walls of Jericho. The High Priest of the Temple could only enter the cube-shaped Holy of Holies, where the Ark was installed, once a year, and then only after a long process of ritual purification. The Ark mysteriously disappeared, however, perhaps whilst Solomon still reigned.

The Ark remained deeply significant to the Jews, and to early

Christians, especially in Alexandria, a city the Jews helped to found. There the Jewish philosopher Philo, in the first century, wrote emphasising the Ark's unique sanctity in Judaism. Philo was also concerned with how the Ark could be used as a key to mystic enlightenment. Influenced by Greek and Gnostic thought, he believed that the spirit could escape the flesh and achieve oneness with God. The Ark, as a metaphor, contained the essence of God. Each part of it, the box, the law treasured within it, the voice, the cherubim above and so on, was a mystical symbol:

> If anyone could really understand the nature of these things, it seems to me that he would be possessed by the most divinely formed beauty, and would be able to renounce every other thing that is desired.[9]

To the medieval mind, whoever found the Ark could well challenge Rome's claim to represent God on earth. The recovered Ark might prove divine favour, and be a great propaganda tool as such (although, arguably, the Church could contend that God's new covenant over-rode the old, and that they were its inheritors).

It seems the Ark was one relic that eluded the Crusaders. Never mentioned during the Templar trials, it would probably not have been something the Templars could have kept secret – or indeed would have wished to, given the potential to profit from the pilgrimage industry that relics generated. That said, however, not all relics were publicised and exploited like this. Some, including those guarded by the Hospitallers, seem to have been kept hidden from ordinary Christians by their owners, and not widely advertised.

A German Freemasonic tradition linked the Templars to the Essenes/ Nazarenes, a sect who had claimed to be heirs to the esoteric mysteries of Moses. Tradition has it that the Templars discovered treasures and Essene scrolls in the Holy Land, and used Jewish scholars to translate them. Essenes were apocalyptic, fundamentalist Jews, based until the first century in a commune at Qmran, near the Dead Sea. They termed themselves 'The Poor' or 'The Living'. John the Baptist and Jesus of Nazareth could have been associated with this group. During the Zealot uprising, the Qmran community concealed their sacred writings (some of which comprised the Dead Sea Scrolls) before being wiped out in AD 70. Two Freemasons, Knight and Lomas, recently hypothesised that the Templars discovered more Essene writings during their early occupation and alleged excavation of the Temple site, and secretly revived their ideas and practices, deeming them closer to the true teachings of Jesus.[10]

A system of cryptography used by the Essenes was discovered by one Dr Hugh Schonfield. This coding, called the Atbash Cipher, figured in the Dead Sea Scrolls. By applying the Atbash Cipher to *Baphomet*, the name

Sophia is supposed to reveal itself.[11] It seems that the Essenes were forerunners of the Gnostics, although dualism was not part of their theology.

If the Templars were open to Jewish influences, this may account for their alleged secret rejection of Christ as the Messiah, worshipping instead one Almighty God. It would little explain the worshipping of a severed head. And yet . . . in the cabbalah, a school of Jewish mysticism, the quest for sacred wisdom and union with God is expressed in the concept of the tree of life, with the godhead at the *Kether*, the crown. This symbol is also represented by the seven-branched candlestick. In a fifteenth-century copy of the *Operea Chemica,* by the philosopher and mystic Raimon Lull, there appears an illustration of a version of the same tree of life. In the diagram the tree rises through an urn with a red-coloured, three-faced, bearded head on it, and another small black head, past two birds through another triple-faced head. The tree then rises to a crowned head (half black, half white), then six branches lead out to more heads from a trunk coiled with a serpent, that leads ultimately to two more human heads at the top, a white one over a black one. The whole is surrounded by a halo of concentric spheres. The diagram is an apparent expression of Hermetic philosophy. The imagery it incorporates closely resembles the idols described in confessions by many Templars. The diagram leads one to wonder whether the various heads were more than the invention of the Templars' enemies, whether they might not rather have been symbolic components in an esoteric, mystical tradition.[12]

The ugly sentiment of anti-semitism was commonly expressed in medieval society. It was sometimes encouraged by the Church, and massacres of Jews frequently coincided with times of Crusading fervour. The Dominicans played a significant part in the persecution of the Jews, and burned many of their writings. Individual Templars had also instigated pogroms, but such events were rare and isolated. The Order as a whole was not given to attacking unarmed, innocent people, and at times it demonstrated remarkable tolerance. In several cities the Templars owned houses that they rented to Jews, such as the Norman era 'Jew's house' that survives in Lincoln. The tenant, called Aaron the Jew, was an important financier to Henry II of England.[13] The tax on The Jews of London was paid at the New Temple. Some of the Templars' banking skills may similarly have been learned from Jewish financiers, a race who were allowed no other profession. Jewish bankers also helped finance the Third Crusade, not that they were given much choice in the matter.

Gnosticism

Gnosticism was a loosely affiliated heretical/occult movement in early Christian times, flourishing in Palestine and elsewhere. Gnostic philosophers rejected the crucifixion and the literal resurrection of Christ. Some have seen in this the origin of the Templars' alleged abuse of the Cross. *Gnosis* is Greek for knowledge, relating to spiritual mysticism. Gnostic gospels recounted the arcane revelations Jesus supposedly brought when he returned as a spirit to Mary Magdalene. In the 'Gospel of Thomas', these teachings were beyond St Peter's grasp. The Gnostics revered Sophia, the Queen of Heaven, personifying holy wisdom, corresponding to the mystic Jewish *Shekinah*.

A significant strand of Gnosticism emerged in Alexandria in the first century, deriving elements of belief from the ancient Egyptian cults of Thoth and Isis, Greek Orphism, Judaism and Christianity. Gnosticism later absorbed Manichean dualism, the belief that God transcended all creation, and that a second god, a false *demiurgos*, had created the material cosmos from debased matter. In human beings this devil trapped a 'divine spark' of the original God. 'Gnosis' was enlightenment to the truth beyond everything. If this epiphany came during life, death released the 'divine spark' back to God. If not, the soul was reincarnated on earth. As a passage from the Coptic–Gnostic Epistle to Rheginos (part of the cache of writings from Nag-Hammadi in Egypt) put it: 'Do not think that the resurrection is an illusion. It is no illusion, but it is the truth. It is more suitable to say, then, that the world is an illusion.'

The early Roman Church suppressed Gnosticism in Europe as heretical, and it died out in the fourth century. Mandaeans/Subbis were surviving Gnostics, in Persia. They practised Christian baptism, and venerated Saint John. They also incorporated Zoroastrian, Indian, Manichean and Muslim elements, worshipping a 'light king'. They indulged in much allegorising of ancient myths, with holy books written in Aramaic. Small Mandaean communities survived in Iraq into the modern era. They used degrees of initiation into their ancient cult, and had ceremonies and secret grips (handshakes) with striking similarities to those used by Freemasons. Knight and Lomas contend that the Templars either encountered such living groups, or found the writings of their ancestors. They adopted their practices and passed them on to Freemasonry in medieval Scotland – where the Order of the Temple secretly survived. If there was substance to the theory that Freemasonry originated in certain vestiges of the Temple, then, in this roundabout way, the idea that the Templars were Gnostics might become more credible. How else could the practices of obscure sects in the Middle East have informed the rituals of a secret society in medieval Scotland?

A Gnostic link to the Templars is that several explanations of *Baphomet* fit the worshipping of 'sacred wisdom'. Friedrich Nicolai, an eighteenth-century German Masonic bookseller, linked the Gnostics and the Templars, citing common symbolism. His work was influential, but is almost forgotten today.[14] Likewise, Joseph von Hammer-Purgstall connected the two movements, though his overriding desire was to smear

Freemasonry. Freemasonry had spread from Britain, and was still seen as subversive by the Austrian Chancellery for whom Hammer-Purgstall worked. He therefore sought to link the esoteric secret society with the Knights Templar and the Gnostic sects. He painted them both in an evil light, as worshippers of all things carnal and as insidious conspirators against Catholic civilisation.

Joseph von Hammer-Purgstall perhaps drew on Ireneus's description of the third-century Capocratian Gnostics. The Capocratians allegedly believed that Jesus achieved union with the unbegotten Father (God) by 'despising' the laws of his society. Inhibitions were the chains that bound people to the prison of the body. Thus Capocratians were said to seek salvation by breaking every social taboo. It was claimed that they also advocated communal living, without social rank, or private property, as well as something aproaching 'free love'. Ireneus naturally decried those who advocated tasting 'all forms of Godless, unlawful and unspeakable things'.

Waldensians

The Waldensians were a group persecuted as heretics, who coincided with the time of the Templars. They originated in southern France, and were founded by Peter Waldo, a Lyonaise merchant who became a preacher. Peter taught that poverty was blessed, and that feudalism was anathema to good Christians. He was excommunicated in 1184 for rejecting sacramental grace and priestly authority. Persecution scattered his followers into Bohemia, where they became a separate church, surviving to support the Protestant Reformation. Enemies, especially the Inquisition, attempted to villainise them with accusations of Devil-worship, involving similar heresies to those of the Templars.[15] Shortly after the Templars were suppressed, the Inquisitor Bernard Gui wrote a manual for Inquisitors, in which he mentioned sexual excesses and cat worship among the Waldensians.

Bogomils and Cathars

Bogomils were Balkan dualists, seemingly influenced by remnants of the Gnostic sects in the Middle East. Bosnia fell for a time to France, and the Knights Templar were established there. Later the Church would sanction the taking of Bogomil heretics into slavery by French Catholics. Before their demise, the Bogomils had some contact with their co-religionists in southern France and parts of Italy, who were called 'Cathars' by the Catholics. For a time they even held councils and, at the conclave in the town of St Félix en Lauragais in 1167, debated theological matters with representatives of the Roman Church.

Matthew Paris mentions the 'suspect sophistries of the Albigensians', another name given to the heretics, from Albi, a home to many Cathars. It used to be supposed that 'Cathar' translated as 'pure one', but the term was never used by the sect itself. 'Cathar' was a term of abuse, which some historians now link to the rumour spread by their enemies that the sect worshipped a satanic cat. Eleventh-century Cathars adhered to Gnostic dualism, but considered themselves 'Good Christians'. To them, human souls were imprisoned in flesh by a fallen angel whom they identified with the jealous Lord of the Old Testament – all of which they seem to have rejected. This world was the only Hell. The worldly Catholic Church was unwittingly serving the Evil One.

Cathar priests, called 'Parfaits', were of both sexes, and wore black robes. During their initiation rite, the *consolamentum*, they received a cord to wear. What actually happened during this ceremony remains a mystery, but it is thought that the newly Perfected were received with a chaste kiss. Cathars rejected the other sacraments. Parfaits had to abstain from all sexual acts and from consuming meat, as they believed in reincarnation. They held that their spirituality and their attained *gnosis* meant that they would be released from the mortal coil, and death would liberate their souls to return to Heaven. Catholic propagandists wrote that some Cathar followers, or *Credentes*, preferred, on account of their beliefs, to copulate in fashions that would not produce more children for the Devil. It therefore became common for the Inquisitors to accuse suspected heretic of buggery (a word linked to Bulgar, or to *Bogomil*).

Other people recognised Cathars as humble people who abhorred violence. This pacifism made them ideological opponents of Military Orders, incidentally. The rejection of violence makes it problematic to link the Cathars with the Templars. They did share a belief in holy poverty, however, and rejected materialism. The Cathars, like the Waldensians, found a sympathetic audience among the religious peasantry and urban poor, disaffected by the overt wealth and luxury of the aristocratic Catholic priesthood. More surprisingly, they also had friends among the nobility. St Bernard preached against the Cathars in southern France, but on this occasion few listened. Catharism's spread became increasingly threatening to papal supremacy. The Languedoc's autonomy also affronted the covetous north of France. The resulting wars against Catharism (waged by barons who served the King of France) thus also served the Capetian dynasty's expansionism.

The Counts of Toulouse, Catharism's defenders, had previously donated generously to the Military Orders. They also maintained their links with their kin around Tripoli in Syria, part of the east that retained a distinctly Provençal character. During the protracted 'Albigensian Crusades', most Templars remained neutral, having sworn only to fight the Saracen. The Hospitallers were even less willing to assail the Cathars, due to their traditional alliance with the St Gilles Counts of Tripoli.[16]

The Cathars were Docetists, believing Christ was a spirit untainted by matter, and that his Passion and Resurrection were illusory. They rejected religious images, and repudiated the Cross. Crucifixes were relatively recent innovations, unknown to Christianity in its early centuries. The Templars, more usually, used the plain *croix pattée* (a cross with arms of equal length that widen outwards), or else the red cross of St George with the Lamb of God at its centre. Although the Albigensian heretics were likewise accused of Devil-worship (and in turn effectively accused Rome of serving the Devil), the worship of idols, especially severed heads, would only have disgusted a Cathar. Fugitive Cathars might have taken refuge within the Temple (as other Cathars were sometimes sheltered by the Benedictines and Cistercians). If evidence of a deeper connection had existed, Philip IV's men would surely have found it.

Montsegur, the last Cathar castle, had fallen in 1244. Its defenders went willingly into the Dominicans' bonfires. They let the flames free their souls from this world. In 1248 Louis IX, whilst passing south on his Crusade, had encountered hostility from his southern subjects, around Avignon, whom his men called Albigensians and traitors. The excessive oppression of Catharism had provoked a resentment in the region that would endure. Ironically, as we have seen, Nogaret himself had a Cathar background, and was under a papal ban throughout the proceedings.

If Nogaret, the King's minister, somehow schemed to be avenged on the Roman Church by causing it to self-mutilate – to turn on its own trusty champions – then it was a subtle and audacious plot. However, if that were the case, the Templars were a strange choice of victims, having done less to the Cathars than certain of the Cistercians and Dominicans. Indeed, the suppression of the Templars gave the Dominican Order – the very scourge of Catharism – a new triumph and new justification. This enabled its Inquisitorial establishment to perpetuate itself on into the era of the witch hunts.

Nogaret's accusations attempted to make it look as if the Order of the Temple had been corrupted by the Cathar heresy, playing on common myths and prejudices. However, certainly for the most part, the world view of a Templar – who served God by taking part in worldly fighting – would have had little in common with that of a Cathar. The Cathars were ordinary people, yet they embraced martyrdom at the hands of Catholics. The Templars were religious soldiers; yet all those Templars whom Philip the Fair caused to be burned, died protesting their innocence and fidelity to the Catholic faith. Not one died defending his supposed heresy.[17]

Copts and the Ethiopian Ark

The Coptic faith preserves Monophysite Christianity, manifested in north-east Africa. The Patriarch governs from Alexandria in Egypt, where the

Copts form a sizeable minority. Ethiopia is predominantly Coptic, with indigenous peculiarities. The situation was similar in the Middle Ages. As believers in a Christ with a single, divine nature, an interpretation of Coptic ideas may have inspired the Templars to reject the importance of the Crucifixion, or to deny the man who died on the Cross.

Like the Templars, the Copts used the Byzantine liturgy, often built round churches, and practised secretive monasticism. Like the Cathars, some Copts believed in Christ as a purely spiritual entity, untainted by worldly matter. Unlike the Cathars, however, the Copts placed great emphasis on the Old Testament, particularly in Ethiopia, where there survives a deep-rooted cult of the Ark of the Covenant.[18] Ethiopians had lived in Jerusalem since the fourth century. Their monastery near the Holy Sepulchre was among the Holy City's most ancient churches. Ethiopia fuelled the Crusaders' 'Prester John' legend of a Christian Empire beyond Islam. In 1177 Ethiopian imperial envoys arrived in Jerusalem, seeking to be granted an altar for their sect in the Holy Sepulchre. (Appeals were sent to the Pope requesting this privilege, although it would actually be Saladin who granted them their altar in 1189, three years after his conquest of the City.)

In the inner sanctum of most Ethiopian churches, a stone called the *Tabot* represents the Ark of the Covenant. Before its conversion by Saint Frumentius, Ethiopians may, in fact, have observed a religion closely akin to early Judaism. Scholars believe Jews from Arabia brought the faith to Ethiopia. The Ethiopians themselves tell that Judaism was brought far earlier, by a prince called Menelik, the son of Solomon and the Queen of Sheba. Ethiopian lore remembers her as Mekida, the Queen of Axum, a city where Coptic monks still guard what they believe is the Ark, taken by Menelik from Jerusalem. The sanctuary chapel where the Ark supposedly lies is quite modern, but stands amid the ruins of much older shrines. Axum lies in the Ethiopian highlands, in the north of the country, and is dominated by ancient obelisks taller than any in Egypt. It is closer to Mecca than Jerusalem is.

A Prince named Lalibela fled from Ethiopia to Jerusalem in the 1160s. Lalibela's brother, the despotic Emperor Harbay, had attempted Lalibela's assassination, having learned of a prophecy that the young prince would one day take the throne. Lalibela returned in 1185, deposing Harbay. Graham Hancock theorises that some Templars might have willingly accompanied him, if they learned of the possibility that the Ark was in Ethiopia. In the city Lalibela founded in the Ethiopian highlands, there are sunken cathedrals excavated from the living rock. Some of these incorporate apparent Templar symbols, including the *croix pattée* within a star of David, and the Cross within a Cross. The Templars were certainly active in Egypt at this juncture, but whether they could have passed south and gained access to the Ethiopian Ark without it being recorded seems questionable. The Red Sea route was another possibility.

Shortly after this time, during the reign of the Ayyubid Sultan al Kamil, Abu Salih, an Armenian chronicler living in Egypt, wrote an Arabic history of the Patriarchs of Alexandria. In it he detailed the diplomatic missions between Egypt and Lalibela's Ethiopia, and mentioned the Ark Cult:

> The Abyssinians [Ethiopians] possess the Ark of the Covenant, in which there are two tablets of stone, inscribed by the finger of God with the commandments which he ordained for the children of Israel. The Ark of the Covenant is placed upon the altar, but it is not so wide as the altar, it is as high as the knee of a man, it is overlaid with gold, and upon its lid there are crosses of gold and there are five precious stones upon it . . . The liturgy is celebrated upon the Ark four times a year, within the palace of the King, and a canopy is spread over it when it is taken out from its own church to the church which is in the palace . . . namely on the feast of the great Nativity, on the feast of the glorious Baptism, on the feast of the holy Resurrection, and the feast of the illuminating Cross. And the Ark is attended and carried by a large number of Israelites descended from the family of the prophet David, who are white and red of complexion with blond hair . . .[19]

The claim that the men who bore the Ark were golden haired could support the notion that some Europeans were in Ethiopia, and were, for a time at least, honoured by the Emperors during religious festivals.

An Ethiopioan diplomatic mission to Europe, on its way to meet Pope Clement V, was recorded by a Genoese chronicler in 1306. Hancock theorises that their purpose was to ask for the suppression of the Templars, who, the Ethiopian Emperor now feared, may have plotted to steal the Ark from Axum. Clement acted, Hancock suggests, because he feared the challenge the Order might make to papal supremacy if they took possession of the Ark and brought it to Europe. Outlandish as the idea of Templars in Ethiopia might seem, the theory is supported by the later activities of the Knights of Christ, a Portuguese chivalrous Order that succeeded the Templars after 1312. The Knights of Christ became great maritime explorers. They expended much of their resources in attempts to sail round Africa, to re-establish contact with the mythical Empire of Prester John. One may speculate that certain Templars believed the Ark to be the divinely powerful secret weapon that could reverse the losses suffered by the Crusaders, and that they desired it for that reason.

The Black Madonna Cult

The veneration of material objects, such as statues of the Virgin and the relics of saints, was a major part of medieval religion at all levels. (Such practices actually caused Jews and Muslims to suspect the Catholics of idolatry and polytheism.) As we have seen, people believed that these fetishistic objects possessed powers to heal, to bestow blessings and even to affect the natural world, much in the way that the Templars' alleged idol was supposed to. The Knights Templar were dedicated to the Virgin Mary, but they have also been associated with the more shadowy 'Black Madonna'. Black Madonna figures seemed to manifest in areas with a Templar or Cistercian presence, many of them near the sites of Roman temples to Isis (the mother goddess the Romans appropriated from Egypt). Depictions of Isis, holding her infant son Horus, inspired later representations of the Virgin and the Christ Child. Some contend, however, that Black Madonna figures represented not the mother of Christ, but instead the Queen of Sheba, or (as it is more commonly held) Sainte Mary Magdalene, to whom many Templar Churches were thought to be dedicated.

During the trials, Galcerand de Teusum, a Neopolitan Templar, admitted denial of Christ. He attested that in the practice of lay absolution, the absolver declared: 'I pray God that he will pardon your sins as he pardoned . . . Sainte Mary Magdalene, and the thief who was put on the cross'.[20] The Templar Latin Rule orders the recruitment of penitent, excommunicated knights. It may be that Mary Magdalene was a symbol of God's redemption of sinners.

In the Bible, Christ cast seven devils from Mary Magdalene (Luke 8:2). She was present at the Crucifixion, and afterwards went to anoint Jesus' body, instead to encounter the resurrected Christ, who sent her to take the news to the disciples. The Church represented her as a whore, who repented to follow Jesus. Pope Gregory the Great identified her as the woman of Bethany who anointed Christ's feet, and washed them with her hair (and also with Mary, the sister of Martha and Lazarus, though the Eastern Church questioned these associations). In religious iconography, she was usually depicted holding the unction jar. Gregory identified her demons as the vices of pride and vanity, from which Christ turned her. 'She turned the masses of her crimes to virtues in order to serve God entirely in penance, for as much as she had wrongly held God in contempt.' This reading became a model for Rome's claim to possess the power to absolve sins.

An account called the 'Golden Legend' filled in the gaps in Mary Magdalene's story. It portrays her as the wealthy fiancee of the disciple John. After he left her to follow Christ, Mary lapsed into promiscuity, but was redeemed after Christ's raising of Lazarus from death. After the death of Jesus, according to the myth, Mary (with Lazarus, Joseph of Arimathea and other companions) was exiled and sailed to Provence, to preach and pray. She supposedly lived out her life as a hermit, clothed only in her long hair, and fed on manna from Heaven. At any rate, the south of France became the epicentre of her cult. She was venerated at Saint-Maximin-la-Sainte Baume, in the Camargue, in the convent of Les-Saintes-Maries-de-la-Mer. Later her relics were moved to Vézelay in Burgundy (the launching place for the Second and Third Crusades). The monks there justified the pious theft of the relics claiming that a saint chose where he or she would bless through their relics and that no relic could be moved without heavenly approval. Vézelay claimed to house her skull kept in a hinged gold reliquary shaped like a woman's head. Meanwhile, a conflicting tradition had Mary Magdalene buried in Palestine.

In a Gnostic Gospel (rediscovered at Nag Hammadi), Mary encountered Christ at his tomb in spirit form, and received his mystic revelations regarding the nature of God. She was symbolically identified with Sophia (Isis too, as some would have it), the feminine spirit of 'sacred wisdom', and a heavenly counterpart to Christ. According to an anti-heretical tract, meanwhile, the Cathar heretics even taught that Mary was Jesus' widow.[21] The premise of Baigent, Lincoln and Leigh's *The Holy Blood and the Holy Grail* is that this supposed union bore fruit, that the 'Davidic' bloodline of Jesus flowed into the Dukes of Lorraine via an ancient Jewish principality in France, and then the Merevingian Kings of dark ages, who were ultimately usurped by the Capetians, with the complicity of the Church. They proposed that this hidden dynasty was one of the secrets the Templars, and a secret society, the Priory of Sion, guarded. The Grail stories are read as veiled accounts of the existence of this supposed bloodline. The authors produce no firm evidence besides these.

There actually seem only to be the most tenuous links between Mary Magdelene and the Templars, despite the speculation of Baigent, Lincoln and Leigh and of Andrew Sinclair. There was no hint in the accusations that the Templars were ever suspected of revering Mary Magdelene or the Gnostic Sophia, or of involving themselves in any form of goddess worship. When he wrote, on behalf of the Templars, that 'In honour of Our Lady our Order was founded and in her honour it will come to end when it pleaseth God', Saint Bernard had the Virgin Mary in mind, a sexless embodiment of purity. His rule, of course, forbade the Templars any association with real women, and made no mention of any Magdalene cult.

Clearly, for St Bernard, feminine powers were dangerous and corrupting, and worked best to lure men's hearts astray. However, during the Templars' trials, Ponsard de Gizy, Preceptor of Payns, confusingly referred to 'Sisters of the Order', and there is some evidence that the anti-feminist clause was ignored.[22] There were many female patrons of the Templars, for example one Lauretta who donated all she owned in the village of Douzens in 1133, and occasionally women were even apparently accepted into the Order, or, at least, attempted to be. In the same year one

Azalais gave herself to the Order, 'to serve God under obedience to the Master'.

The Inquisition, under Guillaume de Paris, had moved against a movement of lay communes of women called the Beguine. The Beguine opposed the patriarchal Church establishment, advancing the view that it was wrong to deny the body, or to demonise creation. Some of their philosophers taught that the Holy Spirit was the female aspect of the Divine. The Inquisition would burn a leading Beguine and her writings for this heresy, which seemed to have its roots in Gnosticism. So Gnostic thought was current in Europe in the early fourteenth century, and the possibility of it influencing the Templars cannot be dismissed out of hand.

Witchcraft

In 1233 Pope Gregory IX wrote to the German Princes about Rhineland heretics, who denied Christ and spat the host – the consecrated bread of the Catholic Eucharist – into latrines. They worshipped toads and black cats. They adored the Devil, perverted the mass, and indulged in obscene kisses and indiscriminate fornication. This is broadly typical of Catholic diatribes against heretics.

It was common, many clerics believed, for the Devil to appear to his followers in animal form. Walter Mapp described Paterines as worshipping a huge cat, who 'descended to them on a rope'. Obscene kisses heralded the usual orgy. In the twelfth century, Allain de Lille accused the Cathars of kissing the hindquarters of a cat. Rome's propaganda, contrived to discredit rivals and enemies, engendered widespread belief in a Satanist conspiracy, sewing the seed of the witch hunts of later centuries. The Inquisitors came to believe every outrageous concoction they tortured out of their victims.

Nogaret called the Templars 'potential witches', and implied that it was Satan who had enriched them. As well as the official accusations, the French government fuelled numerous vulgar rumours. The kiss of a Templar became like a vampire's, something mothers scared their children with to make them behave.[23] The Templars summoned female demons from Hell, for carnal rites. In fact, in one whole series of investigations, sodomy was never mentioned, instead the Templars were supposed to engage in orgies with demons in the form of beautiful young girls.[24] Any children born of these alleged unholy liaisons were burnt before altars, their fat used to anoint idols of *Baphomet*. Meanwhile, *Les Grandes Chroniques de France* would record the treacherous Templars' collusion with the Muslims, and their worshipping an embalmed head, with 'hollow, carbuncle eyes, glowing like the stars of the sky'.[25]

The accusers, in Malcolm Barber's analysis, were exploiting popular beliefs in sorcery, which the Church had given diabolical connotations, creating a climate that believed in Devil-inspired witchcraft. The charges would, therefore, have had a meaning at all levels of society. The accusations show an attempt to suggest contamination with witchcraft, Catharism and Islam as they were (mis)understood, and thus vilify the Order several times over.

Barber concluded that '. . . perhaps . . . it [this demonisation] was only partly conscious, for both Philip's lawyers and Clement's inquisitors were themselves part of the age and . . . imbued with its ideas and traditions'.[26]

Norman Cohn contended that no real sect was ever guilty of such Satanic worship, incestuous/promiscuous orgies, child-murder and cannibalism – things later, unofficially, tagged on to the Templar accusations. Even the Fraticelli (spiritual Franciscans), who argued for Church poverty in emulation of the disciples, would be accused of similar things, and many would be burned. The evidence was derived only from 'polemical tracts and monastic chronicles', written centuries before. These old sources reflected loathsome rumours which, ironically, before the conversion of the Empire, had been used to defame the early Christians.[27]

Conclusion

There is insufficient evidence to make clear links between Templars and 'unchristian' parties, or to identify the unorthodox beliefs which their secrecy may have existed to protect. Certain aspects of the accusations can be rationalised by cultural echoes of a Celtic cult of heads, or else of Gnostic influences. These, however, lose veracity when it is remembered that the spitting on the Cross was supposedly accompanied by a denouncing of Christ as a false prophet; and that the adoration of the head as a saviour went alongside the materialisation of a supernatural cat. From a theological point of view, the things described in the accusations make poor sense.

How likely does it seem that hundreds of knights could join a religious Order through devotion to Christianity, only to discover all these practices on their reception – profane and humiliating as they were – and, after such a shock, would remain? Many scholars have reasonably argued that it is highly unlikely. Yet it is not as impossible as some historians (perhaps too used to peaceful libraries and civilised company) might like to think. It is a paradox, but perverted and bestial behaviour can go on inside human institutions with values that remain (at least outwardly) admirable.

Savage bullies exist undetected in many armies around the world even today, exerting a psychological grip on their victims. Young soldiers, in their own way equally idealistic as the young knights who sought entry into the Temple, join distinguished regiments, only to find themselves subjected to an inescapable regime of terror by comrades. It may be perverse and unreasonable, but it happens. Sometimes the savagery is ritualised, with new recruits being subjected to humiliating initiation rites, involving physical and even sexual abuse. In many cases other participants are swept along and, without meaning to, contribute to the degradation of the victim. The chain of command may demonstrate indifference, or may deny any problems, in order to avoid scandal or repercussions. In some cases, soldiers have committed suicide to escape the shame and torment. Seen in this disturbing context, an abusive cult involving spitting on crosses, obscene kisses and the rest, operating within a brotherhood of soldier-monks, seems less implausible.

The allegations against the Templars may have arisen from abuses only happening at isolated Preceptories (who can say?), but it it difficult to dismiss them entirely as the lies of a tyrant (though a tyrant Philip IV clearly was) and his stooges. (Philip IV's actions can in no way be exonerated by this theory. A modern equivalent might be a ruler, desirous of seizing all the Church's property, arresting every Catholic priest in his country and torturing them until they confessed to paedophilia.) Meanwhile, if any of the accusations against the Templars were true, the hold of the Order on its members – members who joined seeking purity, but found, instead, a den of depravity – must have been strong indeed, for not one of them to sound the alarm before 1307.

A letter (extracts of which were quoted earlier for its account of Inquisition torture) was sent to the 'honourable doctors and scholars of the University of Paris'. It was written by an anonymous source close to the Templars in early 1308, who made the case for their innocence:

> The unheard of and iniquitous proceedings against the Templars contain no justice, but rather savage tyranny, since they were arrested without warning ... shamefully and dishonourably incarcerated with destructive rage, afflicted with taunts, the gravest threats and various sorts of torture, compelled to die or produce absurd lies which they knew nothing about . . . [by] . . . their enemies who forced them through those torments to read a foul, filthy and lying list which cannot be conceived by human ears and should not enter the human heart.

The letter pointedly avoids implicating King Philip the Fair, as chief malefactor ('Oh good Jesus, merciful father, what kind of advice has led such a great prince to act like this – when he always used to rule and be ruled by your will?') Instead it suggests that Dominican 'Jacobin friars – masters of great iniquity' were responsible, deaf to the truth:

> . . . deceived by their ardent hatred, and blinded by their savage cupidity. They hope to enrich their monks and associates at the

> expense of others, to get fat on the Templars' goods, so that they will be able to gain part of their revenue forever. So they order that the Templars who tell the truth should be tortured fiercely for so long until either they die of the punishment, or they are forced to suppress the truth and lie that they denied God, despised Christ's Cross, and produce the other worthless things which not only should not be done, but not even described.

The accusations arose:

> . . . from the accuser's manifest cupidity alone, and nothing can conceal it. For who can believe that a free man . . . would seek to enter a religious Order to the detriment and death of his soul? This would certainly be ridiculous and insane! It would seem . . . impossible that the noble brothers . . . of a religious Order which has spread through the whole world should be ensnared by such crimes, when they have given themselves to the service of the glorious Virgin for the salvation of their souls, and constantly bear the cross out of reverence for the crucified and in memory of his Passion. Moreover, in ancient and modern times, a great many people have left the Order because they lacked the firmness of purpose. After apostatising in this way, they received many taunts from their parents and friends because their religious Order has dismissed them. If such people knew about the blot in the Order, why did they keep quiet, when they could have excused themselves by saying that they did not wish to remain among men of such wickedness?[28]

This document says all that can be said by way of argument for the Order's innocence. Voltaire believed that the accusation that the Templars worshipped a head was so ridiculous and self-contradictory as to destroy itself. Meanwhile, most of the supposed links between the Templars and the various Gnostics and mystic groups only emerged in theories devised centuries after the suppression. Links to the Celts cannot be proved, and the early Grail romances were so arcane as to be filled to the brim with symbols and allegories that are open to an infinite variety of interpretations. Something similar can be said of the Dead Sea Scrolls. As for the beliefs of the Assassins, Gnostics and Cathars, their own writings were mostly destroyed by their enemies, and little besides the biased diatribes of these enemies remain as sources – filled with rumour and exaggeration. What, then, do the Templars' archives tell us? In fact the Templar archives are conspicuous by their absence.

These records must have existed. The Knights Hospitaller of Saint John had an enormous library of documents, including grants of land, letters, accounts, treaties and proclamations. Many dated to the time of Baldwin

I of Jerusalem, and were salvaged from the Holy Land and protected first on Cyprus, then Rhodes, then Malta, where the Order settled after losing Rhodes to the Ottoman Empire in 1522, after five months of heroic battle. The precious and extensive records still sit in Valetta, Malta, awaiting deeper study. The Templars must have accumulated a similar mass of documents. It seems, however, that the myrmidons of the King and the Inquisition could find no Templar writings with which to confront the knights with evidence of their heretical beliefs or practices. The Templar leadership must have hidden or destroyed hundreds of manuscripts, prior to their arrest: and why do so if they had nothing to hide? Why practise secrecy, and why not keep these records as proof of innocence, orthodoxy and long, loyal service to the Catholic faith?

Most of the Templars *were* innocent, and had been suspected of nothing before 1307. If they had been, the proposed amalgamation of the Order with the Knights of St John would have been preposterous, for nobody would join a brotherhood suspected of heretical depravity to one untainted and devout. The Templars who died protesting their innocence surely were telling the truth. Others had confessed whatever their captors had suggested, after great suffering under torture. It was an injustice and a scandal. But if there was nothing more sinister, even if it lay only within an inner circle of the Templars, how are we to explain the esoteric secrecy and the vanishing of the Order's records?

From the confession of the serving brother Jean de Chalons, it seems there was a climate of fear in the Order in France. Chalons, like Etienne de Troyes, was quite willing to attack the Order, and repeat his allegations before the Pope. He testified that if he had not denied Christ, the others would have placed him in the deadly pit in Merlan. Anyone who crossed the senior Preceptors, especially Gerard de Villiers, might end up in that dreaded pit. Chalons denounced his Order as rife with greed and corruption. On the eve of the arrests, Gerard de Villiers had escaped with fifty riders, according to Chalons, and the Treasure of the Visitor, Hugues de Pairaud. Did these riders also whisk away the records which might have shed light on the secrets of the Knights Templars? Or were the Templars who denounced the Order before the Pope, for the King, motivated by private grudges against the Order, by promises of rewards and by fear of being returned to the Inquisition? If so, then it is possible the Templars' archives were secretly destroyed on the orders of King Philip, because, after all, they contained only proof of innocence.

NOTES

1 Frayling, Christopher, *Strange Landscape*, p. 16. The ubiquity of the head of John the Baptist seems to have been something of a joke in medieval times. One pilgrim in France was shown a skull of John the Baptist on two days

running, at different places. When the pilgrim queried this, the keeper of the second relic said: 'Ah, the skull you saw yesterday was obviously the skull of John as a *young man*.'

2 Zaczec, Iain, *The Art of the Celts*, p. 19.

3 Ibid., pp. 19–20.

4 Ibid., pp. 16, 20, 46, 47, 49. Though found in Denmark, the Gundelstrup cauldron is believed by some to have been made by Thracian silversmiths in Bulagaria or Romania. The iconography, however, is entirely Gaulish. The seven outer plates show the heads of deities. The inner part shows the antlered god, surrounded by beasts. In another scene, a goddess appears to be dunking soldiers head-first into a suggestively shaped cauldron. There are also other bizarre scenes. In Celtic mythology, cauldrons were linked with death and regeneration.

5 Anderson, William, *Green Man,* p. 70. The heads look 'unmistakably demonic', perhaps representing the three-headed Beelzebub mentioned in the Apocryphal Gospel of Nicodemus, and in Dante's *Inferno*.

6 Hancock, Graham, *The Sign and the Seal,* pp. 92–5; Laidler, Keith, *The Head of God,* pp. 190–216, 220, 241, 374–5. Laidler's far-fetched argument is that the Templar treasure was the head of Jesus, which was also the Holy Grail. He supposes the existence of a cult of heads dating back to Akhenaten's Egypt, brought to Judah by Moses (one and the same man, according to Laidler, as Akhenaten). That Egyptians saw complete preservation of the body as fundamental for an afterlife, troubles Laidler not. The linking of Moses with the monotheistic Aten cult may be historical. The rest is probably hysterical.

7 Laidler, op. cit., pp. 2, 221, 314. See also Burman, Edward, *The Assassins – Holy Killers of Islam.*

8 Read, Piers Paul, *The Templars*. p. 271. Read cites, rather scornfully, the French writer Michel Lamy's contention about the deeper meanings of the Jewish involvement with the Cistercians. Knight, C and Lomas, R, *The Hiram Key*, pp. 20, 22, 208, 271–3. Some Freemasons have claimed that 'secret knowledge' and certain rituals of Ancient Egyptian origin passed into Freemasonry via the Essenes and the Knights Templar. For instance, the Masonic initiation ceremony involves a symbolic raising of the dead, as it seems that of the Essene may also have.

9 Grierson, R and Munro-Hay, S, *The Ark of the Covenant,* p. 20, quoting Philo.

10 Knight and Lomas, op. cit., pp. 52, 198, 324.

11 Ibid., p. 202.

12 Wheatley, Denis, *The Devil and All His Works*, p. 217.

13 Lord, Eveleyn, *The Knights Templar in Britain*. p. 81.

14 Rudolph, K, *Gnosis.,* p. 56. The Gnostic gospels (rejected by the fourth-century Church) were rediscovered in a cache from Nag Hammadi, Egypt.

15 Maxwell-Stuart, P G, *Witchcraft: A History,* pp. 50–2. Inquisition torture brought out these stories in the 1460s. Waldensians were supposed to kiss the Devil, blaspheme holy objects, and take part in perverted orgies.

16 Read, op. cit., pp. 189–95.

17 Barber, Malcolm, *The Trial of the Templars,* pp. 19–20, 181, 188–9, 191, 243. Barber refers to H C Lea's observation.

18 Hancock, op. cit., pp. 3–4, 13, 25, 37, 105, 121. Also Grierson and Munro-Hay, op. cit., Chapters 1, and 13–21.

19. Grierson and Munro-Hay, op. cit., p. 250.

20 Barber, op. cit., p. 213.

21 Laidler, op. cit., p. 114. Laidler credits Dondaine, A, '*Durand de Huesca et la*

polémique anti-cathare' (Archivum Fratrum, Praedictadorum. Rome, 29, 28–276). He repeats the theory popularised by Baigent, Lincoln and Leigh, *Holy Blood Holy Grail*, that Jesus was of Davidic blood, and that Mary was of Benjamite aristocracy, and may even have been Christ's wife. After the crucifixion, so the legend goes, she and companions including Lazarus, Joseph of Arimathea, and Nicodemus were exiled and cast adrift on the sea. Providence brought them to Marseilles, bearing the Grail. Laidler diverges from Baigent *et al*, suggesting the Grail was Jesus' head. Their idea that she brought Jesus' alleged child may be more attractive, but is equally speculative. They construct a history of this holy bloodline, flowing into the Merovingian Kings, of dark-ages France. After this mystical dynasty was deposed (the Pope condoning the murder of Dagobert II), they claim, a secret society called the *Preure de Sion* materialised – conspiring for the restoration of the 'Holy Family'. The Templars were a creation of this esoteric organisation, which was already anti-Catholic.

22 Barber, op. cit., pp. 127, 245, 267 n. 8.

23 Rogers, Byron, article on Royston Cave in the *Sunday Telegraph,* 14 January 1996. 'In the middle ages mothers are reputed to have told their children, "Beware the kiss of a Templar".'

24 Cohn, Norman. *Europe's Inner Demons*, pp. 88, 89.

25 Barber. op. cit., pp.182–85. Most of the ingredients of the 'black mass' were inferred to exist in heretical groups prior to the Templars' trials, which acted as a catalyst and vindicated the Inquisition's position. It provided an example for the sort of diabolical heresy the Inquisition claimed to be defending the faith against.

26 *Ibid*., p. 192.

27 Cohn, op. cit., pp. 45–9. Cohn discusses the Demonisation of Medieval Heretics.

28 Anon., 1308. *The Downfall of the Templars and a Letter in their Defence*, translated by C Cheyenne in *Medieval Texts and Studies,* 1978, pp. 322–7.

CHAPTER XIV
Trial and Terror

The Defence of the Order

The commission of cardinals appointed to examine the Order of the Temple as a whole assembled in the episcopal hall of the Bishop of Paris in November 1309, following many delays. It certainly cannot be said that the clerical body was predisposed towards the Templars. Most of the prelates involved were Philip the Fair's allies, and Gilles Aicelin, the presiding Archbishop of Narbonne, had even been among those churchmen who denounced the Templars before the Pope at Poitiers.

Ponsard de Gizy was among the Templars who defended his brotherhood before the cardinals' enquiry. He stated that all the accusations were false. Templars had confessed 'through violence and on account of danger and fear; since they were tortured by Floyond de Beziers, Prior of Montfulon, and the monk Guillaume Robert, their enemies'. By this time thirty-four Templars had died from torture in Paris alone. Ponsard had been subjected to torture in a narrow pit, before the Bishop of Paris. If tortured again, he would deny all he now said, and confess whatever anyone wished. Because it took only a short time, he would gladly suffer fire for the honour of the Order. He could, however, face no more protracted tortures, having already endured it for two years.

Jacques de Molay and the other leaders of the Temple were less ready to speak in defence of the Order at the hearing. They feared jeopardising their chances of getting an audience with Clement V. Therefore they dithered. When de Molay testified, Guillaume de Nogaret was hovering in the background, voicing evil rumours about the Templars, including that Saladin had attributed the Order's defeats to their affliction with pederasty. The Grand Master responded that in fact the valour of the Templars had been highly respected by their enemies. He swayed between expressing a desire to defend his Order, which had shed its blood defending Catholicism, and then remembering his confessions. (By now he had already once retracted these, and then retracted his retractions.) Growing emotional, he then crossed himself, and apparently challenged his accusers to trial by combat. Such outbursts hardly impressed the commission, and bore witness to the level of stress the Grand Master was suffering. At de Molay's second hearing, King Philip's other great minister Guillaume de Plaisians was present, disparaging the Order, and generally keeping tabs on proceedings for the King. De Molay, in his confused state, appealed to de Plaisians, of all men, for advice and support. Plaisians warned de Molay, presumably in a sardonic tone of voice, to watch he did not perish by a noose of his own making.[1]

Though the Grand Master consistently offered little leadership, the rank and file Templars showed themselves willing and eager to defend the Order. The hearing reconvened, to hear the brethren from elsewhere in France. Five hundred Templars rallied to the defence, though many expressed ignorance of legal procedure, and most told stories of torture and death. Only about fifteen refused to defend the Order at this stage. The defence was hampered by the Templars being segregated from their brothers in dispersed prisons. The goods of the Temple had also already been confiscated, so they could not pay for any proper representation.

There were several outside witnesses who spoke up for the Templars. A Dominican theologian called Pierre de la Palud testified to having heard confessions from numerous Templars, some of whom had denied the crimes, some of whom had confessed them. He considered that there was 'more faith attached to those denying than confessing'.[2] Priest Jean Robert, meanwhile, said that he had also confessed many Templars, and heard nothing of the offences mentioned in the articles of accusation. Only now did the Templar defendants succeeded in getting these articles read to them. The Templars brought to Paris were kept in dispersed prisons, abbeys, bishops' palaces, private houses and the dungeons of the Paris Temple. The Templars wishing to defend their Order were granted permission to meet together to discuss their situation. There were so many of them, by March 1310, that they were obliged to meet outside, in the episcopal gardens in Paris. After this meeting, two literate Templars, Renaud de Provins, Preceptor of Orléans, and Pierre de Bologna, Procurator to the Roman Court, emerged as spokesmen.

They first complained, on the Order's behalf, about the wretched conditions in which their brethren were being held. They were denied the sacraments, they had lost their religious habits, they were suffering 'vile incarceration in chains' and wasting on poor provisions of bread and water. Those who died in prison had been hurredly buried in unconsecrated ground.[3]

The cardinals told the Templars to nominate procurators, to represent them officially. However, the Templars were reluctant to do so, as this should have been the responsibility of the Grand Master, and he would never dare to disturb matters whilst still in the King's custody. Meanwhile the Templars showed unfailing loyalty to the Grand Master and the other leaders, who were still vainly procrastinating. The tactic had worked before in the east, where prevarication had kept prisoners alive for long years in Saracen prisons, but now the Order had nothing left to bargain with. This the Masters seem never quite to have grasped.

Bologna told the cardinals' notaries, when they visited him in prison at the Paris Temple, that the accusations were outrageous. They were shameful, 'most false, and impious, and were fabrications, invented . . . by witnesses and rivals and lying enemies, and the Order of the Temple was clean and immaculate, and always was, from all these articles, vices and sins.' The confessions were lies, spoken from fear of torture and death. 'The torture of one is the fear of many.'[4] This fear, allied with seductive false promises, had elicited confessions of terrible things from hitherto entirely faithful (though frequently by their own admission simple) Christians.

At the hearings, Renaud de Provins requested money for a defence and Church custody for the prisoners, to secure freedom from royal repression. He went on to expose the arbitrary nature and questionable legality of the initial arrests, listing a number of procedural irregularities. He called the Templars' accuser to appear, and be ready to pay damages if he should lose. If there was a denouncer from within the fraternity, his testimony ought to be questioned, as he should first have gone to his immediate superior inside the organisation with his complaints and whatever evil he suspected.

The Templar Jean de Montreal submitted a document stating that the Order of the Temple was honestly founded, that it had continued without sin and that the Kings of Europe would not have trusted its members as treasurers, were it not so. The document reminded the court of Templar sacrifices for the Christian cause, and of various supposed miracles proving divine approval.[5]

Nine representatives were eventually chosen (though not officially procurators). These defenders, growing bolder, criticised the presence of Nogaret and Plaisians as spies at the Grand Master's hearing. They also argued that all the confessions initially made by the brethren were invalid, because they were so clearly made under duress. Pierre de Bologna argued that it was more wonder some spoke true, given the menaces and outrages the truthful had suffered, and the favourable conditions given to those who told the Inquisitors what they wanted to hear. 'Beyond France no Templars will speak these lies,' he predicted, asserting the Order's orthodoxy, and love for Jesus and the Virgin.[6]

The defenders denied the idolatry and indecent kissing, saying that in the true rite, every entrant was received with the honest 'kiss of peace'. They swore poverty, chastity and obedience, and to fight for Jerusalem. After receiving his cord and white tabard, the entrant affirmed his loyalty to Rome and his veneration of Christ.

The attacks made against the Order were 'horrifying and detestable', and the accusers were 'false Christians, motivated by ardour of greed'. Philip IV had been led to believe falsehoods (no defendant yet dared to directly criticise the King).

The Templar Priests Bologna and Provins, and the Knights Chambonnet and Sartiges, were made procurators, whilst the leaders still waited passively, hoping eventually to see the Pope. Meanwhile, when the Templars appealed for better conditions, they were wasting their breath, as the commission could not access the Order's goods, held by the King, and had no say over where and how the Templars were confined.

The King still controlled the persons of the Templars. He fed into the courts unfavourable witnesses, including laymen who would try to stiffen hostility to the Order. Raoul de Presles, a royal advocate, testified that Gervais de Beauvais, the Templar Preceptor of Laon, had often spoken of a secret part of the Order's regulation book, which he would rather have his head cut off than reveal. There was also a point during the General Chapter that was supposedly so secret that the Templars would kill anyone who discovered it. Other defamatory rumours were heard from other laymen, including Guichard de Marsillac, who had heard rumours of an 'Article 30' of the secret Rule, which concerned the meaning of kissing of the base of the spine. Guichard said that a relation of his named Hugues had been made a Knight Templar, at the Preceptory in Toulouse, and had emerged from a sealed room in Templar robes, 'very pale, as if disturbed and stupefied'.

Bologna defended his Order furiously, in the face of this. Torture, he argued, had killed and maimed many Templars, robbing them of their freedom of mind, memory and understanding. Confessions made in such a state could not be prejudicial. Corruption lay behind the moves against the Order, and '. . . all the aforesaid matters are so public and well known that by no evasion are they to be hidden'. If the Temple had been as riddled with heresy as the accusers maintained, it could not have commanded the loyalty of the most noble and powerful men of the past. They would have spoken out against the 'blasphemies to the name of Christ'.

By this stage, the emboldened defenders had started to directly implicate the King. Philip felt obliged to call again on his theologians at the University of Paris to intervene, and say how right, faithful and noble the King was to bring to justice the depraved Templars. 'Grave presumption' was made, with sophistry, to outweigh proof of guilt. The Order could not be redeemed now, the religious scholars decreed, without 'danger and scandal to the whole Church'. Crucially, Templars could not retract their confessions, without becoming relapsed heretics, and it was unlikely that anyone in the Order was untainted.

The First Burnings of the Templars

Philip was clearly growing tired of the legal wrangling and the long deliberations of the papal commission. He ordered Philippe de Marigny, the 22-year-old, royally created Archbishop of Sens, to re-open the episcopal proceedings against individual Templars, in his province. The see of Sens, by some quirk of ecclesiastical demarcation, included the city of Paris within its boundaries, and gave the Archbishop the power to call Templars for trial from the capital. This would very soon make a mockery of the cardinals' enquiry. The four defending Templars appealed for the Archbishop of Sens's action to be blocked. The prelate was proceeding *de facto*, when he could not proceed *de jure*. Pierre Bologna feared that injuries would be brought to the defendants as the commission sat. It was against God and justice, and would completely undermine the cardinals' enquiry.[7]

Cardinal Gilles Aicelin, president of the papal commission, bowed out of the proceedings, at this point, loathe to risk his standing with the King for the Templars' sake. He made some excuse about having to 'celebrate or hear mass' and never came back. The rest of the commission told the Templars that, though they sympathised with their position, they had no jurisdiction to help.

The young Archbishop of Sens thus condemned the Templars who had sworn to their innocence the moment they were away from the rack and other tortures of the Inquisition:

> As you have revoked your confession, the Church no longer regards you as reconciled but as having fallen back into your first errors . . . you are therefore relapsed heretics, and as such we condemn you to the fires.

So, on 12 May 1310, on the orders of the Council of Sens, fifty-four Templars were carted off and burned to death by slow fire, under the commission's nose. They were executed in open country near the Pont-St-Antoine-des-Champs, near Paris. This was only the beginning of the burning. Sixty-seven would have been burned by the end of May, and many other Templars were perpetually imprisoned. These were the ones who had always denied the accusations, and could not be labelled relapsed heretics. Only those who confessed were absolved, and spared the miseries of prison. Terror served the crown well, reducing the remaining indignant defenders to terrified wretches and the cardinals' hearing to a farce.

The defendants were disappearing as the commission sat. Provins found himself indicted as an individual and degraded from the priesthood by the Council of Sens, so he could no longer represent the Order to the cardinals. Bologna disappeared in sinister circumstances, and the knights Chambonnet and Sartiges gave up the game as lost.

After the burnings, few remained who were brave enough, or able, to defend the Order. The figures, given by Barber, are telling.[8]

Witnesses	Heard before 12 May 1310	Heard after burnings
Defending the Order	597	14
Non committal	12	3 (from outside Order)
Against the Order	15	198

Fear of burning, and the removal of all the chief spokesmen for the defence, crushed the resistance. Pathetically terrified, many reverted to their previous confessions.

The third sitting of the commission heard only more confessions of Cross-spitting, blasphemy, obscene kissing and head-worship. Guillaume Pidoye, the royal custodian of the goods of the Temple, was sent to look for idols in the Paris Temple. All he brought back was the silver-gilt reliquary called 'Caput LVIII m'. Pidoye's report described:

> . . . a certain large beautiful silver gilt head, shaped like that of a woman, within which were the bones of a single head, rolled up and stitched in . . . white linen cloth, red muslin placed over it, and there was sewn in a . . . document, on which was written 'Caput LVIII m', and the said bones were considered as similar to the bones of the head of a small woman, and it was said that it was the head of one of the eleven thousand virgins.[9]

A Templar called d'Arreblay testified to seeing a two-faced, bearded head. He said that there were a large number of ignorant, low-born serving brothers in the Order, lacking the means to get to the Holy Land. High-born Templars were not made to do illicit things, whereas he had once rebuked 'stupid serving brothers' for urinating at the foot of a Cross. In his testimony, Raoul de Gizy described an orthodox initiation, then (perhaps wavering under pressure) added the heretical part on, at the end. Lay Masters absolved sin, he said, by evoking God's pardoning of Mary

Magdalene. He described the cord Templars had to wear as a sign of chastity, but knew nothing about it having touched any heads. Like many, he tried to please his questioners, whilst passing the blame on to others, especially the Grand Master and the Visitor.

A few Templars doggedly maintained the Order's innocence. They surely came under enormous pressure, from the King's brutish jailers, to change their stories. Frightened and pale, they yet maintained that they had heard nothing of the abominable practices before their arrest. Aimery de Villiers-le-Duc, a Templar from Langres, told the commission that the accusations were false, but begged them not to tell the King's officers what he was saying, because he did not want to be burned.[10] Meanwhile, the hold of their captors over the majority of witnesses is in evidence from the ready flow of information from the hearings to the French government. On 5 June 1311 the papal commission wound up after sitting for 166 days, spread over two years. It sent its finding to the Pope.

Aside from the 123 Templars burned at the stake near Paris, others had already been burned by bishops loyal to Philip in the Lorraine, Normandy, Carcassonne and other places. Philip's men had even dragged the remains of dead Templars from their graves to roast as heretics. Torture of the less fortunate living Templars continued, meanwhile. Four perished in the Château d'Alaix, and the twenty Templars remaining confessed to worshipping a head in a chapter in Montpellier, after which a Satanic cat materialised and conversed with the assembly. The cat, they said, had promised riches, good harvests and temporal property. As for the head, some said it was male and bearded, others that it was female and not. They had also adored devils who appeared in the guise of beautiful women.

NOTES

1. Read, Piers Paul, *The Templars*, pp. 277–8; also Barber, Malcolm, *The Trial of the Templars* pp 122–53. The presence of the royal ministers at the Grand Master's interrogation was most irregular. It testifies to the all-pervasive fear of Philip IV that nobody dared to ask the King's men to leave.
2. Barber, op. cit., p. 176.
3. Ibid., p 133. Many of the details of the French trials are known through Barber's extensive research and analysis.
4. Ibid., p. 135.
5. Ibid., pp. 137–8.
6. Ibid., p. 139.
7. Ibid., p. 155.
8. Ibid., p. 161.
9. Ibid., p. 163. The 11,000 virgins were the maidens who accompanied the legendary Ste Ursula of Cornwall, all of whom were murdered by Huns whilst returning from a pilgrimage to Rome during the Dark Ages.
10. Read, op. cit., *The Templars*, p. 281.

CHAPTER XV
The Templars Beyond France

The Templars of the British Isles

The Templars had property in nearly every county in England, but many of their establishments were small and unfortified, managed, in some cases, by as few as a single Templar, and they had no castles. Some 229 Templars lived in the British Isles, mostly in England. Edward II, husband of Philip IV's daughter, Isabella (the so-called She-Wolf of France), was initially sceptical when Philip advised him to arrest the Templars. On 4 December 1307 he wrote in the Templars' defence to the Pope and to the Kings of Portugal, Aragon, Castille and Sicily, saying that the bitter rumours must have been invented by envious liars and criminals:

> Verily a certain clerke [the French agent Bernard Pelatin] drawing nigh unto our presence, applied himself, with all his might, to the destruction of the Brethren of the Temple of Jerusalem. He dared publish before us and our council certain horrible and detestable enormities repugnant to the Catholic Faith, to the prejudice of the aforesaid brothers; endeavouring to persuade us . . . that by reason of premise and without a due examination of the matter, we ought to imprison all the brethren ... abiding in our dominions. But considering that the Order, which hath been renowned for its religion and its honour ... it appeared to us that a ready belief in an accusation of this kind, hitherto altogether unheard of against the fraternity, was scarcely to be expected. We affectionately ask . . . your Royal Majesty that ye . . . turn a deaf ear to the slander of ill-natured men, who are animated not with the zeal of rectitude but with a spirit

> of cupidity and envy, permitting no injury to be done to the persons or properties of the brethren of the aforesaid Order until they have been legally convicted of the crimes laid to their charge.[1]

Edward II had reasonably cordial relations with the Templars, and no particular reason to see them as a threat. His father (Edward I, the Hammer of the Scots) had compelled the leader of the British Templars to swear fealty to him in 1291, which the Master had done; along with other clergy and the Master of the local Hospitallers, at Edinburgh Castle. Seven years later, in 1298, the Templar Master of England, Brian de Jay, had died fighting for his King at Falkirk – a clear sign that the monarchy had reigned in the traditionally independent Order. De Jay broke a long tradition of Templar neutrality in conflicts between Christians. He had, however, fought in his own capacity, leading Edward I's Welsh mercenaries, not the Knights Templar. The impetuous Brian de Jay was among the English knights who charged after William Wallace's fleeing men. He pursued them into the woods of Callander, where his horse became bogged down, and where de Jay was slain – perhaps by Wallace himself.

Brian de Jay, incidentally, was not a particularly charitable man, by all accounts. A record dated to 1354, concerned with earlier events, described an act of uncharacteristic brutality on the part of the Templars. It had it that a tenant farmer of theirs died in about 1295, in Scotland. The Templars wanted the property, and tried to evict the widow, Christaine of Eperon. She clung to the door and refused to go. Then one of Brian de Jay's men drew his sword and cut her fingers off, and kicked her out. Later, the Master was alleged to have had Christaine's son murdered, after he petitioned for the return of the property. Eventually Robert the Bruce would return the land to the youngest son. The mean-spirited Brian de Jay, meanwhile, was succeeded as Master of England by William de la More, who would prove himself a rather nobler soul.

Edward II took no action against the Templars until he received the papal bull *Pastoralis Praeemonentiae*, which had already been issued, and which ordered the arrest of the Templars. The proclamation began:

> Clement, Bishop, servant of God, to his dear son in Christ Edward, the Illustrious King of England, health and apostolic blessing.
>
> Presiding, though unworthy on the throne of pastoral pre-eminence . . . we fervently seek after this one thing above all else, that by shaking off the sleep of negligence whilst watching over the Lord's flock, by removing that which is harmful . . . we may be able . . . to bring souls to God.
>
> . . . There came to our ears a light rumour . . . that the Templars, though fighting ostensibly under the guise of religion, have hitherto

> been lying in perfidious apostasy and in detestable heretical depravity . . .[2]

Clement went on to tell of his initial incredulity, remembering the Templars' former fame and loyalty, but then the same story came from the King of France, animated by zeal, and he had been obliged to take measures to ascertain the truth. He had heard the Templars' confessions of lewd acts, heresy and idolatry, and ordered Edward to take swift action, and to hold the Templars in the name of the Church.

The English brethren were thus arrested on 10 January 1308, in a half-hearted operation. Some were allowed to stay on at their Preceptories. William de la More, the Master of England, was arrested at the New Temple, London. He was held in relative comfort in Canterbury, and was even released temporarily.

Clement sent the bull titled *Faciens Misericoriam* to the English bishops. In it he defended Philip IV's actions and motives, and quoted a number of Templar confessions. He made proposals for the trial arrangements in the British Isles. The British Templars were tried at London, York and Lincoln, and in Dublin and Edinburgh – both occupied by the English at that time.[3] Others managed to slip away, and were tracked down in the wilds of Wales, Ireland and parts of Scotland. Meanwhile Clement criticised Edward for selling off the Templars' land:

> In contempt of the Holy See . . . you have of your own authority distributed to different persons the property formerly belonging to the Order of the Temple, which you . . . ought to have rendered at our disposition . . . We therefore obdure that proper persons shall be sent into your Kingdom and to all the parts of the world where the Templars are known to have had property, to take possession of the same conjointly with prelates deputed to that end, and to make inquisition concerning the execrable excesses which the Order are said to have committed.[4]

The Pope's critical tone revealed that he was nothing like as afraid of Edward as he was of Philip, perhaps because England was farther away. The English (like the Italians and Aragonese, among others) probably recognised the extent to which Clement was dominated by the French King, and in turn paid little more than lip-service to the Pope. Edward's reply to Clement was laconic:

> As to the goods of the Templars, we have done nothing with them up to the present time, nor do we intend to do with them aught but we have a right to do, and what we know to be acceptable to the Most High.

Edward did, however, grant passage to the two Inquisitors sent by the Pope. On 13 September 1309 these Inquisitors arrived. They were Dieudonne, Abbot of Lagny, and Sicard de Vaur, Canon of Narbonne. The Templar prisoners were delivered to the constables of the Tower of London, and York and Lincoln Castles. Crude crucifixes, carved into the stone walls, may still be found in the tower at Lincoln Castle, called Cobb Hall, probably left by the Templars when this tower was used for their imprisonment. The lower chamber of the two surviving is particularly bleak: dank and cold, lit only through narrow arrow slits and entered only through a hole in the vaulted roof. The Templars held here were first tried in the splendid chapter house of the nearby Cathedral. Eight of the Templars imprisoned in Lincoln came from the Order's hospital establishment at Eagle. Of these old soldiers, three died in prison, while two were found to be too infirm to testify.

From 20 October to 18 November, the trial of forty-three Templars took place in Holy Trinity Church, London. All the main articles of the French trial were raised, but all the defendants pleaded innocent. William Raven, Knight Templar, testified that the Order swore poverty, chastity and obedience, and not to lay a violent hand on anyone except in self defence, and against the Saracen. He said that at his reception by William de la More in Templecombe, the Master had reminded him of the strictness of the Order and his duties to God and the Virgin. Joining it, he would have to surrender his will to his Masters. If he wished to do one thing, he would be ordered to do another, if he desired to be somewhere, he would be sent somewhere else. When Raven told his interrogaters no more, and refused to confess to the acusations, he was returned to solitary confinement in the Tower. Another Templar, Imbert Blanke, the fugitive Preceptor of Auvergne, and a veteran of the valiant last stand at Acre, defended the Order he had served for thirty-eight years. He said the secrecy in it was 'through unaccountable foolishness and nothing more'.

English law forbade torture, allowing no place for the Inquisition, which was seen as an undesirable and foreign agency of tyranny. The English clergy assisted the Inquisators unquestioningly, however, and copies of the papal proclamation, virtually condemning the Templars, were read in every church in the land before a single trial had convened. This was the only time Inquisitors darkened England's shores. No torture machinery existed for them to use (even as late as 1605 there was only one rack in the entire realm, locked up in the Tower of London, and even then there were no professional torturers).

No evidence was forthcoming from the trial of the Templars in London, and no more from York or Lincoln. At the Council of Canterbury, the two Inquisitors pushed for investigation 'according to ecclesiastical custom', meaning through use of torture. They were already armed with a papal bull empowering them to excommunicate anyone who disobeyed them or hampered their work.

William de la More and his Preceptors insisted, even after many months of imprisonment and interrogation, that the articles were false, and that if their French brethren had confessed, then they had lied. Before torture was used, there were only a few confessions. These referred only to internal confession and absolution, arising from a misunderstanding of developments in Church law.

The severity of internal discipline in the Temple became apparent from a number of testimonies. A knight called de Barton said the Masters and Chapter could forgive brethren for transgressing the Rule and impose penances, but could not forgive sins, as they were laymen, and not priests. The Master would whip the penitent Templar who went on his knees before the altar, in the presence of his brethren, to be flogged on his bare back. Initiates into the Order were made to swear not to reveal the secrets of the Chapter, meanwhile, or their mode of reception. De Barton had heard nothing of the other crimes, except from Peletin, Philip IV's envoy. Peletin, meanwhile, had shown an interest in the fate of one Walter le Bachelor, the Preceptor of Ireland, who had been punished for some transgression and had died in chains, in the dungeon of the New Temple, London. De Barton said that he had not interfered with the punishment of le Bachelor, having been warned of the danger of doing so. It emerged that Walter le Bachelor's body had not been buried in the Templar cemetery, as he had been considered excommunicated for his disobedience.

Hugh of Tadecaster, meanwhile, said his vows as a Templar involved fighting for Jerusalem with all his might, and living in poverty, chastity and obedience. After taking these vows, at his reception, his brethren had presented him with his white mantle, while the Master had put his red coif on his head. Thomas le Chamberleyn said there was the same mode of reception in Britain as abroad. Secular persons were always excluded, and the doors were closed behind the entrant brother. It was part of the Rule that no outsider could be present. He knew not why. Thirty-three others, heard in October and November 1309, denied that anything heretical occurred.

Such stories were not enough for the Inquisitors, who, under pressure to extract confessions, wanted the Templars to suffer more, or be sent to Pontieu, an English possession in France, unburdened with the niceties of English law. In the event, Edward relented, and allowed more torture, providing there be no permanent mutilation, or 'violent profusion of blood'. Clement V subsequently wrote to Edward, ordering him to allowing far greater levels of torture. France, meanwhile, flooded England with propaganda against the Templars. Rumour-mongering, hostile witnesses were found, telling how the Templars held secret chapters at midnight, showed their posteriors to crosses, and worshipped a calf.[5]

Meanwhile, the prison guards were ordered to give the Inquisitors free access to the Templar prisoners, to do with them as they saw fit.

Nineteen Templars were arrested in Ireland, of whom five must have either died or escaped. The fourteen who stood trial in St Patrick's Cathedral, Dublin, confessed to none of the charges before 1311, perhaps because little torture or intimidation was used on them. Most of them had Anglo–Norman ancestry, and may have fled to Ireland from England or Scotland. A stash of weaponry was seized at the Kilclogan Preceptory, including a ballista, while the Order's Manor at Ballymean was found to be well fortified. The Templars had bred horses in Ireland, as well as overseeing a weaving industry. The inventories of their manors found that, unlike the Preceptories in England, they had suffered little looting. Edward's agents stripped the Order's chapels, and sent their goods to Dublin. At the trial, the Templars persistently pleaded innocence. Monastic witnesses testified to their suspicions – that they had seen Templars appear inattentive at Church services, and cast their eyes on the ground during the elevation of the host, but there were few mentions of heresies corresponding with the articles of accusation.

In Lincoln, Templar Robert de Hamilton, one of twenty examined, referred to the cord as the 'girdle of Nazareth'. He said it was worn as a sign of chastity and traditionally had touched the column of the Virgin in Nazareth, in remembrance of her. Brethren were not compelled to wear these cords, however. At York, one of the twenty-three Templars tried in the Minster chapter house, Steven de Radenhall, refused to speak of his mode of reception, as it was secret. Obviously, not grasping the extent of the Order's vicissitude, he said he feared he would lose his habit and chamber, and be put in prison if he revealed it. The others, however, maintained their innocence of any heresy. On 20 May a council of bishops was held in York Minster. After Mass the archbishop gave a sermon and had the papal bulls against the Templars read. The bishops agreed to meet the following June to pass verdict on the Templars. The Inquisition, meanwhile, closed the Lincoln hearing and returned to London to re-examine the Master and others about the issue of lay absolution. The crux of the matter was whether, after thrice flogging the penitent man with a leather thong in the name of the Trinity, the Master said to the chapter: 'Brothers, pray to God that he may forgive you', or: 'I *absolve* you in the name of the Father, the Son and the Holy Ghost.' There were conflicting accounts of the exact wording.

Only two Templars were tried in Scotland, and these only admitted believing in the power of absolution by their lay superiors. This was in the English-held Lowlands. King Robert the Bruce, in the Highlands, was under excommunication throughout this period, and if anything would have welcomed fugitive Templars to his cause. Brother Walter de Clifton, tried in Holy Cross, Edinburgh, repeated the orthodox description of the initiation ceremony, and said that the Scottish Templars received their orders and ordinances from the London Master, who, in turn, was under the Grand Master. He testified that many of his brethren, on hearing of the arrests in France, had flung off their habits and fled. When other witnesses were called, some monks testified that some Templar receptions were, in fact, public. Other witnesses, however, accused the Templars of miserliness, or shutting their doors to the poor while lavishly entertaining the aristocracy. The Abbot of Holy Cross accused them of appropriating the property of their neighbours, whilst others contradicted the first monks, attesting that the Templars' chapters were often nocturnal and always secret.

The Inquisitors in Britain concluded in a memorandum to the Pope that certain practices had crept into the Order that were not consistent with orthodox Catholicism. Needing more proof, they took charge of the prisoners. The English jailers had apparently taken pity on the Templars, and had to be ordered twice to give them up to the Inquisitors. By the next ecclesiastical council, many of the defendants appeared as physical wrecks. The guardian of the Temple Lands was ordered to supply funds for their detention. In London the Templars were put in the prisons at the four city gates, and in private houses. The Lincoln Templars were also brought in chains to London. The Order had, by now, already been collectively condemned by the Pope, and the Templars had suffered from captivity, cold, chains, violence and starvation – the treatment deemed appropriate for obstinate heretics. The Inquisitors visited them at will and dragged them from their solitary confinement to their torture chambers, but still the Templars protested their innocence.

More hostile testimony was taken down in 1311. William de la Forde had heard that a certain Templar at his reception, having been led in his shirt and trousers through a long passage to a secret chamber, had been made to deny God and spit and defecate on a crucifix, which he did, weeping bitterly. The others had then told him to worship the image of a calf. John de Nasington, meanwhile, had heard from two knights, who attended a feast in Templehurst, that the Templars worshipped a calf at an annual festival. John de Dorrington claimed to have heard from an elderly Templar that the Master had introduced four idols into England, one at London, one at Bisham, one at Temple Bruer and the other somewhere he could not remember. Adam Robert, a notary, claimed to know that the Order's receptions were held in secret, at night, but had never seen any magic himself.

The monk Henry Thanet had heard that a Templar guarded a two-faced head of bronze that could answer any question, while the Rector of Ste Mary's in the Strand believed that Templar receptions contained occult rituals, that gave the brethren power over other men. Sir John de Eure,

Sheriff of York, testified that six years before, Brother William de la Fenne, Preceptor of Wesdall, had lent his wife, the Lady de Eure, a book to read after a banquet. She found in it a loose sheet on which were written such heresies as that Christ was not the son of God, nor born of a virgin, that he was a false prophet crucified for his sins. When William de la Fenne was called in, he remembered lending the book to the Sheriff's wife, but pleaded ignorance of any page fastened in it.

The Franciscan Robert of Oteringham claimed to have seen some strange things on a visit to the Templars' Wetherby Preceptory. He had heard a confused noise from a chapel and peered through the keyhole to see a great light within. The next day he had asked one of the Templars which saint they had been honouring in their nocturnal mass. The Templar had turned pale, thinking he had seen what had been done. 'Go thy way,' he had said, 'and if you love me or have any regard for your life never speak of this matter!'

The Rector of Godmersham claimed that, fifteen years previously, he had spoken to the Templar Stephen Queynterel of his own ambitions to join the Templars. Queynterel had advised him against it, saying there were three deadly secret articles among the brethren, known only to them, God and the Devil.

And according to the monk Richard de Koefeld, indeed, every Templar had to sell himself to the Devil. Koefeld claimed to have heard this indirectly from the ill-fated Walter le Bachelor (the Preceptor of Ireland who died in Templar custody). These were not the most outlandish stories to arise.

Sicard de Vaur, the Inquisitor, exhibited confessions, made by the Templars in France, who had testified to heretical initiation rituals that had allegedly taken place in England. These including the confession of Geoffroi de Gonneville, Preceptor of Aquitaine, made in 1307 but subsequently revoked.

In April 1311 the testimonials were compiled by the notaries. The Templars, when given copies of the dispositions, responded that as illiterate men, denied any opportunity to defend themselves, they desired to proclaim their faith and that of their Order publicly. They had a declaration drawn up in Norman French, which they presented to the Inquisitors and bishops in All Saints Church, Berkingchurch. This was presented by de la More and other preceptors from the Tower.

> Be it known to our honourable father the Archbishop of Canterbury and to all Christians that all we brethren of the Temple . . . are Christians and believe in our Saviour Jesus Christ . . . And we believe all that the Holy Church believes and teaches us. We declare that our religion is founded on vows of obedience, chastity and poverty and of aiding in the conquest of the Holy Land of Jerusalem . . . And we

> firmly deny any . . . heresy and evil doing contrary to the faith of the Holy Church. And for love of God . . . we beseech you who represent our holy father the Pope, that we be treated like true children of the Church, for we have all guarded the faith . . . If we have said or done anything wrong through ignorance of a word, since we are unlettered men, we are ready to suffer for Holy Church like him who died for us on the blessed Cross. And we believe in all the sacraments of the Church. And we beseech you . . . that you will judge us as you will have to answer for yourself and before God.

This affirmation of faith was not helpful to the Pope, who wanted confessions of guilt. He directed that the severity of the Templars' imprisonment be further increased. More French monks were sent to make sure that torture was applied unsparingly. Eventually they broke the will of a couple of Serving Brothers and a Chaplain. On 23 June Stephen de Stapelbrugge cracked. A fugitive Templar who had been captured, de Stapelbrugge testified that there were two initiation rites. One 'licit and good reception', one 'against the faith'.[6] The second ritual was supposed to follow the formula established in the French trials. De Stapelbrugge knew that Templar Walter le Bachelor had died of torture at the hands of his brethren at the London Temple. He confessed to denying Christ and pleaded for mercy.

At his trial, Thomas de Thoroldeby spoke of the late Master Brian de Jay's meanness, and how in the Holy Land, he had seen Saracens let Templars go unmolested. He said he had frequently heard Brian de Jay denying Christ as the Son of God. Thomas de Thoroldeby had also fled from his prison in Lincoln, bribing his guard in order to escape. He had been frightened by the threats of the Inquisitor, the Abbot of Lagny. The Inquisitor had grabbed him, swearing that de Thoroldeby would confess before the Inquisition was through with him. De Thoroldeby was recaptured and made to confess to being made to spit on an image of the Blessed Virgin Mary, though he said he managed to kiss her foot instead. De Thoroldeby and de Stapelbrugge repeated their confessions before the Archbishop and Council, and swore to stand by the Church's judgement.

At a solemn ceremony by the west door of London's St Paul's Cathedral, these Templars presented themselves as penitents and prostrated themselves on the steps. They were absolved of excommunication and reconciled with the Catholic Church. Psalms and praises were sung, including 'Gloria Patria', and 'Kyrie Eleison', as they re-entered the fold. They knew that if they revoked their confessions *now*, then they would be sentenced to burn, *without further trial or judgement*.

The Chaplain John de Stoke was the next Templar to confess. In Garway Preceptory, Herefordshire, Jacques de Molay himself had allegedly ordered de Stoke to renounce Christ before a Crucifix, telling him to believe instead in a great, omnipotent God who created Heaven and Earth, and not in the Crucifixion. The clergy put de Stoke through a similar absolution ritual outside St Paul's Cathedral. When Master William de la More was again interrogated, however, he refused to abjure the crimes he insisted he had never committed, and was sent back to his cell. The clergy, meanwhile, told the remaining Templars that they were guilty, as was clear from the papal bulls, and from their own grievous error over lay absolution. They were again invited to confess. Eventually a compromise was reached.

The clergy in England deemed it sufficient that the Templars simply give declarations of disgrace at the things in the accusations. After making these declarations, the Templars were given penance far less severe than their French brethren. They were required publicly to show repentance, and to receive the following absolution:

> Since you have confessed before the ecclesiastical council of Canterbury concerning the sacrament of repentance in believing that the absolution pronounced by the Master in chapter has as much efficacy as is implied in the words pronounced by him, that is to say 'the sins which you have omitted to confess through shamefacedness, or through fear of the justice of the Order, we, by virtue of the power delegated to us by the Lord Pope, forgive you so far as we are able': and since you have confessed that you cannot entirely purge yourself from the heresies set forth under the Apostolic bull, and taking sage council with a good heart and unfeigned faith have submitted yourself to the judgement and mercy of the Church, having previously abjured the heresies ... we, by authority of the council, absolve you from the chain of excommunication ... and reconcile you once more with the Church.[7]

Through July many English Templars underwent the somewhat farcical ceremony, and were allowed again to attend mass. They retained some vestige of dignity, but had to concede to the people who bore witness that they had been guilty of wrongdoing. Naturally the Order emerged forever shamed from this process. The Templars' display of penitance confirmed the sinfulness of the Order to all and sundry, and reinforced the impression that the dissolution was justified. Some old Templars, too sick to attend the ritual at the cathedral, were helped over to Sainte Mary's Chapel, near the Tower, to be reconciled. After being reconciled, these Templars were scattered around various monasteries to do penance, subsisting on a small pension, at least freed of chains, torment and fear. Yet many Templars, including William de la More and Imbert Blanke, preferred to protest their innocence, regardless. These strongly principled men would not betray the honour of their brotherhood, and died incarcerated for their efforts.

The Templars of the Iberian Peninsula

Unlike their brethren in France and Britain, the Spanish and Portuguese Templars were militarily active, as they made a substantial contribution to the ongoing *Reconquista*. The lords of these places had granted them castles, walled towns and other strongholds. James II of Aragon was initially sceptical of Philip's accusations against the Templars. However, after an abrupt change of heart he turned against them. He arrested most of the Templars on 6 January 1308, more than a month before the papal order for him to do so arrived. He took most of the Order's fortresses in Valencia without resistence. Fugitives, including the Master of Aragon, Exemen de Lenda, were apprehended. Other Templars, however, having sensed danger, had started to prepare precautionary defences on their castles, including Miravet, where the Preceptor Ramon sa Guardia dug in. From these strongholds, the renegade Templars sent appeals to King James II and to Queen Blanche, claiming they were 'loyal, Catholic and good Christians' as well as patriots. It did no good, for James II had hardened his attitude against the Templars. In January Ramon sa Guardia wrote again to his King. 'God knows, that I pity you, [and] the King of France, and all Catholics in relation to the harm which arises from all this, more than ourselves who have to endure the evil.' [8] As the Preceptor saw it, the deluded Princes were actually serving the Devil by attacking his Order. Nonetheless, sieges ensued. Ramon offered to surrender on condition that James II would give his brethren protection, at least while the Pope lay in the power of the despotic Philip the Fair. The Templars in Miravet resisted until November 1308, when hunger, disease and hopelessness caused the sixty-three defenders to surrender. Their last defiant castle, Chalmera, surrendered in July 1309.

No Templars admitted to the heresy charges, when brought to trial before the Bishops of Tarragon and Valencia. Other witnesses told varying stories. Dominican Pedro Olivonis had heard that the Templars worshipped a head, and had seen a small silver-bearded head attached to a cord worn by the Templar priest Ferrario Delileto, his uncle.[9] Meanwhile, the Franciscan, Pedro de Podio, had confessed many Templars, and had heard of no heresy. Aragonese law also prohibited torture, which threw up a major obstacle before papal 'justice'. Clement V ordered torture to be used, in order to get to the 'full truth'. However, for whatever reason, even this failed to secure confessions. The trials ended feebly, as at a local level individual Templars were acquitted.

In Majorca, a lesser Spanish kingdom that included Roussillon, the instruction to arrest the Knights Templar was promptly acted upon, although it was some time before the trials got underway. Ramon sa Guardia was extradited, to be tried in Majorca along with twenty-six other Templars, most of whom had been employed managing small manors. These Templars also pleaded innocent, quoting their Order's harsh regulations against homosexual activity.[10] The hearings in Castile, Leon and Portugal turned up even less evidence of heresy than the English trials.

The rulers of the Iberian peninsula may have had their own reasons for wishing to avoid the conviction of the Templars for heresy. If the Order was found guilty, there was more chance that the fate of its possessions would be decided directly by the Pope. If it was found innocent, the various Kings would be in a better position to maintain the fragmented remnants of the Order; reformed and rebranded into new institutions that would be loyal to the secular powers before the Pope. This nationalistic interest, on the part of the Iberian Kings, saved many of the Templars.

In the lands outside the influence of the Capetians, though some perished in prison, not a single Templar was condemned to death for heresy, and very few confessed to any of the charges. However, in Navarre, ruled by Louis, Philip IV's eldest son, where torture seems to have been used unsparingly, a substantial number of confessions were produced.

The Templars of Italy

Another scion of the Capetians was Charles II of Naples, the uncle of Philip IV and the strongest ruler in Italy. He probably saw to it that torture was used to secure confessions, and a number of Templars in his lands admitted repudiating the Cross and the divinity of Jesus. One serving brother, Jean de Nadro, told the enquiry, chaired by the Bishop of Brindisi, that he had been made to join other Templars in trampling on a Cross, having been threatened by the others that he would be thrown into a latrine if he had refused to join in the abuse of the holy symbol. The others, de Nadro alleged, had wanted him to urinate on the Cross, but he had recently relieved himself and had been unable.

Other Templars pleaded innocent of any such thing, and said that those who had confessed had lied and invented nonsense as a result of coersion.[11] A later hearing at Ravenna acquitted a number of Templars, sparing even those who had initially confessed through fear of torture. Meanwhile only six of the thirteen Templars tried in Florence confessed, despite the Pope's having ordered the use of torture there. Perhaps the order to torture was not acted upon with any great enthusiasm, this being another syptom of resentment of the Pope and the French among parts of the Italian clergy.

The Templars of Cyprus

There were eighty-three Templar knights and thirty-five serving brothers living on the island of Cyprus, who had served in the Order of the Temple for anything from three to forty-three years. King Amaury de Lusignan, who owed his crown in part to the Templars, was initially reluctant to act on the Pope's command to arrest them. The Templars, under their Marshal, Ayme d'Oselier, tried to negotiate with Amaury's agents, including Philip d'Ibelin, the 'Prince of Galilee' and several clerics. The Templars were prepared to surrender their land, but wanted to maintain their arms and their treasure while in the King's custody, until more news of the Pope's intentions arrived. In May 1308 they also read an affirmation of their faith and innocence before the citizenry and the King in Nicosia. By the time the accusations had been publicised, and the inventories of the Templar estates began to be taken, the Templars had already removed their treasure to Limassol, where the Marshal and a sizeable force prepared to resist attack. Amaury's force caught up with the Templars and laid siege to their Preceptory. By June they had persuaded the Templars to surrender. As well as taking food, wine and arms, Amaury seized 120,000 *white beasants*, a considerable fortune, though it was said that the Templars had secretly managed to hide a far greater treasure elsewhere.[12] The leading Templars were imprisoned in the Castle of Khirokitia, then moved to a stronger dungeon in Aquilia, after attempting to escape and arrange with the Genoese the purchase of a war galley.

When the trials commenced, many secular witnesses, including veterans of the Crusades, had praise for the Templars, who were held up as an example of courage, generosity and piety. Philip d'Ibelin did not believe the charges against the Templars, though he blamed any suspicion against them on their reputation for secrecy. Knights such as Jacques de Plany remembered how the Templars had stood against the Saracens while others had fled, and had preferred to be decapitated than to renounce their faith. Others vouched for their orthodoxy, though some accused them of greed. The only important Frankish witness to denounce the Templars was the Prior of the Knights Hospitaller, who may have felt that his own Order would gain by the destruction of their rivals. (The majority of the Hospitallers remained silent during the Templars' trials, in all parts of Europe. They were in a difficult position. If they had spoken up for their old brothers in arms they might have risked facing similar heresy charges from Philip the Fair. If they had spoken out against the Templars, on the other hand, they would simply have seemed keen to profit from their rivals' demise, and would have invited scorn for that.) Even ordinary citizens spoke well of the Templars on Cyprus, however. Perocius, a farmer, had seen a Templar priest use a cross to cast demons from the body of a woman in Nicosia. The Marshal, meanwhile, swore that within the Temple there 'never were any errors'.[13]

In June 1310, a month into the trials, the mutilated cadaver of Amaury de Lusignan was discovered in his palace. Soon Henry II, sworn enemy of the brethren, regained the throne. Pope Clement V sent Inquisitors to Cyprus, with instructions that Henry let them begin torturing the Templars, to get to the truth. The Templars were incarcerated in the castle of Kerynia, in much harsher conditions than they had previously experienced. In 1316 the Marshal and a number of others perished in its dungeons.

The Templars of Germany

The fragmented regions of Germany witnessed some dramatic and farcical events, in the wake of the papal order to arrest the Templars. In May 1310, at the hearing before the Archbishop of Mainz, twenty armed Knights Templar burst in. Their leader, Hugh von Salm, Preceptor of Grumbach, protested against the Pope's plot to destroy the Temple without allowing a fair trial. He declared that God had shown the innocence of the Templars who had been burned, for the flames could not consume the white mantles and red crosses of these martyrs. The unnerved Archbishop promised to discuss the matter with the Pope. Later the Preceptor's brother, Frederick von Salm, declared himself willing to prove their Order's innocence by undergoing ordeal by red-hot poker. He swore that Jacques de Molay had been thought of as an exemplary Christian in the east, and was still highly regarded. The council also heard outside witnesses, who spoke of the Templars' charitable activities. One priest recalled how, during a famine, the Preceptory at Masteire had supplied alms to a thousand paupers each day. The Archbishop's aquittal of the Templars was later overturned by the Pope. Clement had to intervene again, when the Bishop of Halberstadt excommunicated the Bishop of Magdeburg, for infringing his rights – by arresting the Templars in his own diocese. Clement V had to lift the excommunication so the trials could proceed. The papal intervention indicates that the only verdict acceptable to Clement was one of guilt.

NOTES

1 Addison, Charles G, *The History of the Knights Templars*, p. 208.
2 Ibid., p. 210.
3 Ibid., p. 209.
4 Ibid., p. 211.
5 Barber, Malcolm, *The Trial of the Templars*, p. 199. William de la Forde, Rector of Crofton, testified that he had been told by a deceased Augustinian that a Templar, by then also dead, had confessed to denying Christ before pulling

down his hose and baring his backside to the crucifix. He had then allegedly venerated the image of a calf.

6 Ibid., pp. 200–2.
7 Addison, op. cit., p. 220.
8 Barber, op. cit., p. 207.
9 Ibid., p. 210.
10 Ibid., p. 212.
11 Ibid., p. 214. An example was the Templar Andrew of Sienna, one of two tried at Cesena. He said if he had ever heard of the things in the accusations, he would have left the Order and reported it to the Inquisition.
12 Ibid., p. 218.
13 Ibid., p. 21.

CHAPTER XVI
Abolition and Aftermath

The Council of Vienne

The Church Council of Vienne was convened on 16 October 1311. The delegates gathered there, a year after the Council was supposed to begin, in the city's cathedral above the Rhone. Conditions were less than pleasant; for the weather was unusually cold, there was insufficient accommodation or food in the city and disease and discontent were rife. The whole atmosphere seems to have been one more of squalor and rancour than of stateliness and grace.

On the agenda were three matters: the fate of the Templars, plans for future Crusades and Church reform. Both the latter were unrealistic to the point of being pipe-dreams. No King in Europe had the money, manpower or serious desire to lead a Crusade, so that was a non-starter. No priest, meanwhile, could see anything to gain by discussing Church reform (i.e. cleansing the priesthood of corruption) at a council presided over by one of the most notorious nepotists ever to don the papal tiara. The age's cynicism and the decline in respect for the Church was fairly obvious. Though 161 prelates were invited, more than a third did not bother to go, only sending representatives.[1] Moreover, though every crowned head in Christendom was summoned, the only royalty to appear were Philip the Fair and his sons. They showed up six months into the proceedings, and then only for long enough to force their way on the issue of the Templars.

Biased summaries of the trials had been produced, and confessions read out. As an empty formality, to placate the cardinals outside the papal curia and the circles supportive of Philip IV, Clement called the Templars to make a final defence of the Order. Unexpectedly, seven Templars appeared and presented themselves, declaring their readiness to defend their name, and claiming that as many as 2,000 of their brethren would soon be arriving to support them. The guards had to be called, and the bold Templars were put in prison.

The only prelates who favoured the immediate suppression of the Templars were an Italian nephew of Clement and the French Bishops of Rheims, Sens and Rouen, all of whom were King Philip's creatures and had burned numerous Templars in their districts. All the other churchmen held grave misgivings, and many wanted to hear a Templar defence. The English deputy Walter of Hemingborough recorded how afraid many of the French clergy were of the French King. 'Most of the prelates stood by the Templars, except for the prelates of France who, it would seem, did not dare to act otherwise for fear of the King, the source of all this scandal.'[2]

In a repeat of the intimidation tactics Philip IV employed at Poitiers, the King summoned the Estates General, at Lyons, a short way up-river from Vienne. From there he put heavy pressure on the Council, and breathed down the neck of Clement V. Philip wrote to the Pope:

> Your Holiness is aware that I have been informed by trustworthy people of the results of inquiries into the brethren and Order of the Knights Templar ... They committed such great heresies and other dreadful, detestable crimes that the Order should justifiably be suppressed. In consequence, burning with zeal for the true faith, and lest so great an injustice done to Christ remain unpunished, I loyally, devotedly and humbly beg your Holiness to be pleased to suppress the aforesaid Order.

Philip's son, the King of Navarre, along with Guillaume de Nogaret, Guillaume de Plaisians and other persuasive individuals, took the message to the Pope.[3] In March King Philip himself descended on Vienne, with his two brothers, three sons and a strong contingent of troops. All dissent very quickly ended.

The delegates were called to assemble in the cathedral. The Pope sat, sandwiched between Philip the Fair and the King of Navarre, as he read out his controversial bull, suppressing the Knights Templar. He had needed to impose silence on pain of excommunication on the illustrious assembly in order to do so. The bull, *Vox in excelso*, dated 22 March 1312, stated that the Order of the Temple had lapsed against Christ. Because of the infamy, suspicion and noisy insinuation against the Templars, and because of their secrecy and their clandetine receptions, the Order had caused scandal for the Church:

> ... many horrible things have been done by many of the brothers of this Order ... who have lapsed into ... the crime of detestable

> idolatry, [and] the execrable outrages of the sodomites . . . [Therefore] we abolish the Order of the Temple, and its constitution, name and habit, by an irrevocable and perpetually valid decree . . . If anyone acts against this he will incur the sentence of excommunication ipso facto.[4]

Entering the Order and acting as a Templar became criminal offences. Clement abolished the Order by his personal authority, rather than with the Council. The Pope resisted Philip's calls for there to be created a new Military Order to replace the Templars, with one of the Capetian Princes as its Grand Master. In May 1312 the Pope's next bull *Ad Providam* transferred the bulk of the Temple's goods to the Hospital. It seemed the King had been persuaded to relent on this matter, at least, in order to achieve the swift suppression of the Templars. However, the transfer of property and land to the Hospitallers was only to happen after a tenth of the Templars' wealth in France was given to Philip IV for his troubles. It was a substantial pay-off. Shortly afterwards, in England, a heartbroken William de la More died in his bleak dungeon, defending the Order of the Temple of Solomon to his last breath. He was shortly followed by Imbert Blanke, the old campaigner who had fought alongside the defenders at Acre, surviving that nightmare, to die in double chains in an English prison.

The Templars Fade Away

The Church did not release former Templars from their monastic vows when it abolished their Order. Those who had since gone to live as laymen, or who had married, were punished. Subdued veterans were granted pittance pensions, and made to subsist quietly in ones and twos, in dispersed monasteries – some of them Cistercian establishments. It seems the pensions often went unpaid, and starvation threatened some of the ex-brethren. King Edward wrote asking the Hospitallers to assist, while the Archbishop of Canterbury wrote to the possessors of Templar lands: 'We pray and conjure you in kindness to furnish them, for the love of God and for charity, with the means of subsistence.'[5] In England, the Templar lands had been given to royally appointed guardians, who were charged with giving pensions to the erstwhile servants and retainers of the knights, meeting the expenses of the trials and sending what profit remained from the income of the land to the Royal Treasury. They were also called to supply food to the King's castles.

Edward also used parts of the former property of the Templars to reward his favourites. In May 1312 Clement V sent an edict to England repeating the verdict of Vienne, and ordering the bishops to enforce the transfer of land to the Hospitallers, so that it might fulfil its original function. The decree was resisted by secular nobles. Edward II wrote to the Prior of the Knights Hospitaller at Clerkenwell, that the Pope's pretention to dispose of land in England, without the consent of Parliament, was an affront to royal authority. The King commanded the Hospitallers not to touch the Templars' land. Eventually, however, Edward was forced to yield by papal menaces, and in November 1313 commanded his barons to transfer the estates. Not until 1324 was the transfer made official by an act of Parliament.

The Death of the Grand Master

Jacques de Molay, Hugues de Pairaud, Geoffroi de Gonneville and Guy de Charney, the four highest ranking Templars in French custody, were tried afresh in December 1313, by a Paris commission. On 18 March 1314 the papal legate and the Archbishop of Sens summoned Jacques de Molay and the other senior Templars to make yet another confession, before an assembly of prelates and the public. This demand, however, proved one humiliation too many for de Molay. The old man had already been sentenced to unending imprisonment with the three other leaders. With little to lose, the Grand Master finally found his wonted courage, as he mounted the scaffold before Notre Dame Cathedral, and declared to the assembled people something to this effect:

> It is only right that at so solemn a moment, when my life has so little time to run, I should reveal the deception which has been practised and speak up for the truth. Before Heaven and Earth and all of you who are here my witnesses, I admit that I am guilty of the grossest iniquity. But the iniquity is that, to my shame and dishonour, I have suffered myself through the pain of torture and the fear of death, to give utterances to falsehoods in admitting the disgusting charges laid against the Order, which has nobly served the cause of Christianity. I declare, and I must declare, that the Order is innocent. Its purity and saintliness are beyond question. I disdain to seek wretched and disgraceful existence by grafting another lie upon the original falsehood.[6]

The Preceptor of Normandy, Guy de Charney, showed solidarity with his Grand Master, before they were dragged down by the provost's men and hurled back into prison. The other two Preceptors distanced themselves from these suicidal declarations. Philip IV was enraged to hear of so public a recantation. He immediately ordered the two men's burning as relapsed heretics, without consulting the Pope or any other cleric. Before that day closed, the two Templars went into the flames, on the Ile-des-Javiaux, a small island on the Seine between the King's gardens and the

Convent of St Augustine. The serenity, bravery and will they showed (*Beauseant*) earned the admiration of the witnesses, many of whom thought them martyrs. Some people afterwards sifted through the ashes for their charred bones, to keep as holy relics.

Settlement

The Pope and the King had, by then, joined to pull off one final scam. In April 1312 Clement V had gathered an assembly at the Cathedral of St Maurice in Vienne, and preached a new Crusade, a 'general passage' (a large-scale campaign involving combined armies led by the foremost men in Christendom), just as the unfortunate Jacques de Molay had wanted to see. The following year, amid solemn ceremony, Philip the Fair and his sons took the Cross (for the second time in the case of Philip) and swore to rescue the Holy Land for Christ. Money was raised from a tax on the Church and from the donations of the faithful. Pageants were held in Paris, to celebrate the revival of the Crusading dream. No armies were ever gathered, however. Between them, the King and the Pope embezzled nearly all the money raised. They did not have long to enjoy it.

Clement V died on 20 April 1314, less than a month after the burning of Jacques de Molay. It is said that he died of dysentery, related to his cancer. A copy of the Rule of the Templars was found among the Pope's possessions, in the room where he died. It is said that his body was laid in a church in Carpentras, which caught fire that very night and destroyed his remains. His relatives argued over his fortune, which was stored in a chapel in Lucca. Whilst they wrangled, these treasures, which may have included the Pope's share of booty from the Temple, were stolen by a band of Italian and German brigands. Clement left the Catholic Church in such disarray that it was over two years before the conclave managed to elect his successor.

Esquin de Floyran, meanwhile, the man who had sold his stories of the Templar heresy to Philip the Fair, was apparently hanged for fresh crimes shortly after. Philip IV himself managed to squeeze more money out of the Knights Hospitaller of Saint John (including 200,000 *livres tournoise* from the Venice Hospital). He exacted so much money from the Hospitallers, that they ended up poorer in capital than they had been before the suppression of their rivals, the Templars. Then, it is said, the King caught a strange, lingering disease, which some sources link to a hunting accident. He died in November 1314. Philip's son, Louis X demanded another 60,000 *livres tournoise* from the Hospitallers for the trial expenses, although he did not live to reign long, dying in 1316. His brother and successor, Philip V, demanded a final pay-off of 5,000 *livres tournoise* from the Hospitallers. Interestingly, all the wives of Philip's sons were convicted for adultery. None produced a surviving heir, and within two decades the Capetian line, which had seemed so healthy in the reign of Philip the Fair, was extinct on the male side.

The French and English aristocracies wanted to recover land they had given to the Templars. In England King Edward had already sold some of it back to them. Edward II, like the heirs of the donors, who claimed Templar land by right of escheat, was reluctant to hand over seized lands to the Hospitallers. He had to be bribed (and even threatened with excommunication) before he would relinquish them. The Hospitallers, it is reckoned, still never received a twentieth of the Templars' late holdings.

Edward II demanded heavy contributions from the former Templar estates in England and Ireland, to support the continuing wars in Scotland. Other Temple lands he gave to Scottish lords, such as John of Argyle, in exchange for support against Robert the Bruce. The wars did not go well, nonetheless. Edward II's army of 23,000 was defeated by Robert the Bruce's Scottish army of 6,000, at the Battle of Bannockburn in June 1314.

A recent theory, that has gained popularity, and which is supposed to lend credence to the survival of the Templars in Scotland, relates to a mysterious event during the fighting at Bannockburn. A strange body of reinforcements appeared at the battle to turn the tide in favour of Robert the Bruce. A comtemporary legend was that these were patriotic Scottish camp followers who joined the affray with banners made from sheets, when they saw things were going against their compatriots. Some, though, have hypothesised that this phantom cavalry were really fugitive Templars from France. However, if the Knights Templar did unfurl *Beauseant* one last time at Bannockburn, and rode to the aid of Robert the Bruce, one must wonder why the vanquished English kept so quiet about it. A body of renegade Templars helping the interdicted Scots would have greatly mitigated Edward II's defeat; and England would have been able to show the excommunicated Bruce to be in league with condemned heretic knights – heretics who had once enjoyed renown as the elite fighting force of Christendom.

After Bannockburn, the Scottish forces poured south of the border, subjecting the English populace to similarly brutal treatment as that to which the English armies had subjected the Scots. Six years later the Scots sent their passionate declaration of independence, from Arbroath, to Pope John XXII, the successor of Clement V. Things went from bad to worse for Edward, in the years after he fled from Bannockburn. He and his two favourites, Hugh de Spencer and his son, the younger de Spencer, had humiliated and antagonised the passionate Queen Isabella, who had evidently inherited her father Philip the Fair's guile and vindictiveness. With her lover, the Welsh warlord Roger Mortimer, she invaded England from the Netherlands and raised a revolt supported by many barons, in the name of her son, the future Edward III. The elder de Spencer was hanged, drawn and quartered, shortly followed by his son. Edward II was captured and deposed by Parliament. His captors tried to asphyxiate him, locking him in a cell above a well filled with rotting carcasses in Berkely Castle, Gloucestershire. When this rotting carrion failed to kill the King, they tortured him to death with a hot iron. Edward III, on his coming of age, had Mortimer executed, and his mother, Isabella, imprisoned for her part in the murder of her husband. She died a lonely and demented prisoner in Castle Rising, twenty-seven years later. Her Capetian blood gave rise to the English claim on the throne of France, which was the major cause of the Hundred Years War. It was easy for some to see these deadly events as the culmination of the curse of the Templars, a curse supposedly voiced by Jacques de Molay, with his dying breath.

Some German and Italian Templars had to be dislodged by force from their Preceptories, but the transfer of property to the Hospitallers was reasonably smooth in Cyprus. In the Iberian kingdoms, meanwhile, Temple property, rights and duties were generally transferred to newly constituted Orders, the Grand Mastership of these Orders being annexed to the various crowns. James II of Aragon enriched the Order of Calatrava, and also the Orders of Alcantara and Santiago, which continued to fight, reconquering land from the Moors. In Portugal, the Order of Christ arose, under King Diniz. The Knights of Christ, confirmed as an Order by John XXII, were, to some extent, the Templars by a different name, although without the same autonomy. Though secretive and credited with much arcane wisdom, they were never accused of spitting on Crosses or suspected of worshipping disembodied heads. They extended the Templar *Convento de Christo* at Tomar, which remained their headquarters. They exchanged Crusading for maritime exploration and imperialism. The Knights of Christ were later to produce many illustrious seafarers, including Prince Henry the Navigator (1394–1460), their Grand Master and a patron of explorers.[7] They also included Vasco da Gama, who reached India in 1497, and his son, Don Christopher da Gama, who was killed in Ethiopia in 1542. Establishing contact with Prester John, the fabled Christian Emperor beyond the Islamic world, was always a dream of the Knights of Christ. Whether they hoped to forge an alliance with him against the old enemy Islam, or whether they had inherited the Templars' interest in and knowledge of the Ethiopian Ark of the Covenant, are matters for debate. The Knights of Christ, like the other Iberian Orders, gradually became secularised, and grew closer to the monarchs. They would wane as Spain grew to dominate the peninsula.

After the suppression of the Order of the Temple, some former Templars naturally sought a less tedious life than banishment in a monastery. The former Preceptor of Corbens turned up in Barcelona as the Ambassador of the Sultan of Tunis. Others fared less well, losing all pride, discipline, faith and respect for authority, and becoming petty criminals. Other Military Orders absorbed some, but for the most part the Templars had a rather prosaic end. Not to be forgotten are those Templars who remained prisoners of the Muslims in the orient, in the decades after the fall of Acre. One knight, at least, gained his freedom eventually and it is said, ended up as a humble wood-carver for a Sultan.

NOTES

1 Read, Piers Paul, *The Templars*, p. 292.
2 Ibid., p. 293.
3 Ibid., p. 294. Also Maxwell-Stuart, P G, *Chronicle of the Popes*, p. 127, letter from Philip to Pope Clement V. Clement is remembered chiefly for his nepotism, for his subservience to Philip the Fair, for abandoning Rome in favour of Avignon, and possibly as the Pope who excommunicated Robert the Bruce after his murder of John Comyns. More to his credit, this Pope also founded the universities of Orléans and Perugia, and the chairs of oriental languages at Paris, Oxford, Salamanca and Bologna, contributing something to the intellectual life of Europe.
4 Barber, Malcolm, *The Trial of the Templars*, pp. 228–9, quoting *Vox in Excelso*, ('Voice in Heaven').
5 Addison, Charles G, *The History of the Knights Templars*, p. 145.
6 Seward, D, *The Monks of War*, p. 170, quoting the recorded declaration of Jacques de Molay.
7 Hancock, Graham, *The Sign and the Seal*, p. 57.

EPILOGUE
The Shadow of the Crusades

There were no major Crusades after the suppression of the Templars. Popes were diverted by Italian wars. There were a few maritime engagements, but nothing on the scale of what had gone before. In the 1360s King Peter I of Cyprus toured Europe raising support for a Crusade. His armada managed to capture and plunder Alexandria, but held it for only a few days. There was much indiscriminate butchery, after which most of these Crusaders were keen quickly to be off with their booty. This raid owed less to the Crusading spirit than to a Cypriot desire to cripple a trading rival. The Mamelukes afterwards inflicted cruel reprisals on the local, Coptic Christians, and also closed the Holy Sepulchre, or what was left of it, to pilgrims.

The destruction of the Templars facilitated the advance of the Mamelukes and then the Ottoman Turks in the east. The Ottomans, descendants of the Seljuk Emir Othman, made themselves masters of Asia Minor, then expanded their territory westward, bypassing Constantinople and sweeping through the Balkans, as far as the Danube. They defeated the Serbs in battle at Kosovo in 1386.

The Teutonic Knights waged yearly Crusades from Marienburg, their castle near Danzig, against the Livs, the pagan Slavs who inhabited Lithuania. The Order, which never again contributed to the struggle against Islam, was much criticised for being more interested in killing and enslaving than in converting in their northern campaigns. In 1386 the Lithuanians converted to Christianity of their own accord, under their Grand Duke Jagiello. In 1410 the Teutonic Order met with terrible defeat by the Slavic armies at the battle of Tannenberg, and dwindled as a power thereafter.

The Hospitallers continued to fight the Muslims in the name of Holy War, but were restricted to the Levant. They heroically repulsed the attacking Turks a number of times from Rhodes. It was a form of Crusade, but it was a cause deplorably neglected by the greater part of Europe. Rhodes finally fell to the Ottomans in 1523. (Seven years later they received the small island of Malta from the Emperor Charles V. They continued their activities from there, holding it until robbed of it not by the Turks but by Napoleon.) The Avignon Popes would even relax trading restrictions with the Ottoman Turks and with Egypt, and for Venice and Genoa it was business as usual. The Cypriot-led Crusade against Alexandria had also looted the storehouses of Italian merchants there, and these merchants later contrived the commercial ruin of Cyprus, in revenge.

The Ottoman Empire pushed up through Bulgaria and Serbia; and the west did little to prevent it. Many merchants brokered trade treaties and actively profited from it, and only aided the Crusaders on the rare occasions when it suited them. In 1396 French and Transylvanian knights, under King Sigismund of Hungary and Count John of Neves, were defeated at Nicopolis on the Danube. The Ottomans decapitated their prisoners except for those under 20, whom they took into slavery.

The penultimate Byzantine Emperor, John VIII, toured Europe attempting to rally support against the Turkish threat. At the Council of Florence in 1439, he even accepted ecclesiastical union and subordination to the Roman Church. Very few Crusaders took the Cross, even so, and those who did met with annihilation at the battle of Varna, in Bulgaria, in 1444.

In 1453, when the Ottomans massed to overwhelm Constantinople, no Crusaders came to the once glorious city's aid. Mehmet II's Ottoman forces attacked from land and sea, equipped with massive cannons. The walls were reduced and stormed by Janissary units. Janissaries were warriors more terrible even than the Mamelukes. Whenever the Ottomans had captured a place, they had taken the eldest sons of all the Christians living there and made them Janissaries – slave conscripts, indoctrinated from youth with the feverish creed of *Jihad*. The Janissaries slew the last Emperor, Constantine XI, on the walls of Constantinople. His body was never found.

The aggressively capitalistic Italian merchants, meanwhile, were loath to risk disturbing their profitable trade with the Muslims. Long before, the Templars had warned that the Crusading venture ought not to depend on the maritime republics. The Knights Templar, however, rather than the Venetians and Genoese, were blamed for the loss of the Holy Land, and punished accordingly with their destruction. This (in the long term), the loss of another half of Christendom, was a consequence. The Hospitallers alone, diminished and out of sight and mind on their island, could not capture the west's imagination, and failed to keep the Crusading cause alive and vital. The west, full of apathy, left the war against the encroaching forces of Islam to those in immediate peril.

The politics of nation states had replaced the politics of Christian solidarity. The international destruction of the Templars was the dissolution of one of the bonds that had held Christendom united. After the fourteenth century, the rulers of Europe's evolving nation states would expend infinitely more energy fighting each other than any common enemy. The Ottoman Empire continued to dominate the Mediterranean. They would have taken Malta in 1565 but for the spectacular resistence offered by the outnumbered Knights of St John, under their Grand Master, la Valette. Six years later the Order contributed galleys to the fleet of Spanish, Venetian and papal ships that defeated the Turks at Lepanto and reduced the threat to Europe posed by the Ottomans. By then, however, the Protestant Reformation had already splintered Europe, and soon Christians would fight 'holy wars' against other Christians, as bitter and costly as any fought against Muslims. Each side in the sectarian divide believed the other to be in league (consciously or not) with the Devil.

This relates to another reason why the destruction of the Templars was damaging for Europe in general. It left an enduring legacy of demonological anxiety, causing the Devil to loom larger than ever in both learned theology and the beliefs of ordinary people. When Philip IV succeeded in portraying the brethren as heretics and Devil-worshippers, there were obviously many who came to believe it. This helped to entrench society's acceptance of the existence of dark forces. It seemed possible that heretics and black magicians were working in the shadows to overthrow good Christians. It became accepted that the Anti-christ could secure his minions in the highest places and that brutal methods were necessary to combat them. The resulting suspicion was like a madness, or a disease, and was easily exploited as a tool of oppression.

The accusations against the Templars vindicated those who believed in a Satanic conspiracy, and kept sharp the tools of the Inquisition. The witch/heretic hunting frenzies that plagued Christendom from time to time thereafter might not have been so brutal, had not the persecution of the Templars, for Devil-inspired heresy, set a legitimising precedent for torture and burning. The events surrounding the ending of this once exalted Order seemed to justify the darkest superstitions and paranoia that could inhabit the soul of a civilisation.

APPENDIX A

Modern Templars – Survival or Revival?

Modern societies exist, claiming to be contemporary manifestations of groups that ceased to be centuries ago. Among these are societies claiming that the Order of the Temple survived its suppression for heresy in the 1300s, and that they, themselves, are the living heirs of the Knights Templar.

The lawyers who took over the Inner and Middle Temple in London inherited certain ways and customs of the previous occupants, and sometimes called themselves Templars. Many of the traditions of apparent Knights Templar origin were certainly still alive in 1842, when Charles G Addison wrote his history of the Order and its legacy. The Templar device of the Lamb of God within a Saint George's Cross was retained as the arms of the Middle Temple, and the Law Society still uses the device. The red cross on white field also became part of the badge of the Order of the Garter. This Order of twenty-six knights was founded by Edward III and his son, Edward the Black Prince, in 1348 (incidentally, on the eve of the great plague called the Black Death). Also devoted to Sainte Mary and Saint George, the Knights of the Garter became England's premier Order of Chivalry, appearing as if to fill a psychological gap created by the destruction of the Knights Templar. One later honorary Knight of the Garter was Prince Henry the Navigator, the Grand Master of the Knights of Christ, a practical and learned man who would employ the skills of Moorish and Jewish cartographers.

The Knights of Christ in Portugal also built on a Templar tradition, as an active Military Order, comprising adventurous, skilled and pious individuals. However, these are not the people with whom this Appendix is specifically concerned.

Two other long-standing organisations lay competing claim to true Templar continuity. The first of these is part of Freemasonry, a fraternal society pledged to mutual support, and having secret signs, such as handshakes, by which fellow Masons recognise one another. Masonry is credited with preserving various occult traditions. Members meet at halls called Lodges, which represent the Temple of Solomon (which is in turn seen as a metapor for the human soul). In these Lodges, they enact elaborate rituals. The three basic degrees of initiation are Entered Apprentice, Fellow Craft and Master Mason, though there are side orders with more chivalrous sounding titles. Freemasonic rituals include symbolism based on the tools of medieval stonemasons, though other elements have quasi-Roman, Egyptian or biblical themes. The 'Grand Lodge' the governing body of Freemasonry, was formed in London in 1717, and its coat of arms incorporates the Ark of the Covenant. Freemasons have included such luminaries as George Washington, Wolfgang Amadeus Mozart, Henry Ford, Rudyard Kipling and numerous members of the British aristocracy and royalty since at least Victorian times.

The other large society claiming to have inherited the Templars' legacy is the Sovereign and Military Order of the Temple of Jerusalem (SMOTJ). The SMOTJ, and certain of the Masonic groups, produce contradictory lists of clandestine Grand Masters – succeeding two different men Jacques de Molay allegedly nominated to succeed him as Grand Master, whilst in prison, before his execution at the stake in 1314.

There was little hint or question of the Knights Templar surviving until the Enlightenment, the eighteenth-century philosophical movement that rejected the religion-dominated culture of earlier times. The name 'Templar', in that era, somehow acquired mystical connotations. Suddenly two societies went public, with claims to continuation. It may be said that if Jacques de Molay had nominated any successor, and given him orders to rally whatever fugitive Templars were around, this would have been a breach of the Order's custom, as Grand Masters were traditionally elected at a General Chapter. However, in those turbulent and exceptional times, the occurrence of such a transfer of authority cannot be ruled out entirely.

In France, most of the Templars who were not burned died in prison, or were pensioned off to isolated monasteries. A number of others evidently slipped the net. The question is whether these fugitives could have gone on to preserve their Order in secret, for unknown reasons, in defiance of the Papal bull *Vox in excelso* (which excommunicated anyone 'acting as a

Templar') and perpetuated the Order undetected for the next four centuries. This would have been a clandestine Order without property, prestige, privileges or obvious purpose. Indeed, because of the Pope's excommunication, any men joining it would have been risking their souls.

Modern Templars do not bind themselves with monastic vows of poverty, chastity and obedience, and obviously neither go on Crusade, nor observe the clauses of the Latin Rule. Rather, these modern Templars, the self-styled 'knights' and, interestingly, 'dames' of the SMOTJ have functions, publish magazines, perform ceremonies in Templar robes, and raise money for eye charities (among others), emulating the philanthropy of the old religious Order. (Freemasons likewise patronise worthy charities and hospitals.) The SMOTJ, on their Internet sites, introduce themselves as an autonomous Order, welcoming men and women of all Christian traditions as well as being ecumenical, apolitical and non-Masonic. They are, however, disavowed by the Roman Catholic Church. During the papacy of Paul IV (1963–78), the Vatican declared that the historical Knights Templar were abolished, after their trials, by Clement V in 1312. The Order was never subsequently revived; ergo nobody could legitimately call themselves a Templar.

The response of SMOTJ is that there were places (Portugal and Scotland, notably, and perhaps also Scandinavia and Switzerland) where the Order was never successfully suppressed. They hold that, before his execution in 1314, Jacques de Molay secretly nominated one Jean Marc Larminius as his successor as Grand Master of the Templars. Larminius allegedly rallied the remnants of the Order covertly. There was said to be a secret line of Grand Masters until 1705, when a convention of French nobles elected Philip Duke of Orléans, the '41st' Grand Master. Subsequently the Order 're-emerged' as a 'secular Order of Chivalry'. The Order supposedly survived the Revolution, going public in 1804, under Bernard Raymond Fabre-Palaprat. It seems Palaprat, during the French Revolution, had been a member of a Masonic group in Paris, called the Lodge of the Knights of the Cross. He produced (or forged) the *Carta Transmissionis*, a constitution purporting to have been written by Larminius in 1324. Palaprat appointed himself Grand Master, and re-organised the Templar Order, which, it seems, was subsequently accepted into the occult subculture. They went on to expand worldwide in the nineteenth century. Unlike their supposed ancestors, it seems the modern Templars could not preserve their unity, and have suffered numerous petty rifts and schisms. The SMOTJ appear to be one of these branches. If this is the case, they can be identified, after all, as a Templar-revivalist offshoot of Freemasonry.

Christopher Knight and Robert Lomas, in *The Hiram Key*, admit that modern Freemasonry, for them, and most other 'brother Masons' they knew, was little more than a social club, providing the opportunity to indulge in some amateur theatricals, followed by a good meal and plenty of alcohol. However, when investigating the origins of their rituals concerning Hiram Abif (the legendary murdered architect of Solomon's Temple), they quickly rejected the theory that had Freemasonry originating from medieval stone-masons' guilds. According to their speculations, ideas and rituals from pharaonic Egypt were passed via Moses into ancient Israel. These rituals, they believe, related to the sanctification of kingship. They were preserved by Solomon and passed down to Jesus and the Essenes, to end up in writings buried under the Temple, to await discovery by Hugues de Payens and his fellow knights. The Templars then, supposedly, incorporated these beliefs and rites into their new Order, and passed them on into Freemasonry – hence the quasi-Egyptian character of certain Masonic rituals and the use of the Temple as the basis for the Masonic Lodge. The transition had occurred in Scotland, the supposed cradle of Freemasonry, which later spread to England, and from there abroad.

Claimants for the Templar inheritance are found in York Rite Freemasonry. A Master Mason, having passed through the lesser grades (or *degrees*) of initiation, might attain the *Knight Templar* degree. This is the only segment of Masonry requiring the profession of Christianity, as opposed to simply belief in God,*the Supreme Architect*. Ironically, perhaps, enemies of Masonry (especially American evangelical Christians) also link Freemasonry with the Templars, seeking to cast the former in a sinister light, as worshipping the demon *Baphomet* (rather as the Catholic Joseph von Hammer-Purgstall had tried to do, in the nineteenth century).

It was an exiled Jacobite Scot, Andrew Ramsey, who suggested the Freemasons were descended from Crusaders. In Germany (where Masonry also became established) the idea that the Crusaders in question were the Templars became popular. In 1754 Baron Karl von Hundt created the Masonic 'Rite of Strict Observance'. He claimed that Jacques de Molay nominated one Pierre d'Aumont to succeed him, and that the Order continued in Scotland, where d'Aumont's men fled disguised as stone-masons.

Logically both the stories about Jacques de Molay nominating a successor (one naming Larminius, the other d'Aumont) and the two lines of continuity based on them, cannot be correct (unless, of course, there was some sort of split). There is little concrete evidence (although arguably there is some circumstantial evidence) for secret knowledge existing at the Temple's core. Some sort of heretical teaching, probably based on Cabbalism or Gnosticism, is, perhaps, the only thing that would have been worth preserving, when all else that constituted the Order was lost.

Many popular books on the Templars have emphasised the Order's association with the site of Solomon's Temple – that eternally potent location. They all aver that the knights dug there for something precious, and relate the quest to the occult and to ancient mysticism. Though the books generally accept that the Templars worshipped something called *Baphomet*, they speculate it symbolised Sacred Wisdom. Philip IV's persecution is still shown as motivated by cupidity, superstition and lust for plunder. Such books accept the Knights Templar as the forerunners of the Freemasons, and attribute to this the traditional hostility between Masonry and the Catholic establishment.

The Templar Order in Scotland supposedly went 'underground' and became Freemasonry, to protect its body of esoteric traditions, according to several authors of revisionist histories. They assign to the St Clair/Sinclair clan, Lords of Rosslyn and Earls of Orkney, a pivotal role in these secretive proceedings (despite the fact, pointed out by Evelyn Lord, that two members of the clan actually bore witness *against* the Templars in Edinburgh). The family were long supposed to have links with the Templars. One of their daughters allegedly was married to the founder of the Order, and the Sinclairs went on, it is claimed, to provide a dynasty of Grand Masters for Scottish Freemasonry. Earl William de St Clair built Rosslyn Chapel, in the village of Roslin, south-west of Edinburgh, between 1450 and 1480 (therein, as some assert, to secrete the treasure of the Templars) and had it filled with intricate and strange carvings. These images incorporated fruit and vegetables, feeding endless speculation about the secrets of the Templars. The vegetables take the form of apparent carvings of maize, sweetcorn and cacti, plants only found in the new world, suggesting to some that the Templars had sailed to America two centuries before Columbus. (Columbus would sail, incidentally, with three ships procured from the Knights of Christ, and bearing the Order's red crosses on their sails.)

Spurious evidence to support the idea of a medieval colonisation of north America is cited in the elusive Westford Knight, in Massachusetts and the nondescript Newport Tower in Rhode Island, thought to resemble a round Templar tower chapel. In fact, the Newport Tower, though enigmatic, is a crude structure bare of any symbol to link it directly to the Templars, whereas the Westford Knight – an image allegedly punched into a rock face, resembling a Crusader tomb effigy – was discredited in a geological report as being mostly natural formation. Perhaps in time, better evidence will emerge that will establish whether such fantastic voyages, as writers including Andrew Sinclair and Knight and Lomas have envisaged, truly took place, and whether the Templars had any connection with them. In the meantime doubts are probably justifiable. The Portuguese Knights of Christ may not, however, have been the only organisation to continue the quest of the Templars. The explorations of the Scottish aristocrat James Bruce in Egypt and Ethiopia in the 1760s, and the excavations of the English Lieutenant Charles Warren in Jerusalem in the 1860s, both men having been committed Freemasons, may be interpreted as having some relation to the Templars, or at least to interest in the Ark of the Covenant.

The Holy Blood and the Holy Grail is the catalyst of many later 'Templarist' books. Its authors, Baigent, Lincoln and Leigh, began writing it after investigating the treasure supposedly found in the village of Rennes-le-Château in the French Pyrenees, by the priest Berenger Saunier. In 1891, while renovating the church of Ste Mary Magdalene, Saunier apparently discovered coded documents concealed in the eighteenth century by a predecessor, the Abbé Bigou, who had been chaplain to the Blanqueforts – the family of an early Templar Grand Master – who were the supposed guardians of a 'very great secret'. Saunier took his find to his superiors in Paris, and returned a rich man (evidenced by his commissioning of roads for the village, a neo-Gothic tower folly, and curious statues for his church including the demon Asmodeus, the legendary guardian of Solomon's treasure). Allegedly, whatever Saunier had to declare on his death bed so shocked the attending priest, that he refused to deliver the last rites.

The writers argue that an ancient, esoteric brotherhood called the *Priure de Sion* had bought Saunier's silence about his discoveries. The *Priure de Sion* supposedly linked the Black Madonna to the Egyptian goddess Isis. This secret society (predating the Crusades) had created the Knights Templar, to guard the secret of Jesus' marriage to Mary Magdalene, and that their 'Davidic-blooded' descendants were the Merevingian dynasty, the Visigothic Wizard-Kings of Dark-Ages France. This Jewish 'Grail family' produced Godfrey de Bouillon, Duke of Lorraine, and when Godfrey took Jerusalem, he was reclaiming his Davidic inheritance! (De Bouillon is never recorded as having boasted of any such ancestry, though he did claim descent from Charlemagne.) At any rate, the 'Davidic' bloodline survived in secret, guarded by the Templars. It flowed into the Habsbergs, a dynasty which the *Priure de Sion* aspire one day to restore to power as priest-kings. This would be *almost like a second coming*, as they are the alleged descendants of Christ and the Davidic line. The end message seemed to be, then, that we should be waiting for Jesus' secret family to come out and to put the world to rights for us.

The Holy Blood and the Holy Grail also linked the Templars to the Freemasons, and paints the Masonic involvement in the French Revolution as the taking of a belated revenge on the French monarchy and the Church. It spawned this whole popular literary genre, turning the Knights Templar into enlightened sages, worshipping sacred wisdom, advanced in science and preserving progressive philosophies, in the face of Catholic spiritual tyranny. The concept of mystic Templars does not always stand up to the available evidence, but may be attractive to some of the modern 'Templars', adding to their mystique. Many of the details, however, could be hoaxes – for example, some of the obscure documents cited as sources, mysteriously deposited in various bibliotheques by the supposed 'Priure de Sion' contain lists of alleged Grand Masters that seem mere jokes. (Everyone famous from Botticelli to Victor Hugo was a Grand Master, and the latest one is a Frenchman called Plantard de St Clair.) The angles of the sticks held by two of the Arcadian shepherds in a painting by Poussin are supposed to be clues to the location of buried Templar or Cathar treasure in the Languedoc. Who is duping whom? That is the question.

The bizarreness of the phenomenon of 'Templarism' is becoming apparent, as is how far removed it can become from the reality of the historical Knights Templar. The Templars' name has additionally been hijacked by a number of dubious cults, including the Solar Templars. The Order of the Solar Temple was set up in 1984 by two unhinged ex-Rosicrucians, namely Luc Jouret and Joseph di Mambro. They recruited as many as 400 members, many from the professional classes. The charismatic Luc Jouret had met Julian Origas, a former Gestapo agent who had founded the Renewed Order of the Temple, combining neo-Templarism with Rosicrucian mysticism. After he joined di Mambro, the Solar Temple spread into Switzerland, France, Canada and Martinique. It evolved three grades, progressing from lecture meetings to esoteric and further esoteric, apocalyptic levels. Di Mambro pretended to be the vessel of otherworldly 'hidden Masters'. His own son, Elia, suspected him of being a fraud. Di Mambro frequently used projectors to make visions appear at Solar Templar ceremonies. He had brainwashed his followers into seeing themselves as a chosen people, destined to be reborn on another world orbiting Syrius. In 1995 most of the group committed suicide by setting themselves on fire, though some who died had apparently been murdered by their tragically delusional companions.

There is also a bridge between Templarism and modern witchcraft, or Wicca. Englishman Gerald Gardner (1884–1964) was among Wicca's founders. He had belonged to quasi-Masonic organisations, the Rosicrucian Order and the *Ordo Templi Orientalis* (OTO). The OTO combines Masonic and Templarist elements with tantric sex-magic. It was founded in 1895 by Karl Keller, a wealthy Austrian, on the fringe of Freemasonry, interested in eastern mysticism and the occult. The OTO credited the Knights Templar with arcane knowledge. In 1915 they were taken over by the notorious occultist Aleister Crowley, who liked to be known as the Beast. Another of the names Crowley adopted for himself was *Baphomet*. After his death in 1947, the controversial Order dwindled, but revived in the 1980s, and seems to survive as little more than a Crowley appreciation society. It must seem an insult to the long-dead followers of Hugues de Paynes that such modern crackpots and hedonists would usurp the name of the Templars.

The more respectable modern Templars, that is the Freemasons and SMOTJ, are social groups, that would be more given to washing their meals down with a few good glasses of wine – or, at least, that is the impression one gets. Their initiates, in fairness, are not unanimous in what they believe about the origins of their societies. Yet modern 'Templars' seek to restore honour to the extinct Order by reviving its name. They find something worthy and romantic in emulating the old knights. They seem content to let the truth remain shrouded in mystery. Their rituals and their fantasising do not seem to do any harm. However, the historical Knights Templar were real people who lived and died. All of them chose to relinquish the consolations of family and worldly luxuries for monastic austerity or self-sacrifice. Some bore extremes of suffering in a faraway land, ultimately giving up their lives (as they saw it) for the sake of their religion, their brethren and their God. There was nothing trivial about that.

Of course, as the Order of the Temple of Solomon expanded, like other monastic Orders, it lost some of its original purity and grew more complex. Their warlike function was always, it may moreover be argued, somewhat at odds with the pacifism preached by Jesus. It is ironic, too, that the spiritual knights whom Saint Bernard of Clairvaux praised for purifying the Temple in Jerusalem with their presence ended up themselves as money lenders. However, despite this, for two centuries the Templars remained broadly true to their founding ideal, and overall remained a force for moderation in their times. It is most ironic that many of the Templars who survived fighting for the Cross overseas returned home only to suffer and die at Christian hands. Meanwhile, other military and religious institutions, more prepared to prey on and oppress vulnerable citizens, survived.

We, in the modern world, should not lose sight of that, and no one should take the Templars' name in vain. However, above all, it should be our duty to try our best to seek to appreciate them for what they truly were, rather than what we would like to imagine they were.

APPENDIX B

Grand Masters of the Knights Templar

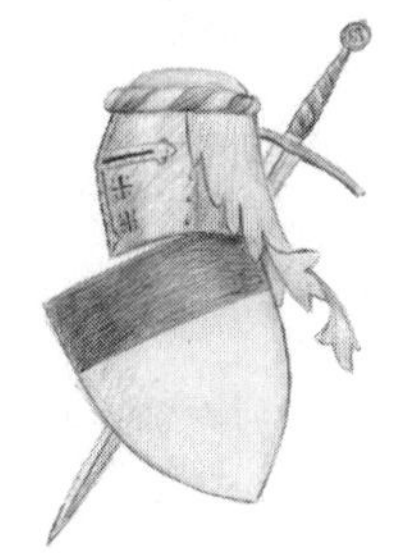

I	1119	Hugues de Payen
II	1137	Robert de Craon
III	1149	Everard des Barres
IV	1152	Bernard de Tremelay
V	1153	André de Montbard
VI	1156	Bertrand de Blanquefort
VII	1169	Philip de Millay of Nablus
VIII	1171	Odo de St Armand
IX	1180	Arnold de Torroja
X	1185	Gerard de Ridefort
XI	1191	Robert de Sablé
XII	1194	Gilbert Erail
XIII	1201	Philip de Plessiez
XIV	1210	Guillaume de Chatres
XV	1219	Peter de Montaigu
XVI	1232	Armand de Perigord
XVII	1244	Richard de Burres
XVIII	1247	Guillaume de Sonnac
XIX	1256	Thomas Bérard
XX	1273	Guillaume de Beaujeu
XXI	1291	Theobold Gaudin
XXII	1293	Jacques de Molay

APPENDIX C
Timeline

AD	
1098–9	First Crusade. Jerusalem taken by Godfrey de Bouillon
1118	Hugues de Payens and original Templars arrive in Jerusalem
1128–9	Council of Troyes. Templar Order recognised
1130	Hugues de Payens leads his new Templars to Jerusalem
1136	Hugues de Payens dies
1147–9	Second Crusade, led by Louis VII. Loss of Tripoli
1160	Papal bull against people pulling Templars from their horses
1163–9	Amalric's expedition in Egypt. Amalric accuses Templars of surrendering 'impregnable cave' to Shirkuh, and hangs twelve of them
1168	Templars refuse to support Amalric's third Egyptian adventure
1173	Templars kill Assassin envoy to Amalric, worsening relations
1174	Saladin comes to power in Syria
1179	Third Lateran Council. William of Tyre attacks Templars
1185	Leprous King Baldwin IV succeeded by his sister Sybilla, and Guy
1187	Hattin. Templar prisoners beheaded. Jerusalem falls to Saladin
1189–92	Third Crusade. Richard I wins victory at Arsuf. Fails to take Jerusalem

1202–4	'Fourth Crusade' sacks Constantinople. Much despoliation and plunder
1207	Innocent III criticises Templar abuses, pride and hautiness
1208–29	Albigensian Crusade in Languedoc. Liquidation of 'Cathar heresy'
1221	Fifth Crusade flounders in Egypt
1228	Sixth Crusade. Frederick II regains Jerusalem by diplomacy
1231	Gregory IX founds the Inquisition (Holy Office)
1239	Crusade of Theobold de Champagne and Richard of Cornwall
1240	Strife between Military Orders. Templars sack Nablus.
1243	Templars' faction drives Frederick II's deputies from Outremer
1244	Khorezmians take Jerusalem and slaughter Christian populace
1258	Mongols (Tartars) arrive in Middle East. Sack Baghdad
1260	Mamelukes enter Palestine. Defeat Mongols at Ain Jalut, Nazareth
	Baybars seizes Aleppo, expels Assassins and masters Syria
1261	Christian army defeated by Mamelukes
1265	Clement IV warns Temple that it would perish without the Church
1266	Baybars takes Safed. Castle ringed in severed heads of Templars
1268	Baybars takes Jaffa and destroys Antioch
1267	Louis IX takes Cross again
1270	Louis IX dies during indifferent campaign in Carthage
1271	Edward of England comes Crusading. Negotiates truce with Baybars
1274	Council of Lyons. Little interest in or optimism about new Crusade
1291	Loss of Acre to Mamelukes, under Al Ashraf. End of Outremer
1305 Nov	Clement V's coronation. Crusade proclaimed, but never happens
June–Sep	Return to good money (i.e. not devalued) of Louis IX in France
1307 14 Sep	Philip IV issues secret orders to arrest the Templars
13 Oct	Arrest of Templars
19 Oct	Paris hearings begin
24 Oct	De Molay confesses. Repeats next day at Paris University

27 Oct	Clement V expresses papal indignation
9 Nov	Confession of Hugues de Pairaud
22 Nov	*Pastoralis Praeminentae*
24 Dec	De Molay revokes confession
1308 Feb	Clement suspends Inquisition
late Feb	Philip sends seven constitutional questions to Masters of Theology
24–9 Mar	Meeting of the Estates-General in Tours
26 May	Philip and Plaisians intimidate Clement at Poitiers
27 June	Philip sends Clement seventy-two chosen Templars, to hear their confessions
5 July	*Subit Aassidue*
13 July	Clement leaves Poitiers
17–20 July	Cardinals hear Templar leaders at Chinon
1309 Mar	Clement establishes curia in Avignon
Spring	Beginning of episcopal enquiry
8 Aug	Papal commission constituted to enquire into entire Order
22 Nov	First hearing
26 Nov	De Molay makes first appearance
2 Mar	De Molay's last appearance
14 Mar	127 articles of accusation read to defending Templars
28 Mar	Meeting of defenders in episcopal palace gardens, Paris
1310 7 April	Bologna and Provins lead legal defence
12 May	Fifty-four Templars burned
1311 5 June	End of cardinals' hearing
16 Oct	Council of Vienne opens. Later seven Templars appear to defend Order
1312 20 Mar	Philip IV descends on Vienne
22 Mar	*Vox in excelso* disbands the Knights Templar
1314 18 Mar	Burning of Jacques de Molay
1314 20 Apr	Clement V dies
1314 29 Nov	Philip IV dies

Addendum

Subsequent to completing this book I learned of the discovery of a document perporting to be part of a secret Vatican archive, and relating to the trial of the Templars, previously thought to have been lost in the Napoleonic era. The parchment supposedly shows that Pope Clement V sent his own emissaries to question Jaques de Molay and other Templar grandees held prisoner in the castle of Chinon. Astonishingly, it is claimed that, at what amounted to a secret trial, the Templars were exonerated but, fearing Church schism (or more probably I would say, the wrath of Philip IV), the Pope kept this verdict secret. These findings were published recently by a researcher named Frale, it seems, and were also reported in *The Times*.

It is further alleged that the Templars at Chinon claimed that the practices of denying Christ and spitting on the Cross were enacted to prepare Knights for what they may be made to do if captured by the Muslims in the Holy Land. The humiliations they may be subjected to were played out and they were taught to renounce their religion with their lips but not with their hearts.

This seems to contradict the prevailing view among historians that the charges against the Templars were fabricated, for financial motives, by Philip IV and his chief minister Guillaume de Nogaret. The idea of the Templars role-playing the unpleasant things that they could expect if captured by the enemy does not seem entirely far-fetched, as something similar is still done by élite forces such as the SAS (indeed it forms a core part of their selection process). Moreover, I was put in mind of the medieval Assassin sect's doctrine of *taqiyya*, or caution. This was the belief that it was acceptable, nay, desirable, for Ismaili *da'is* to deny every part of their creed if it was expedient, or in order to pass undetected by their Sunni enemies. There is, of course, ample evidence of Templar/Assassin contact. However, this said, feigning apostasy goes against the Christian attitude to martyrdom, that it was better to be killed for one's beliefs than to sin by repudiating them. Because of the way the Knights Templar had embraced martydom at Islamic hands after the defeat at Hattin, for example, I would have to question the assertion that the Templars would actively rehearse renouncing Christ. It would also surprise me if the Church had pardoned such a practice.

Bibliography

Primary Sources

Anonymous lament: 'The Downfall of the Templars and a letter in their defence', 1308, translated by C R Cheney, in *Medieval Texts and Studies*, 1978.

Bernard of Clairvaux, *In Praise of the New Knighthood* (*Liber ad milited Templi: De laude Novae Militaie*), early twelfth century, translated by Conrad Greenia. [website: http://orb.rhodes.edu/encyclop/religion/monastic/bernard.htm]

Paris, Matthew, *Chronicles of Matthew Paris* (*Observations of Thirteenth-Century Life*), translated from Latin, edited and with an Introduction by Richard Vaughan, Cambridge, 1984 & 1993.

Upton-Ward, Judith (trans.), *The Primitive Rule of the Templars*, ORB: The Online Reference Book for Medieval Studies. [website: http://orb.rhodes.edu/encyclop/religion/monastic/T_Rule.htm]

Warren, C and Reigner Conder, C, *The Survey of Western Palestine*. 1884 [website: http://www.templemount.org/warren1.html]

William of Tyre, *Historia rerum in partibus transmarinis gestarum* (*A History of Deeds Done Overseas*), XII, 7, *Patrologia Latina* 201, 526–7: The Foundation of the Order of Knights Templar (Internet medieval sourcebook), translated by James Brundage. [website: http://www.fordham.edu/halsall/source/tyre-templars.html]

Secondary Sources

Addison, Charles G, *The History of the Knights Templars, the Temple Church, and The Temple*, London, 1842.
Anderson, William, *Green Man*, London: HarperCollins, 1990.
Baigent, M; Leigh, R and Lincoln, H, *The Holy Blood and the Holy Grail*, London, Cape, 1982.
Barber, Malcolm, *The Trial of the Templars*, Cambridge: CUP, 1978.
——— *The New Knighthood, A History of the Order of the Temple*, Cambridge: CUP, 1994
Barlett, Robert (ed.), *Medieval Panorama*, London: Thames & Hudson, 2001.
Billings, Malcolm, *The Cross and the Crescent*, London: BBC Books, 1981.
Brega, Isabella, *Egypt, Past and Present*, Tiger Books International, 1998.
Burman, Edward, *The Templars: Knights of God*, Aquarian Press, 1986.
——— *The Assassins – Holy Killers of Islam*, London: HarperCollins, 1988.
Cohn, Norman, *Europe's Inner Demons*, Sussex University Press, 1975.
Currer-Briggs, Noel, *The Shroud and the Grail*, London: Weidenfeld & Nicolson, 1979.
Dafoe, Steven A, *Unholy Worship: The Myth of the Baphomet, Templar/ Freemason Connection*, Templar Books, 1998.
Duhmus, Joseph, *The Middle Ages*, History Book Club, 1969.
Farmer, David, *Oxford Dictionary of Saints*, Oxford: OUP, 1997.
Frayling, Christopher, *Strange Landscape: A Journey Through the Middle Ages*, London: BBC Books, 1995.
Forey, Alan, *The Military Orders from the Twelfth to the Early Fourteenth Centuries*, Basingstoke: Macmillan, 1992.
George, Leonard, *The Encyclopedia of Heresies and Heretics*, London: Robson, 1995.
Godwin, Malcolm, *The Holy Grail, its Origins, Secrets and Meaning Revealed*, London: Bloomsbury, 1994.
Greenwood, Susan, *The Encyclopedia of Magic and Witchcraft*, London: Anness, 2002
Grierson, Roderick and Munro-Hay, Stuart, *The Ark of the Covenant*, London: Phoenix, 2000.
Haagensen, Erling and Lincoln, Henry, *The Templars' Secret Island*, Moreton-in-Marsh: Windrush, 2000.
Haldon, John, *Byzantium. A History*, Stroud: Tempus, 2000.
Hancock, Graham, *The Sign and the Seal*, London: Mandarin, 1992.
Jones, Terry and Ereira, Alan, *Crusades*, London: Penguin/BBC Books 1996.
Knight, Christopher and Lomas, Robert, *The Hiram Key*, London: Century, 1996.

Laidler, Keith, *The Head of God. The Lost Treasure of the Templars*, London: Orion, 1998.
Lea, H C, *A History of the Inquisition in the Middle Ages*, Vol. III, New York, 1888.
Lord, Evelyn, *The Knights Templar in Britain*, Harlow: Longman, 2002.
Maxwell-Stuart, P G, *Chronicles of the Popes*, London: Thames & Hudson, 1997.
——— *Witchcraft. A History*, Stroud: Tempus, 2000.
Newman, P, *A Short History of Cyprus*, London: Longman Green, 1940.
Nicholson, Helen, *The Knights Templar: A New History*, Stroud: Sutton, 2001.
Oldenbourg, Zoé, *The Crusades*. London: BCA 1998.
O'Shea, Stephen, *The Perfect Heresy*, London: Profile Books, 2001.
Partner, Peter, *The Murdered Magicians: the Templars and their Myth*, Oxford: OUP, 1981.
Read, Piers Paul, *The Templars*, London: Weidenfeld & Nicolson, 1999.
Riley-Smith, J (ed.), *The Oxford Illustrated History of the Crusades*, Oxford: OUP, 1995.
Robinson, John J, *Born in Blood. The Lost Secrets of Freemasonry*, London: Evans, 1990
Rudolph, K, *Gnosis*, Edinburgh, 1983.
Schonfield, Hugh, *The Essene Odyssey*, London: Element Books, 1984.
Seward, Desmond, *The Monks of War*, London: Methuen, 1972.
Sinclair, Andrew, *The Discovery of the Grail*, Crown Publishers, 1998
Strayer, Joseph, *The Reign of Philip the Fair*, Princeton University Press, 1980.
Vessay, Norman, *The Medieval Soldier*, London: Arthur Barker, 1971.
Wheatley, Denis, *The Devil and All His Works*, Peerage Books, 1983.
Zaczec, Iain, *The Art of the Celts*, London: Parkgate Books, 1997.

Useful Internet addresses

http://www.fireplug.net/~r.shand/streams/masons/blood.html.
(Trial by Blood and Fire)

http://www.intranet,ca/~magicworks/knights/head.html
(Stephen Dafoe's History and Myths of the Knights Templar. This contains much data, including primary sources such as the Templar Rule, as well as a wealth of images)

http://www.albino.com/circle/pos/booknotes/revelations.html
(John the Baptist/Templars)

http://www.veiling.nl/anne/templars/2_7.htm
(Catholics, Heretics and Heresy Part 2: The Templars)

http://orb.rhodes.edu/encyclop/religion/monastic/templar.htm.
(Malcolm Barber's essay on the Templars)

http://www.kingmere.demon.co.uk/SMOTJ/temple/temp_1-1.html
(*Temple*, magazine of the Modern KT)

http://www.templars.org.uk/history.html

http://www.web-site.co.uk/knights-templar/templar2_5.html
(The excavation by the Templars of the Temple of Solomon)

http://members.xoom.com/_EMCM/doru_gavril/accusations.htm
(Overview of the trial of the Order)

http://www. thornr.demon.co.uk/kchrist/tomar.html
(Tomar, HQ of the Order of Christ)

Index

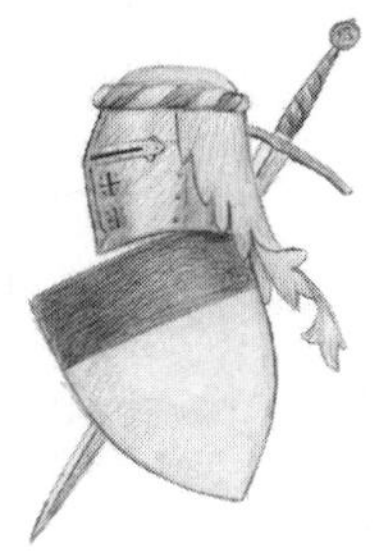

Abbasids, 9
Absolution, 119, 138, 159, 160, 164
Acre, 32, 41, 45, 59, 61, 63–6, 70, 71, 73, 81, 84, 86–90, 114, 158, 178
Adam de Wallaincourt, 34
Addison, Charles G, xiv, xv
Ad Providam, 173
Agnes (Queen), 60
Aimery (King of Jerusalem), 75
al-Adil, 72, 75
Alan Marcel, 52, 80
Al Aqsa mosque, 12, 17, 45, 49, 65
al-Ashraf, 89, 90
Albigensian *see* Cathars
Alexandria, 73, 85, 130, 132, 135, 137, 179, 180
Alexius Comnenus, 9
Alexius III, 74
Alexius IV Angelus, 74
Alexius V Ducus, 74
al-Kamil, 81, 137
Allah, 7, 8, 128
Amalric (King of Jerusalem), 51, 52, 56, 57
Amaury de Lusignan, 97, 167
André de Montbard, 18, 40
Anglo Saxon Chronicle, 30
Antioch, 11, 20, 45, 56, 60, 65, 82, 87, 88
anti-Semitism, 10, 131
Antonio Sicci de Vercelli, 116
Aragon, 97, 155, 165, 166
Archembald de St Amand, 19
architecture, 19, 44–7
archives, 143, 144
Ark of the Covenant, 3, 4, 20, 21, 117, 127, 129, 130, 136, 137, 177, 184, 188
Armand de Perigord, 81–3
Arnold Amaury, 75
Arnold of Torroja, 58
Arsuf, battle of 72
Arthur, King, 126
Ascalon, 57, 66, 73
Assassins, 22, 51–2, 56, 72–3, 86, 127–9
Atlit *see* Pilgrim's Castle
Augustine of Hippo, 6, 25
Avignon, 111, 135, 180
Axum, 136, 137

Ayme d'Oselier, 167, 168
Ayyubids, 72, 79

Babylon, 4, 80
Bagras (castle), 45
baillis, 99, 109, 110, 116
Balak, 21
Balcanifer, 33
Baldock (Herts), 43, 46
Baldwin I, 12
Baldwin II, 12, 17, 18, 20, 21, 37
Baldwin III, 55, 56
Baldwin IV, 57, 59
Baldwin V, 59
Baldwin of Flanders, Count, 74
Balin of Ibelin, 64, 73
Ballentradoch (Temple), 30
banking, 43, 48–50
Bannockburn, 176
Baphomet, xiii, 115, 117, 124, 132, 186, 187, 189
Barbarossa *see* Frederick I
Barber, Malcolm, xv
Barcelona, 178
Baybars, 83, 85–7
Beaufort (castle), 58
Beauseant, 33, 176
Beguine, 140
Beit Allah *see* Dome of the Rock
Belbeis, 56
Belvoir (castle), 45
Benedict, Saint, 6, 25
Benedict XI, 100, 113
Berengaria of Navarre, 70
Bernard, Bishop of Pamiers, 102
Bernard de Tremelay, 40
Bernard de Vado, 111
Bernard of Clairvaux, 1, 8, 19, 25, 28, 39, 40, 47, 127, 129, 134, 190
Bible, The, 3–6, 9, 32, 138
Bibliothèque Royale, xii
Bisol, 19
Black Madonnas, 137, 140
Blanquefort, Bertrand de 56
Bogomils, 135
Bohemond of Toranto, 11, 12
Bohemond III of Antioch, 56
Bologna, xiv
Boniface VIII, 100, 112, 113
Boniface of Montferrat, 73
Bornholm, 47
Brian de Jay, 156, 163
Bristol, 47
Bruer (Temple), xiv, 161
burning of the Templars, 151–3, 174
busses, 48
Byzantium, 6, 8, 9, 11, 12, 37, 39, 55, 58, 65, 69, 74, 75, 88, 97, 179, 180

Cabbalism, 131, 186
Calatrava, Order of, 117
calf worship, 159, 161, 169
Canterbury, 38, 46, 58, 69, 74, 75, 88, 97, 180
Capetians, 84, 88, 99, 101, 134, 166, 173, 176, 177
'Caput LVIIIm', 116, 152
Carcassonne, 75, 117, 153
castles, 44–6, 64, 73, 82, 115, 127
Cathars, xv, 75, 76, 96, 100, 114, 119, 133–5, 141, 189
cat worship, 115, 118, 133, 134, 140, 141, 153
celibacy, 6, 27
Celts, 124, 125, 141
Cernunnos, 124, 125
Chambonnet, 150, 152
Charles of Anjou, 84, 88
children's Crusade, 79, 87
Chrétien de Troyes, 16, 117, 126
Christopher de Gamma, 177
Church of the Nativity, 7
Church of the Resurrection, 7, 17
Cistercians, 18–29, 46, 127, 129
Cîteaux, 19
Clairvaux, 19, 40

Clement V, 97, 101, 102, 111–15, 137, 147, 156, 157, 159, 163, 165, 168, 172–5
Clermont, 10
Cluny, 50
Cohn, Norman, xiv–xv
Comnenus, John, 37
Comnenus, Manuel, 41
Conrad III (of Germany), 39
Conrad of Montferrat, 65, 66, 71, 72
Constantine, 5–7
Constantinople *see* Byzantium
Coptic Christians, 135–7, 179
cords, 2, 3, 106, 118, 134, 160
Crowley, Aleister, 198
Crusades, xi, 10–12, 15, 16, 20, 31, 38, 39, 55, 58, 66, 69, 70, 73 –5, 80, 95, 105, 171, 175, 179–81
Custos Chapellae, 46
Cyprus, 55, 60, 70, 71, 88, 95, 96, 98, 101, 116, 144, 167, 168, 177, 179, 180

Damascus, 4, 8, 11, 37, 39–41, 57, 58, 63, 80, 82, 83
Damietta, 79–82, 85, 86
Dante, xii, 106
David (King of Judah),3, 188
David I (of Scotland), 30
defence of Order, 144–5, 147–52, 162, 163, 172
de Joinville, Lord, 85
de Mowbray, Roger, 40
demons, 19, 26, 29, 47, 105, 117, 118, 129, 138, 140, 167, 188
denial of Christ, 106, 113, 114, 129, 138, 140, 141, 143, 153, 162, 163
Devil worship, 106, 107, 115–18, 120, 125, 133, 135, 140, 141, 162, 181
de Vitry, Cardinal, 41
Dieudonne, Abbot of Lagny, 158, 163
Diniz (King of Portugal), 177
Dinsley (Temple), 43, 108
Dome of the Rock mosque, 8
Dominicans, xii, 75–7, 111, 112, 131, 135, 142, 148
Dublin, 157, 160
Du Puy, Pierre, xii

Eagle (Essex), 27, 40, 158
Edessa, 38, 39, 82
Edward I, 83, 88, 100, 156
Edward II, 155–8, 174, 176, 177
Edward III, 176, 183
Egypt, 21, 51, 56, 57, 72, 79, 80, 85, 86, 118, 132, 186
Eleanor of Aquitaine, 39, 58, 70, 135, 136
Elephas Levi, xiii, 118, 125
England, 27, 30, 40, 46–8, 53, 58, 73, 75, 83, 84, 88, 127, 131, 155–65, 176
Enrico Donaldo (Doge of Venice), 74
Eschiva (Countess), 61
Esquin de Floyran, 106, 175
Essenes, xiii, 130
Estates General, 112, 172
Etienne de Troyes, 106, 115, 116, 144
Ethiopia, 51, 97, 98, 177, 187
Eugenius III, 39, 50
Everard des Barres, 39, 40
Exemen de Lenda, 165

Falkirk, 156
Fatimids, 11, 56
Feudalism, 33, 34, 43
Finke, H, xiv
Franks, 7, 9, 12 21, 37, 49, 51, 55, 58, 63, 87, 89
Frederick I (Emperor) 'Barbarossa', 69
Frederick II (Emperor), 81–4
Frederick von Salm, 168

Freemasons, xii, xiii, 130, 132, 133, 184–90
Fulcher of Chatres, 12
Fulk d'Anjou (King of Jerusalem), 17, 19, 37

Galceron de Teusum, 138
Garter (Order) *see* Order of the Garter
Garway (Temple), 125, 163
Gaza, 40, 57, 66, 72, 82, 83
Genoa, 47, 79, 87, 88, 97, 167, 180
Geoffroi de Gonneville, 114, 162, 174
Geoffroi de St Omer, 16, 19
Gerard de Pasigo, 110
Gerard de Ridefort, 59, 61, 63, 66
Gerard de Villiers, 110, 144
Germany, 168, 186
Gilbert d'Assaily, 56
Gilbert Horal (or Erail), 73
Gilles Aicelin, Archbishop of Narbonne, 147, 151
Giovanni da Carignano, 97
Glastonbury, 126
Gnosticism, xiii, 6, 21, 114, 127, 131–3, 139, 141, 143, 186
Godfrey de Bouillon, 11, 12, 188
Godfrey Wedderburn, 34–5
Gondemar, 18
Goral, 19
Gorgon Medusa, 117
Greece, 74, 88, 140
Gregory VIII (Pope), 66
Gregory IX, 52, 76, 83, 140
Guichard, Bishop of Troyes, 102
Guichard de Marsellac, 150
Guillaume de Beaujeu, 88, 90
Guillaume de Chatres, 79, 80
Guillaume de Nogaret, 100, 106, 112, 113, 135, 140, 147, 149, 172
Guillaume de Paris, 102, 110, 140
Guillaume de Plaisians, 112, 148, 149
Guillaume (or William) de Sonnac, 85
Guillaume Pidoyne, 152
Guillaume Robert, 147
Guy de Charney, 174
Guy de Lusignan (King of Jerusalem), 59–61, 63, 66, 70–2

Harbay Zagwe, 51, 136
Harding, Stephen, 129
Hattin, battle of, 61–2, 64, 66, 83
heads worship, 106, 107, 109, 114–16, 123–5, 131, 152, 153, 161, 165
Helena, 7
Henry, Count of Champagne ('the Liberal'), 73, 126
Henry II of Cyprus, 96 97
Henry I of England, 30
Henry II of England, 58, 59, 64, 66, 70, 131, 168
Henry III of England, 46, 47, 52, 53, 75, 83, 97
Henry VI (Emperor of Germany), 73
Henry the Navigator, 177
Heraclius, Patriarch of Jerusalem, 58–60, 62, 65, 66
heresy, 5, 6, 76, 77, 100, 106, 113, 127, 140, 141, 143, 144
Herod, 4, 21
Hertfordshire, 43, 46
Hiram, King of Tyre, 3
Holy Grail, 20, 125–7, 143
Holy Land, 3, 7, 12, 29, 30, 34, 39, 41, 44, 47, 53, 74, 79, 82, 84, 88, 89, 95, 128, 180
Holy Office *see* Inquisition
Holy Roman Empire *see* Germany
Holy Spear (or Lance), 20, 74, 126
homosexuality *see* sodomy
Horal, Gilbert, 73
Hospitallers, 21, 30, 31, 34, 56, 58, 63, 65, 70, 72, 81, 83–5, 88–90, 96,

98, 123, 127, 134, 167, 173–7, 180, 181
Hugh, Count of Champagne, 16, 19, 20
Hugh von Salm, 168
Hugues de Pairaud, 112, 115, 117, 144, 174
Hugues de Payens, 15, 17, 19, 20, 28, 30, 37, 46, 115
Humphrey of Toron, 71

Iberia, 8, 45, 46, 165, 166, 177
idolatry, 115, 117, 123, 138, 173
Ilgazi, 21
Imbert Blanke, 158, 164
Innocent III (Pope), 73, 74, 75, 76
Innocent IV (Pope), 77, 84
Inquisition, xii, 75–7, 102, 107, 110, 111, 133, 135, 140, 144, 158, 159, 160, 151, 163, 168, 181
Ireland, 157, 160
Isaac Angelus, 69, 74
Isaac Ducas Comnenus, 70
Isabella (Queen of Jerusalem), 71, 73
Isabella (the 'She-Wolf') of France, 155, 176, 177
Isis, 132, 138, 139
Islam, 7–9, 38, 41, 114, 117, 128
Israel, 3, 186
Italy, 166, 179

Jacob's Ford, 58
Jacquelin de Mailly, 60–1
Jacques de Molay, 96, 98, 102, 110–12, 120, 147–9, 163, 164, 168, 174, 175, 184
James II or Aragon, 109, 165–7, 177
Jean de Challons, 110, 144
Jean de Joinville, 85
Jean de Montreal, 149
Jean de Nadro, 166
Jean-Marc Larminius, 185, 186
Jerusalem, 3, 4, 6, 8–12, 15–17, 32, 40, 56, 57, 59, 63–5, 72
Jerusalem Church, 4, 5
Jesus Christ, 4–5, 6, 8, 12, 15, 20, 26, 29, 80, 82, 84, 106, 113–14, 130, 138
Jeune, Canon R P M, xiii
Jihad, 8, 38, 57, 58, 60, 180
Johannes Michaelensis, 28
John (Saint) the Baptist, 21, 74, 114, 117, 128, 130
John XXII, 176
John (Prince, later King) 'Lackland', 73, 75, 99
John Comnenus (Emperor), 37
John de Eure, Sir, 161, 162
John de Stoke, 163, 164
John of Neves, 180
Johnson, George Frederic, xiii
Joscelin de Courtney, Count of Edessa, 38
Joscius, Archbishop of Tyre, 66
Joseph of Arimathea, 4, 126, 138
Judaism, 3, 9, 129–31, 136
Justinian, 8

Kemel ed-Din, 21
Khorezmians, 82–4
Knights of Christ (Portuguese Order of), 177, 183, 187
Knights of Lazarus, 89
Koran, The, 7, 9

La Forbie, 83, 84
Lalibela, 51, 136
Languedoc, 75, 76, 134, 139
Laon, 150
La Rochelle, 47, 110
Lea, Henry Charles, xiv
Les Grandes Chroniques de France, 140
Levi *see* Elephas
Lincoln, 131, 157, 158, 160, 163
London, 30, 34, 46, 50, 52, 59, 83, 97, 157, 163, 164, 183

London Temple, 59
Longinus, 23 n9
Louis VII, 39, 41, 70
Louis VIII, 76
Louis IX, 84–8, 99, 123, 125
Louis X, 175
Lull, Raimon, xii, 131
Lyons, 88, 101

Malek el Afdul, 60
Malta, 123, 144, 180, 181
Mamelukes, 38, 57, 83, 85–90, 179
Mandaeans, 132
Mansel, Robert, 41
Marguerite (Queen of France), 85, 86
maritime activity *see* ships
Mary (the Virgin), 19, 32, 44, 127, 138, 139, 150, 158, 160, 163
Mary Magdalene, 4, 21, 39, 75, 132, 138, 139, 188
Matilda (Queen), 40
Matthew le Sarmage, 116
Mecca, 7, 8, 49, 50
Melisende (Queen of Jerusalem), 17, 37, 40, 55
Merlan (prison), 110, 144
Merovingians, 139, 188
Milicia Dei, 44
Milites Templi, 44
Mohammad, 7, 8, 65, 82, 117
monasticism, 6, 19, 25, 32, 46, 136
Mongols, 86, 87
Montguisard, 57
Montsegur, 135
Moses, 3, 21, 125, 145 n6, 186
Muslims, 7, 10–11, 15, 21, 33, 48–50, 55, 114, 123

Nag-Hammadi, 132
Napoleon, xii, 123, 180
necrophilia, 116, 117
Nero, 5
New Temple (London), 49, 50
Nicolai, Friedrich, xiii
Nicolas IV, 89, 95
Nicopolis, 180
Normans, 9, 11, 20
Nur ed-Din, 38, 40, 41, 52, 55–7, 60, 65

Odo de St Armand, 52, 56, 57, 58
Omar (Caliph), 8, 9
Omne Datum Optimum, 43, 44
Order of Teutonic Knights, 70, 81, 89, 96, 179
Order of the Garter, 183
Ordo Templi Orientis, 189
Othman (Caliph), 8
Ottomans, 144, 179–81
Outremer, 15, 40, 55, 65, 72, 86, 88

papacy, 7, 9, 10, 43, 51, 75, 76, 83, 100–11, 171, 175, 179
Paris, 30, 39, 45, 102, 111, 112, 120, 147–9, 151, 174
Paris, Matthew, 51, 82, 86, 133
Paris, University of 109, 111, 112
Pastoralis Praeeminentatiae, 112, 156, 157
Paterines, 140
Paul of Tarsus, 4–6
Payen de Montdidier, 19
Pedro II of Aragon ('the Catholic'), 76
penances, 26, 34, 58, 159, 163, 164
pentagrams, 118
Peter de Montaigne, 80
Peter the Hermit, 10, 16
Philip II Augustus (King of France), 59, 66, 70, 71, 99
Philip IV ('the Fair'), xii, 98, 100–5, 107, 109–12, 115, 121, 142, 144, 147, 151, 157, 165, 167
Philip de Plessiez, 74
Philip d'Ibelin, 167
Pierre d'Arbeley, 117

Pierre de Bologna, 148, 149, 150, 152
Philip of Nablous, 56
pilgrimage, 6, 7, 9, 15, 16, 18, 20, 48, 79, 130, 138
Pilgrims' Castle, 45, 47, 73, 84, 89, 127
Poitiers, 112, 115, 121, 147, 172
Poitiers, Battle of, 9
Ponsard de Gizy, 139, 147
Portugal, 40, 155, 165, 166, 177, 183
Prates, Hans, xiii
Prester John, 51, 136
Priure de Sion, 139, 188
privileges, 44, 45, 46, 48–53
Prussia, 96

Qalawun, 88, 89

Raimon Lull *see* Lull
Ramsey, Andrew, xiii
Raoul de Gizy, 117, 152
Raoul de Presles, 150
Raven, William, 158
Raymond de St Gilles, 11, 12
Raymond of Toulouse, 11, 12
Raymond VI of Toulouse, 75
Raymond II of Tripoli, 39
Raymond III of Tripoli, 57, 58, 59–62
Raynouard, François, xiii–xiv
Reconquista, 45, 46, 165, 177
Reginald de Vichiers, 86
Renaud de Provins, 148, 149, 152
Rennes le Chaeau, 188
Reynald de Chatillon, 55, 60, 61, 63, 71
Rhodes, 96, 144, 180
Ricault Bonomel, 114
Richard I (Lionheart), 70–3
Richard of Cornwall, 81, 82
Robert de Craon, 37–8
Robert de Sable, 70, 73
Robert the Bruce, 156, 160
Roger de Flor, 97
Roger de Molines, 61
Rosslyn Chapel, 187
Royston, xiv, 107
Rule, 25–8, 30, 119, 175

sacraments, 115, 135, 148, 163
St Clair (or Sinclair) family, 20, 30, 187
St John-Hope, William, xiv
Saladin, 57, 58, 60–6, 69, 70, 73
Saphet (castle), 45, 82, 87
Sartiges, 150, 152
Scirra Colonna, 100
Scotland, 20, 30, 34, 132, 156, 157, 160, 176, 187
secrets, 32, 24, 118, 121, 122, 186, 188
senechaux, 99
Sens, 151, 152, 172, 174
Sheba, Queen of, 136
ships, 47, 48, 65, 66, 70, 86
Shirkuh, 57
Sicard de Vaur of Narbonne, 158, 162
Sicily, 55, 83, 84
Sidon, 89, 166
Sigismund of Hungary, 180
Simon de Montfort (the Elder), 75–6
Simon de Montfort (the Younger), 53, 83, 97
Sinan, 52, 72, 127
Sinclair *see* St Clair
Sisters of the Temple, 27, 139
sodomy, xii, 32, 116, 119, 120, 134, 142, 173
Solar Templars, 189
Solomon's Temple, xi, 3, 4, 8, 17, 20, 29, 129, 184, 186
Sophia, 118, 127, 132, 139
Sovereign and Military Order (SMOTJ), 184–6, 190
Spiritual Franciscans, 141

Stephen (King), 40
Stephen de Stapelbrugge, 163
Stephen of Blois, 11
Suger of St Denis, 39, 60
Sybilla (Queen of Jerusalem), 59, 64, 65, 71

Tancred (King of Sicily), 70
Tancred de Hauteville, 12
'Templarism', xiii, 139, 185–8, 190
Temple Church (London), xiv, 34, 46, 47
Temple Cressing (Essex), 46
Temple Denny (Cambs), 27
Temple Wetherby, 162
Terric (Preceptor of Jerusalem), 63
Tertullian, 5
Teutonic Knights, Order of, 70, 81, 89, 96, 179
Theobold Gaudin, 90
Theodora (Greek Princess), 55
Theodoric, 45
Thomas de Thoroldeby, 163
Tibald, Count of Champagne, 73, 81
Tiberias, 41, 64
Tiscelin Sorrel, 18
Titus, 4, 21
Tomar, 177
torture, 77, 110, 111, 142, 147, 149, 150, 151, 153, 158, 159, 161, 163, 165, 181
Tours, 112
treasure, 107, 110, 167, 177, 187
Troyes, 16, 19
True Cross, 7, 20, 61–3, 74, 81, 123
Turin Shroud, 117
Tyre, 21, 65, 66

Umayyads, 8–9
Unur, 38
Urban II, 10
Urban III, 66
Usama ibn-Munqidh, 49, 50

Vasco da Gama, 177
Venice, 47, 73, 74, 87, 88, 96, 180
Vézelay, 39, 139
Vienne, 171–3, 175
von Hammer-Purgstall, Joseph, xiii, xiv, 132, 133
Vox in excelso, 172, 184

Waldensians, 133
Wallace, William, 156
Walter, 66
Walter de Mesnil, 52
Walter le Bachelor, 159, 162, 163
Walter Mapp, 51, 140
Walter of Hemingborough, 172
Walter Sans-Avoir, 16
'Westford Knight', 187
Wilcke, W F, xiii, xiv
William de la Fenne, 162
William de la Forde, 161
William de la More, 156–9, 162, 164
William of Montferrat, 59
William of Sonac *see* Guillaume de Sonac
William of Tyre, 15, 38, 41, 50, 52, 56, 57, 60
William Raven, 158
witchcraft, xv, 35, 77, 100, 102, 107, 118, 120, 140, 141, 181, 189
Wolfram von Essenbach, 126
women. 5, 6, 8, 27, 28, 35, 38, 41, 44, 64, 65, 90, 120, 139, 140

Yolande, Princess, 81
York, 157, 158, 160
Yousuf ben-Acoub-ben-Saladi *see* Saladin

Zenghi, 22, 37–8
Zion, 10, 30, 37
Zoroastrianism, 132